Breaking the Codes

Female Criminality in Fin-de-Siècle Paris

D1416338

BREAKING THE CODES

Female Criminality in Fin-de-Siècle Paris

Ann-Louise Shapiro

Stanford University Press

Stanford, California 1996

Stanford University Press, Stanford, California
© 1996 by the Board of Trustees of the
Leland Stanford Junior University
Printed in the United States of America

CIP data appear at the end of the book

Stanford University Press publications are distributed
exclusively by Stanford University Press within the
United States, Canada, Mexico, and Central America;
they are distributed exclusively by Cambridge
University Press throughout the rest of the world.

ACKNOWLEDGMENTS

The time of my work on this book—from initial conceptualization to extensive revisions and rewritings—coincides almost precisely with the years I have spent at Wesleyan University. In both direct and more subtle ways, this book is the product of the intellectual stimulation, critical attention, and generous support that I have received from an unusual group of colleagues—in the History Department, at the Center for the Humanities, and most especially in the Women's Studies Program. My good fortune in being part of this vibrant and creative community of scholars has enhanced not only the content of this book but my pleasure in its production.

Historians of France from the United States share stories about the notorious difficulties of negotiating the procedural and bureaucratic hurdles presented by the various archives. My experience, however, was transformed by the invaluable assistance I received from two archivists at the Archives de la Ville de Paris et du Département de la Seine, Brigitte Lainé and Philippe Grand, who walked me through the early phases of my work in the judicial archives and provided interest, encouragement, and access to documents through many years of research. I want also to thank M. Gabion, formerly director of the Dépôt des Archives de la Seine, for facilitating my access to the judicial archives, and to acknowledge further the staff who assisted me at the Bibliothèque Marguerite Durand, the Bibliothèque Nationale, the Bibliothèque Historique de la Ville de Paris, the Bibliothèque de l'Ecole de Médecine, the Archives de la Préfecture de Police de la Ville de Paris, and the Interlibrary Loan Office at Wesleyan University.

I am especially indebted to the National Science Foundation, Program in Law and Social Science, which provided the funds for research trips to Paris and a year-long leave to work on the manuscript. This project was also supported with smaller grants by the National Endowment for the Humanities, the American Philosophical Society, the American Council of Learned Societies / Ford Foundation, and by Wesleyan University.

Many colleagues and friends provided thoughtful critiques that encouraged me to try to meet their high expectations for clarity, focus, and cogency. I am grateful especially for the insightful comments and careful readings of the manuscript offered by Bonnie Smith and Sylvia Schafer. I have been the beneficiary of both their generosity and their unrelenting intellectual rigor.

Joan Scott has been a mentor for nearly all of my professional life; this time I want to turn the acknowledgment around in recognition not only of her attentiveness to my work, but, even more, of the benefits I have derived from my attentiveness to hers. She has been an inspiring teacher whose work has energized my thinking as she first pushed out the boundaries of conventional historical research and then pushed further to extend the parameters of feminist interventions.

I want also to thank Norris Pope of Stanford University Press for his support at every stage as this project moved from an amorphous set of ideas to a finished manuscript. And, finally, I am indebted to friends and family who have listened to my criminal stories and shared my interests and concerns, especially to Michael Shapiro, whose listening and sharing have been immeasurably important to me for so long.

A.-L.S.

CONTENTS

Illustrations

BREAKING THE CODES

Female Criminality in Fin-de-Siècle Paris

Introduction

Paris in the fin-de-siècle seemed a city dedicated to pleasure. For the first time, workers as well as the wealthy could patronize a wide range of leisure institutions, including music halls, circuses, cafés, dance halls, and street fairs. In 1878, 1889, and 1900, Paris hosted Great Expositions that both celebrated national accomplishment and material progress and seemed to confirm, in their opulence and accessibility, the democratization of leisure. The Eiffel Tower and the Galerie des Machines, exhibited in 1889, and the elaborate pavilions of consumer goods and military technology on display in 1900 were spectacular diversions that invoked the new republic's idealized self-image as a unified national community of producers and consumers, giving material form to the fraternal consensus that constituted the implicit promise of republicanism. In place of monarchical pageantry, Church rituals, and class divisions, the secular republic substituted national spectacles and civic *fêtes* that announced the inclusiveness of the republican regime—an inclusiveness that was to be realized not just in political democracy, but in the shared experience of a "dream world of mass consumption."[1]

But for many contemporary observers, the pleasures of the city were merely a fragile façade that concealed its more potent dangers. As at least one Parisian commentator observed, it seemed likely that the French were "dancing on a volcano."[2] While the government promoted republican myths of democratic progress, more skeptical voices warned of national decay. In their eyes, electricity might make a shining fairyland of the urban environment, but the dark underside of the modern city belied these chimerical visual effects. Instead of pleasure they saw increased fatigue, neurasthenia, restlessness and ennui, especially among the upper classes, while the participation of workers in the new institutions of popular entertainment inevitably suggested vice. In fact, physicians and social scientists had identified a national disease, *dégénérescence*—a condition characterized by physical deterioration and by parallel moral and intellectual decline—that captured their sense of the modern age as afflicted by a self-reproducing pathological process.

In the context of anxieties focused on the possibility of devolution, crime and criminality became imaginative preoccupations, leading one anxious critic to lament the fascination with which his contemporaries pursued the vicious and depraved aspects of contemporary life, to bemoan "*le prestige du mal*." The culture seemed saturated with accounts of sensational crimes and infamous criminals. Mass-circulation newspapers entertained a wide popular audience with criminal stories, even as crime became the focus of scientific inquiry and the subject of articles that moved rapidly out of professional journals into more popular formats and general social criticism. Medical and legal experts as well as professionalizing social scientists began to think of crime as a mirror held up to society, exposing the tendencies of the day writ large.

For the past three decades, social historians have echoed these nineteenth-century perceptions, finding in their own pursuit of crime historical markers that point to a broad range of social conflicts and ideological struggles. The study of the processes that defined and punished criminal behavior in the nineteenth century has, for example, opened investigations into the effects of industrial and urban growth and the various social confrontations through which these transformations were expressed. In searching for the historical meanings of criminality, scholars have explored conflicting systems of belief, shifting class relations, the new roles of the state and its administrative apparatus, the development of the professions and professional expertise, the impact of the organs of mass culture, and contests for power and authority within the ruling classes. As wide-ranging as this investigation has been, however, it has largely ignored the implications of gender. Most of these initial studies of crime assume that the criminal is male, or at least that the sex of the offender is not particularly relevant or revealing.

Following the early work of Louis Chevalier, for example, scholars have studied the conditions of the urban environment as the actual and metaphorical ground for the emergence of social pathologies.[3] But this urbanist model cannot adequately explain the cultural codes that made women's crime particularly meaningful in fin-de-siècle Paris. Women's crime did not, in fact, arouse the same fear of lawlessness and anxieties about recidivism as did crimes committed by men. Because female criminality was only a small and declining percentage of prosecuted crime and did not seem actually to threaten public order, it is necessary to look beyond the unsettled and unsettling urban context to grasp the contemporary significance of crimes committed by women.

Others working within a Marxist tradition have explored the effects of changing legal practices in articulating and securing the authority of various elites. In this analysis, the legal system emerges as both an ideological instrument that expresses and enforces the will of the ruling classes and a primary means by which to regulate working-class behavior: to proscribe customary practices in favor of behaviors ordered according to formal legal principles; to protect property; and to authorize a pattern of surveillance and supervision.[4] The "law as ideology" model is not, however, particularly useful when applied to the criminal behavior of women. Although it has been invoked more generally to demonstrate the substitution of formal rules for popular custom, it is clear that responses to female criminality in the fin-de-siècle continued to draw substantially on customary assumptions, as jury decisions flagrantly, or even carelessly, ignored legal principles in favor of outcomes that more closely followed popular opinion. No unified ideology structured responses to female crime, nor did practice mirror prescription.

Perhaps the most powerful inspiration for recent studies of criminality has derived from the work of Michel Foucault.[5] Directing attention to the complicated techniques by which discipline is promoted and enacted, Foucault emphasized the normalizing functions of penal practices designed not primarily to punish the offense but rather to neutralize the danger of the deviant individual. The center of Foucault's analysis described the coming into being of the modern individual through interlocking networks of disciplinary techniques—invisible, internal ones as well as public, functional ones—techniques that emerged in the deployment of specialized modes of knowledge. In Foucault's terms, the criminal, not crime, became the object of a new disciplinary apparatus of power/knowledge. While Foucault's discussion of normalizing strategies and his critique of the social sciences have been extremely useful in focusing attention on the systems of meaning that underpin institutional practices, it is evident that his failure to consider the implications of gender difference assumes a unitary discourse, producing relatively predictable effects, which does not stand up to close examination.

This book arose out of my growing conviction that there were different stories to be told about (and through) an examination of women's crime. Female criminality raised quite specific issues for nineteenth-century society; the discussion of women's crime joined some social debates and was quite distant from others. The very fact that contemporaries wrote extensively about the problem of the female criminal in the absence of statistically important criminal behavior by women seemed to point to "female criminality" as a code that condensed, and thus obscured, other concerns. In the turbulent social environment of the new Third Republic—a world in which the meaning of democracy and citizenship remained unresolved and the fate of the family seemed to have become precarious—the judicial system with its array of professional experts provided an arena for negotiating new standards that might repair perceived disorders in public and private life.

In looking at the judicial system as a filter through which these developments passed, my interest has been to break open the various codes that structured criminal stories, to discover precisely what kind of discussion the "problem" of female criminality invited and how contemporaries imagined that they might solve this problem. For example, to what degree and in what ways did the symbolic overtones of female criminality connect to the substantive issues that appeared over and over again in the stories of women's crimes? How were the crimes of domestic violence, infanticide, and abortion interpreted in the context of broader debates about marriage reform, depopulation, sexuality, and women's roles in the public sphere? What was the role of expert commentary—from the forensic psychiatrist, the criminologist, the legal scholar—in producing a normative code for female behavior? And how did this code accommodate or resist the newly recognized voice of popular opinion? How does a look at female criminality reveal the tensions within republican ideology about mass society, democracy, and mass culture? And why did the stories of female defendants, produced and retold in the courtroom, make at least as compelling theater as dramas created specifically for the stage?

The perceived Otherness of women has, historically, allowed the metaphoric Woman to stand in for a wide and contradictory array of qualities, values, and meanings—has endowed femaleness with a special symbolic resonance. I have been interested, further, in exploring these mythic, fantasmatic valences of femaleness, reinterpreted in the late nineteenth century, as they intersected and inflected the stories of ordinary life that were produced in the discourses of crime. Catherine Clément has written that "societies do not succeed in offering everyone the same way of fitting into the symbolic order; those who are . . . between symbolic systems, in the interstices, offside, are the ones who are afflicted with a dangerous symbolic mobility."[6] Such anomalous creatures—the sorceress and the hysteric, for example—are both threatening and conservative, representing that which is outside or unacceptable and simultaneously providing mechanisms for cordoning off or removing the threat. The female criminal was a comparably ambiguous figure in the social imagination of the fin-de-siècle. (What might we make of the fact that St. Lazare had been, sequentially, a leprosarium, a convent, an asylum for the insane, and a revolutionary prison before its incarnation as a prison for women in the fin-de-siècle?) In her "offsideness," the criminal woman provided an opportunity for drawing distinctions—between good and bad women, between women and men, between natural and unnatural mothers, between the sick and the criminal—as well as for codifying both the rules of social relations and the range of gender-appropriate behaviors.

I am seeking in the first instance to set the discussion of female criminality within the frame of nineteenth-century obsessions about sexual difference, to examine how assumptions about female criminality worked to consolidate and legitimize the practices and conventions of both domestic and public life. In her study of the ways in which the nineteenth-century domestic novel articulated a new bourgeois subjectivity, Nancy Armstrong described the strategic move whereby novels turned political information into psychological and moral truths.[7] Politics disappeared, she argues, in favor of stories of sensibility and a domestic ideal that effaced struggle and obscured relations of power. In expanding on Armstrong's insights, I am describing here the various strategies of different groups—bourgeois professional men, journalists, politicians, and social critics—who attempted to define and, in effect, domesticate the female criminal. In their stories of female crime—stories that were invariably couched in individual rather than social terms—they searched for a kind of closure on the problems of social inequity and unstable gender hierarchies that lay embedded in incidents of female criminality.

In moving beyond these overlapping efforts to produce a knowledge of the *femme criminelle*, however, I have focused on the incompleteness of this project. It has been important to examine the uncertain effects of discourses about the female criminal as they circulated, in their various incarnations, outside the judicial process via different paths of diffusion. It is much more difficult to draw definitive conclusions about these latter processes; it is less complicated to analyze the texts and subtexts of the prescriptive and descriptive information that issued largely from professional men trying to solve "the woman question" than it is to discover how ordinary men and women interpreted and responded to this material. Yet the judicial dossiers and commentaries on individual cases that provide much of the evidence for this study suggest both collisions and complicity between different cultural worlds.[8] "Scientific" testimony about female deviance was not homogeneous; popular renditions of scientific testimony altered its implications; and the actual effects of scientific pronouncements could rarely be predicted in advance. Moreover, women offered their own stories that drew largely upon familiar narratives, identifying expectations that were at once conventional and potentially radical. It seems evident that women did not merely accept the cultural information about femaleness that proliferated across such a broad discursive field, but they could not ignore it either. They did not merely act out male fantasies of female deviance, but they did sometimes follow specific cultural scripts. Women were not simply passive respondents to male authority; neither were they free agents. To escape from the exclusions implied in these dichotomous possibilities, criminal women are presented in this study as both central to the *imaginaire* of fin-de-siècle culture and as participants in and shapers of the debates that surrounded them.

An analysis of the disparate effects of stories about female criminality suggests something about how cultural tensions are expressed, accommodated, and resisted—allowing us to see in this complex negotiation the actual struggles, as change (in gender relations, in the locus of cultural and political authority, in politics, in culture) was both resisted and forthcoming. I am arguing that the discussion of women's crime and the judicial, literary, scientific, and popular responses to the female criminal were deeply implicated in the profound transitions that marked the fin-de-siècle.

This book draws its inspiration from recent studies of culture, informed especially by feminist theory, that bring together questions of power relations in the public sphere and the processes that define the common sense of private behaviors—that which goes without saying in the ordinariness of daily life. The primary objectives of this collective project are to demonstrate the inadequacy of histories that reinscribe the nineteenth-century vision of separate spheres and gendered roles and expectations, substituting instead a more nuanced vision of the permeability of prescribed boundaries and the tensions and adjustments that were necessarily a part of this permeability. Especially relevant in laying out new possibilities for studying culture is the work of Judith Walkowitz. In *City of Dreadful Delight*, she has recently mapped the cultural world of late-Victorian London in terms of "a series of multiple and simultaneous cultural contests and exchanges across a wide social spectrum . . . [highlighting] a shifting pattern of cultural and social perspectives, set in dynamic relationship to each other."[9] I have tried similarly in this study to work out the kind of complex interactions that kept the female criminal at the center of cultural debates in the closing decades of the century: to explore the disparate effects of the preoccupation with female criminality, to analyze how particular explanations of femaleness gained discursive and cultural weight, and to discover under what circumstances (and in what terms) the voices and behaviors of women could and did matter. By focusing on women's criminal behavior, I have been able to examine how the circulation of very different kinds of stories about criminal women marked out an arena of debate over women's place in French society and culture. In this analysis, the proliferation of stories—conservative and normalizing stories as well as more disruptive ones—itself becomes a motor of change that facilitated the loosening of patterns long-anchored by the discourse of difference and the tenacity of gendered norms.

In Chapter 1, I situate the subject of female crime in the several contexts that made it culturally important in the fin-de-siècle: worries about the consequences of urban growth and the implications of a new, perhaps subversive, mass culture; the increasingly theatrical ambiance of the Cour d'Assises; and the growth of the *sciences du moi*, including criminology, which were producing knowledges that sought authority to cure the social pathologies of the modern world. In all of these concerns, I argue, the figure of the criminal woman was symbolically and practically central, a lightning rod that gathered the social and cultural tensions of the period.

The construction of the stories that explained female criminality is the focus of Chapter 2. This chapter examines the production of criminal stories through the procedures and practices of the judicial system, looking especially at the intersections of available myths about femaleness with the testimony of expert witnesses, and at the interactions between the defendant and her various interrogators. Criminal stories are shown to have been generated in the judicial process through a kind of enforced and stylized collaboration. In describing the state's construction of its case, it is necessary to consider what principles governed the inclusion or suppression of information and which genres gave shape and nuance to the narrative. How is it that women's crimes came to be seen in such formulaic terms? What were the consequences when defendants refused to repeat the expected formulas? And how did popularized versions of a case affect its cultural meaning?

Underpinning the entire discussion is the assumption that culture is an arena of exchange, that cultural boundaries are inevitably porous. In looking at the circulation of criminal stories beyond the courtroom, what we see are inevitably stories-in-tension, shaped by the diverse expectations of the producers and consumers of criminal stories, by contemporary social relations, and by institutional practices.[10] Because not all stories commanded equal authority, I suggest the factors that endowed certain stories with intelligibility and cultural weightiness while marginalizing others. Although the evolution of official policies and the ideological basis of practices of punishment have been ably studied by Robert Nye, Patricia O'Brien, and Michelle Perrot,[11] until quite recently court dossiers have been almost entirely ignored by scholars working in the areas of crime and punishment in nineteenth-century France.[12] In focusing on the production of a story in the criminal dossier, I am hoping to expand on existing work by exploring the interface between institutional practices and the construction of cultural meanings.

Chapter 3 examines the ways in which medical discourse provided a language for interpreting female deviancy. By drawing tight conceptual links between female reproductive biology and various disordered behaviors—codifying, for example, the diseases of menstrual psychosis, puerperal insanity, and menopausal mania—physicians succeeded in making femaleness itself into a kind of pathology. Women, disordered in their bodies, were, in effect, potentially criminal. The "problem" of female criminality provided, then, the opportunity for new medico-legal experts to enter the penal system as privileged interpreters of disorderly women. Because medical discourse moved outward from the clinic to the courtroom and, finally, into popular culture, the hysterical female became a widely recognized type; women's erratic, overexcited constitution, often driven by biology, became the acknowledged source of criminal acts. It is my contention that medical discourses had more profound effects in social theory than in individual therapeutics and clinical practice or even in the courts. What seems crucial in understanding the cultural consequences of medical expertise is the way that medical opinion spoke simultaneously about the individual defendant *and* about all women. In looking at how physicians provided the language for asserting female incapacity, I am exploring a medical redefinition of femaleness that raised broader questions about women's roles in public life.

I turn next, in Chapter 4, to an examination of female crimes of passion. These, the crimes that achieved the greatest notoriety, constituted female defendants in familiar symbolic imagery as furies, zombies, harpies —unnatural women, sick women, out-of-control women. It is possible to see in these "love stories" the (re)presentation of stereotypes of femininity, what Michèle Ouerd has called "the persistent fantasies and formulaic nightmares" that inform discourses about the deviant woman.[13] But I am arguing further that these formulaic fantasies performed specific cultural work. In reinventing female stereotypes in the fin-de-siècle, bourgeois authorities were seeking to secure the traditional bourgeois family as the basis of the social order and to normalize the working-class household.

Chapter 5 traces the emergence of the feminist in the 1890s, a new and dangerous "type" that was increasingly conflated with the criminal woman. In effect, contemporaries were so preoccupied with an alleged disorder of women, manifest in variously interpreted challenges to a traditional gender hierarchy, that distinctions between feminists and female criminals began to disappear. Both increasingly came to be seen as the embodiment of a dangerous gender ambiguity that threatened male authority and signaled national decadence. This convergence, emblematically realized in Alexandre Dumas's tract *Les Femmes qui tuent and les femmes qui votent* (Women who kill and women who vote), placed *la femme criminelle* on the cusp of the social changes she had symbolized for decades. What would women's rights be in the new republic? Were women to be citizens, French(men?) after all?

Because assumptions about gender difference often provided the normative, organizing principles by which contemporaries made sense of both cultural and political life in the fin-de-siècle, a study of female criminality reveals the specific ways in which female behavior had become a key interpretive grid that measured nothing less than the viability of the society. In confronting *la femme criminelle*, the bourgeois society of the fin-de-siècle was forced to address the unsettling effects of shifting patterns of gender relations and the inability of traditional authorities to suppress or contain the cultural and ideological uncertainties of contemporary life. In the social imagination of the fin-de-siècle, the female criminal was never very far from debates about divorce reform and civil rights for women, or from heightened national anxieties about the viability of the traditional family and conventional gender roles on the one hand, and the perceived crises of depopulation and national decadence on the other. In sum, the story of female criminality was a story about the pain of social change. It was a story that often read like melodrama, casting deviant women in leading roles. It is just possible, however, that in their move from the domestic space of the household into the public arena of the courtroom, criminal women turned melodrama back into politics.

CRIME AND CULTURE

The "Problem" of the Female Criminal

The serialized novel is able to create that frightening thing that is a popular mentality. . . . It is said that the life of a man ends always in resembling his dreams. Will the life of the people end in resembling their fictions?

Maurice Talmeyr, "Le Roman-feuilleton et l'esprit populaire," *Revue des Deux Mondes*, 1903

In 1880, Georges Grisson donned his frock coat and hat, armed himself with a revolver, and embarked on an investigation of the vicious and criminal elements of Paris. In the chronicle of this adventure, he invites his readers on a "voyage of exploration" that promises to be "sinister and grotesque, distressing and droll."[1] Grisson's announcement of his enterprise warns of the real danger represented by the city's debased population (witness his weapon), while engaging his readers with the titillating offer of scenes that are filled with "gross amusements," "ferocious joys," and "frightening pleasures." The particular appeal of this writing lay in the explicit mingling of pleasure and danger. Grisson's audience would immediately recognize the invitation to share in the voyeuristic, transgressive pleasures of the criminal story. In fin-de-siècle Paris, crime had become an imaginative obsession. Vignettes such as those Grisson promised proliferated across a broad cultural field that included journalistic, literary, legal, medical, and social scientific writings.

Criminals were the subjects of popular ballads; they wrote memoirs from prison and figured prominently in illustrated supplements to mass-circulation newspapers. Forensic psychiatrists probed the medical dimensions of criminality in published case histories; former chiefs of police wrote multivolume memoirs that celebrated, in ironic juxtaposition, both crime and its containment; a specialized daily newspaper, the *Gazette des Tribunaux*, reported on the most intriguing or scandalous court cases, quoting the texts of criminal indictments and providing a reconstructed version of the interchanges of the courtroom; the *faits divers* of the new popular press—those condensed stories about terrifying accidents, natural disasters, sensational crimes, mysterious disappearances, miraculous escapes, and otherworldly occurrences—came more and more to focus on violent and criminal events; popular theater featured criminal melodramas in its staple fare; novels and serialized *romans feuilletons* elaborated on real and fictional crimes, blurring the distinction between them; and professionals in law and criminology issued a steady stream of expert testimony in the courtroom and in journals, monographs, and reports from international conferences.

Michelle Perrot has argued that "there are no 'facts of crime' as such, only a judgmental process that institutes crimes by designating as criminal both certain acts and their perpetrators. In other words, there is a discourse of crime that reveals the obsession of a society."[2] My schematic listing of the variety and diffusion of criminal stories attests to a generalized preoccupation whose meanings for contemporaries need to be unraveled. Crime was the focus of both science and art; it evoked fear as well as fantasy. Not only did criminal stories make good press in the fin-de-siècle, providing the occasion for vicarious psychic and social adventures, but they seemed to promise access to deeper, more unfathomable truths. In evaluating this mass of documentation, we need to know how different narratives about crime worked in cultural terms and how different communities articulated and appropriated criminal stories. A crime always has the status of a symptom, in Dennis Porter's terms, a symptom that functions as an insistent question, inviting a discussion of causes and motivation.[3] It is the purpose of this study to explore the ways in which contemporaries responded to the "question" of crime in the final decades of the century and in so doing to discover, along with Grisson and his readers, the various obsessions that gave crime its particular cultural resonance.

The problem of crime seemed on one level a quintessential marker of a crisis in modern urban society. To contemporary observers, political and social stability in the final three decades of the nineteenth century appeared to be profoundly threatened by a range of pressing and apparently intractable urban problems: an organized working class espousing ideologies of resistance; the persistence of poverty and the unsettling presence of people who could not become bourgeois and did not revere bourgeois values; a mass society, apparently endangered from above by the decadence of the wealthy and from below by the pathology of unruly crowds. Many focused on crime as the symptom par excellence of these various social threats. The most striking aspect of contemporary discussions of crime was not, however, the fear of physical danger that they evoked, but rather, anxieties about a new and disturbing experience of cultural anarchy. It seemed increasingly evident to politicians and professional men that laws, institutions, and the most basic customs of the society were being renegotiated through the somewhat haphazard processes of criminal trials. Traditional institutions appeared unable to guarantee traditional mores. According to one jurist, "one day it is the issue of the right to bring paternity suits, another day divorce . . . or the right to vengeance, the impotence of justice to rectify certain injuries, the unequal distribution of wealth—all pass before the court."[4] Those accustomed to thinking of themselves as arbiters of contemporary practices worried that the social problems signaled by well-publicized accounts of criminal activity appeared to be moving toward resolution in serendipitous ways, linked as much to the idiosyncrasies of the penal process and the volatility of popular opinion as to the dictates of law or established custom.

The production and dissemination of criminal stories through emerging vehicles of mass culture similarly posed an unprecedented challenge to traditional authorities. New forms of popular entertainment—including especially the *café concert*, popular theater, and the mass-circulation press— suggested the possibility of an autonomous culture unsupervised by, and even resistant to, the values of traditionally dominant groups. Bourgeois critics deplored the theaters and music halls of the popular classes as agents of "the invading march of filthy licentiousness," while government censors attempted to expunge lyrics deemed politically dangerous from the popular repertoire.[5] It was not accidental that a scientific literature on crime developed alongside a growing mass audience for criminal stories, as self-appointed experts worried over the uncertain effects of suggestion on behavior and of pleasure on discipline. Actual criminal activity seemed less threatening than the domestication, if not the celebration, of crime that found expression in new organs of popular culture. For the established classes, it remained unclear on what terms social stability and a democratized mass culture could coexist.

The contemporary concerns that produced this preoccupation with crime found their clearest expression in the figure of the criminal woman, who became in the closing decades of the century a pivotal character in the eclectic repertoire of criminal stories, factual and fictional, that circulated so widely throughout the period. Nothing in the criminal statistics of these decades, however, accounts for this new obsession with criminal women. Women constituted a declining percentage of those arrested for crimes over the course of the nineteenth century, and, by the closing three decades, represented approximately 14 percent of all defendants—this low number including arrests for infanticide and abortion, categories in which women were highly overrepresented.[6] Rates for violent crime by women were especially low: women constituted 5.7 percent of those indicted for homicide; 6 percent of indictments for theft with violence; 8.7 percent of assault and battery cases; and 13.3 percent of premeditated murders.[7] It is possible that a certain amount of female lawlessness was masked by the criminal statistics. Between 1860 and 1890, the percentage of crimes heard in the main criminal court of Paris, the Cour d'Assises, declined from 24 percent to 18 percent, and continued to drop in the next two decades.[8] As magistrates worried especially about the increasing willingness of juries to acquit women, female offenses were frequently transferred to the lower courts where, tried as misdemeanors rather than felonies, they received less harsh but more reliable punishment. In fact, Marie-Jo Dhavernas has speculated that French women were so marginalized within their society that they could not even violate its laws, making them regularly the recipients of "*ces touchants faveurs.*"[9] Thus, she argues, women made up a larger proportion of "apparent criminality" (that is, recognized but not pursued) than of legal criminality (crimes actually brought before the courts), and would probably have constituted a larger share of real crime (all infractions committed) if these figures could be known.[10] But even if the official statistics distorted figures for female criminality, it does not seem that women's crime was perceived as growing alarmingly in this period. Acquittal rates remained high for women, passing 50 percent in the 1890s (in contrast to acquittal rates of about 30 percent for men), and female offenders were celebrities as well as pariahs.

In her recent study of the discipline of criminology, Carol Smart notes that, historically, there has been little interest in women's crime because it could not be understood as a pressing social problem: there were too few offenders; most did not commit repeat offenses; female criminals were seen essentially as anomalies. In contrast, she observes, there is no shortage of research on topics such as female insanity and maternal deprivation, subjects that have been identified as having greater social relevance.[11] It seems that the female criminal of late-nineteenth-century France should have been similarly consigned to a marginal space. What is particularly interesting about the French case is this very disparity between a low-steady or declining rate of female criminality on the one hand and the explosion of a discussion about female crime across a broad discursive field on the other. What accounts for the outpouring of interest in criminal women in the fin-de-siècle?

The work of Joan Scott, Mary Poovey, and others, has suggested that "those issues that are constituted as 'problems' at any given moment are particularly important because they mark the limits of ideological certainty," pointing to cultural tensions and ongoing struggles.[12] In following this lead I am seeking to situate the problem of crime—especially women's crime—within larger processes of cultural definition. The discussion of female crime was on one level about the fixing of sexual difference in a time of considerable challenge to conventional norms. Explanations of female criminality took as their starting point the disparity of crime rates between the sexes. Experts sought to determine whether women were more moral than men. They assessed women's lesser participation in crime in terms of their closer connection to religion, their role as nurturers, their ostensibly more childlike qualities. They suggested that low rates of female criminality derived from women's reduced intelligence, limited imagination, and more restricted access to opportunities for transgression. What was it, they asked, that moved women to commit violent crimes? Were there quintessentially female crimes? This set of issues that constituted the female criminal as a social problem invited a clarification of difference—an attempt to codify and stabilize gender identities in a period of unsettling social change. But on another level, the use of gendered understandings of crime provided the conceptual tools for evaluating contemporary culture. The attention to female criminality put into circulation a broad discussion of a syndrome of pathologies that were represented through—indeed, embodied in—the criminal woman. The emergence of the "problem" of female crime in the fin-de-siècle points, then, to the intersection of two areas of cultural tension: new uncertainties about the role and place of women, and concerns about the nature of modern mass culture.

It is my purpose here to explore the ways that the female criminal figured in the cultural transactions of fin-de-siècle Paris. In Perrot's terms, what obsessions of the society were revealed through the various discourses on women's crime? How did the female criminal come to stand at the center of anxieties about mass culture and shifting social relations as she stood before the bench of the Cour d'Assises? And what was the discursive and cultural place of the criminal woman as she circulated through and participated in the construction of the various stories about her? In seeking to answer these questions, I will be looking at collisions and collusions between the stories told by professionals in law and the new social sciences—attempts both to make sense of the cultural changes of the period and to secure their expertise—and those emanating from the more popular forums in which criminal stories became part of the public domain. This chapter will suggest how the female criminal became the most resonant site for exploring the implications of a perceived moment of cultural anarchy in which traditions and traditional authorities seemed to be losing their hold.

Crime attracted so much attention in the fin-de-siècle because it had become one of the primary symptoms of what physicians and social scientists described as a new national disease: *dégénérescence*—a condition characterized not only by physical deterioration but by parallel moral and intellectual decline. In terms that provided a counter-discourse to the rhetoric of progress, degeneration was understood as the disease of particular individuals as well as the condition of modernity itself, manifest in persistent social divisions, the irrational behavior of crowds, urban crime, and insanity. According to Daniel Pick, theories of degeneration "flirted and flitted between the dreams of purity and danger . . . in socially specific ways," suggesting sometimes that "degeneration involved a scenario of racial decline (potentially implicating everyone in the society) and [alternatively] an explanation of 'otherness,' securing the identity of, variously, the scientist, (white) man, bourgeoisie against superstition, fiction, darkness, femininity, the masses, effete aristocracy."[13] Concern about degeneration permeated social criticism precisely because it could not be reduced to one message or one context; rather, it emerged to conceptualize "a felt crisis of history" that could be seen equally in the national defeat by Prussia in 1870 or in pervasive and intractable social problems.[14]

Conservative moralists identified the national crisis as one provoked by relativism and materialism—a loss of faith that was epitomized in the "egoism" and individualism of republican ideals. Other commentators from diverse religious and political positions blamed the luxuries and commercial pleasures proliferating in the city for undermining the physical and moral integrity of the upper classes on the one hand, and for generating the envy, taste for luxury, and sloth of urban workers on the other. In the terms of this argument, the urban environment was responsible for an increase in nervous disorders among the wealthy, while workers, unsupervised in the midst of temptations, succumbed to vice. In effect, they construed the urban world of the late nineteenth century as the breeding ground for defective beings whose tainted hereditary pre-dispositions were released by the disintegration of older, safer social struc-tures and practices. We can see a good example of this kind of linkage in the work of one legal scholar who explained degeneration as the result of "alcoholism, the indifference of the law toward human reproduction, an excess of civilization, and urban congestion."[15] With such a diffuse etiology, degeneration theorists could link political fears about repeated revolution, unruly crowds, anarchism, and violence to anxieties about depopulation, alcoholism, crime, prostitution, insanity, and feminism.

Criminology emerged in the fin-de-siècle as part of the new social sciences that aspired to provide the modern cure for the pathologies of modernity. Informed by a medical model of social analysis, it presented it-self as a kind of public hygiene for the "epidemic" of crime, promising a scientific solution to the problems of social defense. Although a crimi-nologist in 1899 described this preoccupation with the study of crime as evidence of an unprecedented expansion of "the prestige of evil" (le pres-tige du mal)[16]—an exaggerated interest in things degenerate that was per-haps itself unhealthy—he softened his alarm in the end by granting crime a privileged status as a source of profound knowledge. According to the professor of legal medicine Alexandre Lacassagne, "societies have only the criminals they deserve."[17] A dissection of the corpus of crime would therefore provide an anatomical sketch of the social body. In this con-ceptual frame, studies of crime and criminality (le virus criminel) could address a broad range of perceived social pathologies—including alco-holism, venereal disease, prostitution, degeneration, suicide—while pro-ducing a prophylactic knowledge of human sentiments—hate, greed, vengeance, love, despair—and a normative description of healthy and vi-able social arrangements, including appropriate relations between men and women and among social classes. These goals were to be accom-plished by a new army of professionals whose separate and collective ex-pertise could be deployed across the broad terrain claimed by criminology. The criminologist Gabriel Tarde made this point explicitly, boasting that a revitalized study of crime stood just at the intersection of the new hu-man sciences—statistics, anthropology, psychology, physiology—which would illuminate "social facts . . . [that are] no longer confused and doubtful like the generalizations of earlier times, but are now as precise and certain as their details."[18]

Crime came to be thought of as the most vivid and accurate reflection of social customs and inclinations. The prison, along with the asylum, could be understood as "a living museum that enclosed a pathologically enlarged version of the tendencies of the day."[19] The criminologist was assimilated, in this discourse, to the photographer (or the developer, *le révélateur*) who merely reproduced with absolute verisimilitude the precise image before him. As if to confirm this perspective, Marie François Goron, a former chief of police in Paris, described the accounts of his professional exploits as "social photographs that, without retouching, by their unadorned simplicity and horror, conveyed the truth."[20] In the world of his subjects, "savage and vile as it was," one found oneself, Goron insisted, "closer to nature." Similarly, a reviewer for *Le Radical* spoke of former prefect of police Gustave Macé's autobiographical reflections, *Un joli monde*, as "a powerful study of social physiology [in which] the vices of our society are laid bare with a documentary exactitude."[21]

Criminology's claims to "photographic exactness" were, then, part of an effort to garner authority for the new disciplines, enhancing the appeal of expert knowledge that would be closer to nature, truer, and more authentic than ordinary knowledge. We seem here to be in the presence of what Denise Riley has recently described as the emergence of "the social," that is, of an intermediary ground between the old public and private arenas.[22] This reconceptualized "social" became, in Riley's terms, a space in which newly defined sociological categories ("women," "the working class," "the criminal," and so on) were spread out, dehistoricized, and opened to remedial interventions. In their growing professionalization, social scientists produced "a total geography for comprehension and reform" that endowed them with responsibility for curing social ills and covered them with the mantle of disinterested, scientific humanitarianism. The discourses of the new social sciences envisioned a world managed by scientific experts, men of probity and discernment, protected from self-interest by a shield of class and profession:

The dream of a truly evolved and civilized human society would be one in which each crime (committed by the proud, by the rich as well as by the poor), each illness and each madness, each pathological case, would be examined in the severe and serene halls of science by competent and capable men for whom the sole goal would be that of defending society against those who compromised the conditions of its existence, and who would cure, whenever possible, those who had offended it.[23]

This was an expertise that claimed authority not only to assess the viability and health of social arrangements but to plumb the depths of the human psyche. We can hear something of the scope of this aspiration in a description of the near-mystical insights of the famous defense lawyer Charles Lachaud who

had descended, step by step, into the mysterious underground of contemporary existence where he had seen every misery, known every horror, borne every shame, found every limit, examined all motives, reached the bottom of all suffering and of every social degradation. . . . Like the professor of surgery who makes use of his surgical practice to give an anatomy lesson, in each of his cases—by digging among feelings and human passions to their very roots, by sounding, even beyond consciousness, the silent depths of instinct—he finds the means to construct a veritable lesson in moral anatomy.[24]

Insisting that the study of crime was, for professionals, more than a vulgar curiosity, the criminal anthropologist Scipio Sighele claimed that "it is precisely in the analysis of evil that we find the explanation *de notre moi*."[25] To many, the knowledge excavated from the dark underside of human life seemed to promise a means to understand, and then to control, the dangers hidden in the human heart. These were secrets, mysteries that could be unlocked only through a new kind of professional scrutiny. It is perhaps no coincidence that criminology and psychoanalysis emerged in tandem: parallel beginnings in the late nineteenth century of the *sciences du moi*.[26]

In his discussion of the development of the discipline of criminology, Foucault has charted the emergence of this preoccupation with the nature of the accused criminal. Although nineteenth-century criminologists remained divided in their assessments of the relative importance of sociological, psychological, and physical factors in provoking crime, he argues that in spite of these differences they increasingly focused on the character of the criminal.[27] The crime itself seemed to carry less meaning than the defendant's personal tendencies. Foucault has offered a recent example that captures the implications of this late-nineteenth-century shift: "A man who was accused of five rapes and six attempted rapes between February and June 1975 was being tried in the Paris criminal courts. The accused hardly spoke at all. Questions from the presiding judge—

"Have you tried to reflect upon your case?"
—Silence.
"Why, at twenty-two years of age, do such violent urges overtake you? You must make an effort to analyze yourself. You are the one who has the keys to your own actions. Explain yourself."

— it would be normal for him to speak for volunteously

—Silence.
"Why would you do it again?"
—Silence.
Then a juror took over and cried out, "For heaven's sake, defend yourself!"[28]

The juror's outburst makes visible the extent to which the fact of a crime and the apprehension of the individual responsible for the act had become merely the opening moment in a judicial process that was finally about something else—that is, about a dangerous or deviant individual whose condition of delinquency might even precede the commission of a criminal act. The business of the court, Foucault argues, increasingly replaced the question of "What must be punished, and how?" with the question "Whom do you think you are punishing, and why?"[29] In terms of penal practice in the late nineteenth century, this shift was apparent in the expanding use of the concept of extenuating circumstances to mitigate formal legal penalties, in efforts to "individualize" penalties so as to create a two- or three-tiered system that responded directly to the issue of motivation, and in the introduction of the expert testimony of psychiatrists who would situate the crime within a comprehensive, "scientific" portrait of the criminal so as to calibrate precisely the social danger and possibility of rehabilitation presented by the accused.

Foucault's analysis does not, however, account for the particular determination to dissect the nature of the female criminal in the fin-de-siècle. In his neglect of the ways that assumptions about gender difference fractured discussions of criminal character, Foucault's analysis misses the convergence of anxieties about social disorder and cultural anarchy in the figure of the female criminal, the quintessential unruly woman of the fin-de-siècle. This focus on femaleness, which I wish to underline, was grounded in patterns of thought that conceived of women as uniquely capable of reflecting back the contours of social life—as the mirror through which society would recognize itself. The poor working-class women who passed through the Cour d'Assises suggested, in a well-entrenched model of social analysis, all that was wrong with modern urban society.[30] The prostitute, the seduced and abandoned unmarried mother, the unreliable domestic servant, and the thief each brought into focus the unresolved social problems of the urban agglomeration: social anarchy, unregulated sexuality, poverty, class envy.

This use of a female figure to represent urban social realities was not new; it had typified nineteenth-century social criticism. Throughout the

[handwritten: Bourdieu: Q as keeper/repository of cultural capital]

century, bourgeois investigators had discussed the perceived pathology of
the city in terms of the condition of working–class women. At least from
the time of the publication of Jules Simon's *L'Ouvrière* in 1860, the social
debris of modern urban society had been represented by descriptions of
the impoverished and degraded working woman. Lurid evocations of
her situation stirred endless speculation on questions of moral and political economy, calling forth "scientific" analyses to account for her condition and remedial strategies to cure it. Commentators who wrote about
the lives of working-class women nearly all described a prototypical de-
scent into *une vie déséquilibrée* as the conditions of urban life exacerbated
women's inherent or inherited weaknesses. In a kind of classic formula-
tion, one author suggested that there were two types of *ouvrière*: the first,
a woman born in the city and endowed with "appropriate female qualities" who became a seamstress, milliner, hairdresser, clerk, florist, or laundress, married a worker capable of supporting his family, and worked
only until the arrival of children; or the second, a migrant woman, sep- *[handwritten: migrants]*
arated from her family, who arrived in the city either as a domestic or
industrial worker and, *bouleversée* by poverty and city ways, slid fatefully
into prostitution.[31] This double image produced an imagined "before"
when urban life was less fraught with moral dangers, when workers found
their natural place and lived settled, responsible lives. At the same time, it
condemned both the new type of city woman and the new city.

   With similar intent, one medical commentator diagnosed the scourge
ravaging French society as "the unrestrained luxury of women," who,
seduced by the false glamour of clubs, cafés, spectacles, and public dances,
deserted their homes, abandoned their modesty, and, in imitation of cour-
tesans, were fatefully thrown onto the public thoroughfare.[32] In this analysis, working women's susceptibility to corruption derived in large part
from an acquired refinement, "superior to their condition," that was typical of aspiring urban working women. These pretensions, which allegedly made them unsuitable partners for members of their own class,
turned them into the easy prey of upper-class men.[33] In the hyperbolic
language of one criminologist, "The wolves [*loups ravisseurs*] seek to de-
vour this victim, so pure, but so frail, so isolated. No matter where she
turns . . . the peril is everywhere . . . she is lost. . . . Oh! each year there
is a long and wretched list of martyrs."[34] Another commentator lamented
the decline of the small workshop and the loss of the protection of the *patron*, which, he argued, led to "unsupervised lunches, solitary evenings,
and the suggestions of loneliness," ultimately the ground for theft and

infanticide. Working women, deprived of familial or *patronal* supervision, were then trapped. Either, he speculated, the novelties that they needed to attract men would lead them to shoplift in a department store or to some kind of swindling, or an unwanted pregnancy would force an abortion or infanticide.[35] Dangerous in both her autonomy *and* her dependence, the working girl became a permanent fixture of studies of the urban social landscape, one that often merged discussions of criminal behavior with overtly sexual concerns.

In Denise Riley's terms, this working-class woman who emerged in the rhetoric of social criticism was a strange hybrid who stood in a somewhat ambiguous position to both "class" and "women." She was more, according to Riley, than the female section of her class; her femininity filled a distinctive space, overflowing class, that provided the "point where 'society' could best endeavour to meet the threatening and threatened class in its intimate form."[36] It was, then, not only the working-class woman but the prostitute who most acutely came to represent the actual and symbolic center of anxieties about class and gender relations, about sex and power. The collapsing of the working woman into the prostitute—the quintessential figure of overflowing femaleness and the social equivalent of the criminal—is most evident in contemporary usage of the same term, *femme isolée*, to name both the unregistered prostitute and the female wage-earner living alone in furnished rooms.[37] *Femmes isolées* suggested together "the domain of poverty, a world of turbulent sexuality, subversive independence, and dangerous insubordination."[38] The condensed and popularized version of these assumptions is evident in Zola's famous (1880) description of Nana:

[She was] a girl descended from four or five generations of drunkards, her blood tainted by an accumulated inheritance of poverty and drink, which in her case had taken the form of a nervous derangement of the sexual instinct. She had grown up in the slums, in the gutters of Paris; and now, tall and beautiful, and as well made as a plant nurtured on a dungheap, she was avenging the paupers and outcasts of whom she was the product. With her the rottenness that was allowed to ferment among the lower classes was rising to the surface and rotting the aristocracy. She had become a force of nature, a ferment of destruction, unwittingly corrupting and disorganizing Paris between her snow-white thighs.[39]

Nana became the prototype of the prostitute saturated with depraved sexuality—the "seminal drain" and "putrid body" that inserted itself into bourgeois households, corrupting bourgeois patrimony. But she also evoked a more specific political danger that had come to be represented in terms of a (sexually) threatening woman.[40] In accounts of the civil war of 1871 and the revolutionary government of the Commune, these potential political dangers became explicit. Although there was considerable evidence that pointed to men as the incendiaries who had set fire to Paris during the upheaval, contemporary opinion, fueled by rumor and sensational press reports, latched tenaciously onto the figure of the *petroleuse*, a "hideous and fierce but sexually compelling female figure," as the vengeful perpetrator who allegedly set the fires, enacting literally the latent female threat to overturn the political order.[41] Contemporary social scientific literature similarly cast women as agents of political upheaval. In the words of one crowd theorist, "by its routine caprice, . . . its credulity, its excitability, its rapid leaps from fury to tenderness, from exasperation to bursts of laughter, the crowd is woman, even when it is composed, as almost always happens, of masculine elements."[42]

By the 1880s, then, there was a well-established pattern of representing social and political disturbance by images of dangerous women, or, put slightly differently, contemporary popular and social scientific writing understood the changes that were transforming modern urban life in terms of a specifically feminized problem of disorder. The figure of the criminal woman both borrowed from and added to this rhetorical tradition. She, like the other images of disorderly and dangerous women, was both real and imagined. And like other unruly women, she pointed to all that was wrong with modern urban society. Descriptions of this modern deviant female in the writings of fin-de-siècle criminologists were in fact largely formulaic, following a larger pattern that produced taxonomies or physiognomies to describe a set of criminal "types." In the words of the criminologist Camille Granier, female criminality highlighted women's nature: "To put into relief the feminine entity, the study of her dark side, her criminality, is as useful to the sociologist as shadowing is to the graphic artist."[43] Underpinning this general project were two deeply held assumptions: that female nature was timeless and eternal, and that women, unlike men, constituted a homogeneous category. Lombroso and Ferrero were repeating a broad consensus when they wrote that "all women fall into the same category, whereas each man is an individual unto himself; the physiognomy of the former conforms to a generalized standard; that of the latter is in each case unique."[44] Much like Freud's nearly contemporaneous posing of the riddle of femininity, the discussion of the female criminal would, it was hoped, produce a knowledge of Woman in both her normal and more aberrant forms.

The specificities of the female criminal type thus derived from older assumptions about dangerous women and worked to reinforce those perceptions, while adding more contemporary concerns. What was new in the discussions of fin-de-siècle criminology was an expanded cast of dangerous women. The concerns of criminologists extended beyond earlier preoccupations with the alleged pathologies of working women to include female criminals who belonged to the upper classes: the murderesses, adulteresses, and kleptomaniacs who, through their criminal acts, stepped out of their protected social positions and became the centerpieces of notorious *causes célèbres*. This enlarged constituency of criminal types was understood to point especially to a dangerous instability in the traditional family, to shifting gender expectations, and to problems of supervision and authority in a mass society. Fin-de-siècle *femmes criminelles* became the signs and instruments of a particularly modern malaise. Henri Thulié provides us with a fairly complete description of a set of assumptions about national decline, provoked and made visible by criminal women, that had by 1885 gained considerable currency:

Scientists have finally aroused public attention. Cries of alarm are heard everywhere: the size of the population is diminishing; infant mortality is increasing; infanticide and abortion have become, as in America, routine phenomena of daily life; prostitution is growing; people seek shameful and sterile pleasures; the vitality of France has been undermined. . . . From another perspective, women defend themselves against men with vitriol and with the revolver. They no longer seek legal justice, which does not have the power to protect them; hence they take vengeance. This weakening of the nation, these vices and violences, are symptoms of a profound sickness from which France is suffering.[45]

National anxieties were, in Thulié's analysis, collected around the "vices and violences" of women. The new divorce law of 1884, reintroducing divorce after nearly a century in which it had been illegal, raised the spectre of domestic chaos. And, as national anxieties in the fin-de-siècle became increasingly focused on the size of the population, the female-identified crimes of infanticide and abortion and the apparent growth of unregulated prostitution, the "pursuit of shameful and sterile pleasures," seemed to be at the heart of issues of national strength. In contemporary minds, women's growing demands for greater rights in marriage and greater protection for irregular liaisons, including the right to bring paternity suits (*la recherche de la paternité*), as well as the emergence of a small but worrisome feminist movement, confirmed anxieties about a disturbing tendency toward gender slippage. All threatened to profoundly destabilize traditional family patterns and masculine authority. The female offender could be seen, then, as one link in a chain of disruptive women whose social place needed to be restabilized. For cultural critics and a wide range of professionals, the malaise of modernity and the malady of the modern female converged.

The perennial "mystery" of women invited experts to produce a knowledge capable of ordering and making sense of social relations. By invoking "the eternal feminine" and linking women's behaviors to nature, bourgeois experts could construct a set of expectations that they deemed timeless and universal, remaking social norms according to their own deepest wishes. Gérard Wajeman has described the nineteenth-century incarnation of the disease of hysteria as a kind of pas de deux, a collaboration between patient and doctor that enacted the conditions by which a mystery produces a knowledge. According to his analysis, the hysteric posed the enigma of herself in such a way as to necessarily evoke a response from the person who had the position and power to respond.[46] The cultural importance of the criminal woman may be understood in similar terms: in her antisocial behavior she raised disturbing, unresolved questions about gender and class relations in the early Third Republic; and in her symbolic mobility, she provided the material and discursive site for bourgeois authorities to attempt to address these issues, to "solve" the problems. She was, literally, a source of knowledge. I am using "knowledge" here in the sense described by Joan Scott, when she speaks of knowledge as "the understanding produced by cultures and societies of human relationships":

Such knowledge is not absolute or true, but always relative. It is produced in complex ways within large epistemic frames that themselves have an (at least quasi-) autonomous history. Its uses and meanings . . . are the means by which relationships of power—of dominance and subordination—are constructed. Knowledge refers not only to ideas but to institutions and structures, everyday practices as well as specialized rituals, all of which constitute social relationships. Knowledge is a way of ordering the world; as such it is not prior to social organization, it is inseparable from social organization.[47]

The examination of the criminal woman must be understood as part of efforts to stabilize social relations and practices through the ordering potential of knowledges that were widely held and broadly diffused.

Scientific pretensions notwithstanding, criminologists could neither control criminal behavior nor attain a monopoly on interpretations of criminality. Their expert knowledge worked to construct, in D. A. Miller's apt phrase, convictions about "the normality of normativeness";[48] it did not produce social discipline or certain, uncontested knowledge. Most important in undercutting scientific authority was the way that the discussion of crime escaped from the purview of experts and percolated through popular culture. The kind of mastery over crime aspired to by criminologists seemed, in their minds, to be continually thwarted by the serendipity of an intrusive mass culture that glorified crime and defied professional wisdom, producing alternative discourses on both criminality and the criminal. The jurist Guillot noted, for example, that modern crime had become "veiled," transformed in some sense, so that it was no longer understood as a brutal act, but had become the subject of conversation in salons and the inspiration for novels, its dangerousness masked by its pervasive presence in contemporary life.[49] According to another legal scholar, contemporary society had been "split open by literature"; social questions were no longer addressed in the privacy and silence of the professional's study, but had become part of the democratized public domain. So, he argued, issues of grave social import were discussed not only in the academies and ministries of state but in "the tumult of workshops and in conference rooms which placed their podiums indiscriminately at the disposition of popular orators."[50]

Thus, although criminologists had hoped to provide a kind of social hygiene for modern urban society, their professional and cultural aspirations were always tempered, and indeed compromised, by what they perceived as the cultural anarchy of mass society—"unauthorized" authors and proliferating interpretations that deprived experts of the final word. Not only were the public spaces of conference rooms sites of challenge and confusion, but private acts of reading seemed also to have grave public consequences. The novelist Paul Bourget claimed, for example, that Stendhal's *Le Rouge et le Noir* had caused an incurable moral poisoning among young people of his acquaintance,[51] and criminologists and doctors noted that suicides often were found with underlined copies of Goethe's *Werther* in their pockets. Such poison-by-novel could also spread beyond individuals to institutions. One magistrate worried that novelists (especially Zola) had fatefully vulgarized scientific material, particularly the tenets of criminal anthropology, spreading complicated philosophical doctrines among people ill-equipped to perceive the subtleties of the argument. He argued that even educated people could be seduced by the entertaining mise-en-scène that drove the novel's plot, and would fail to see the ways in which a vulgarization that weakened belief in the efficacy of free will could disarm society in its time of great peril.[52] Making the point even more directly, a legal critic observed that the minds of jurors had been irremediably contaminated by exposure to intellectual currents they could not assimilate:

All the ideas of the century are introduced so as to reflect in a troubled mirror. The school, the army, the novel, and the newspaper have acted on the minds [of jurors] so that they carry within themselves all the philosophical doubts that lawyers or experts can awaken. . . . Today, with the jumble of systems, with vulgarized theories spreading everywhere, announcing the fateful persistence of atavistic traits, determinism, the corrupting influence of the social milieu, how is it possible for juries to declare with any serenity or assurance that this person is guilty?

In retaliation against this implied call for censorship, the literary critic Ferdinand Brunetière—disdaining the pretensions of jurists "who spoke of their science in the same terms as did physiologists and astronomers"—quipped that neither Rousseau nor Voltaire had looked to official authorities for permission to write about social organization![53]

The Chambige affair in 1886, however, seemed to confirm in particularly vivid detail the perils of novelistic suggestion. Mme Grille, a thirty-year-old mother and wife of a respected bourgeois functionary, was murdered at a villa near her Algerian home by her lover, twenty-two-year-old Henri Chambige, a minor literary figure who insisted that they had acted together in a double-suicide pact that had literally misfired. The ambiguities surrounding Chambige's story, the pristine reputation of Mme Grille, the disparity in ages between the alleged lovers, and the exotic ambiance and hint of sexual disorder all gave this case a high degree of visibility, inviting, in its suggestive disarray, the intervention of professional authorities to bring order to the story. Several experts focused on the medical aspects of the case—the apparent irrationality of Mme Grille's actions and the personal pathology that might have linked her to Chambige.[54] But other criminologists were quick to point to this event as "truly a literary crime."

These commentators understood the "facts" in a way that foregrounded Chambige's connection to literary circles. In their version of the affair, Chambige had been especially influenced by Taine's *Histoire de la littérature anglaise*. Of particular importance were Byron's reflections, recorded by Taine, that he "would be curious to experience the feelings that a man must have when he has just committed a murder." Shortly

HISTOIRE AFFLIGENTE DE DEUX AMANTS
ou suites funestes de la lecture des mauvais livres.

"The tragic story of two lovers; or, the deadly outcome of evil books," an illustration from the popular press.

before the crime, the argument concluded, Chambige had told friends that "he would like to experience the feelings of an assassin in order to analyze them."[55] Enhancing this literary allusiveness, Chambige, condemned to seven years of forced labor, wrote a prison autobiography in which he claimed, "I often told Mme Grille that people admired the lovers created by Alfred de Vigny who died together, that it would be a great beauty to die in this way, and that we would be admired."[56] Chambige became, in this interpretation, neither a cynical killer nor a man driven by an impossible passion, but rather the instrument of an artificial or imitative passion that was, at bottom, literary. By drawing out and brooding over these connections, contemporaries linked literary decadence to a cultural pathology that rendered reading dangerous for the most impressionable segments of the population.

Criminologists came to understand the effects of this seepage of criminal stories into popular venues as a problem of "contagion."[57] The presumed vectors of contagion were multiple: the family, tainted by bad heredity and a sordid environment; the collection of already susceptible people in milieus such as prisons where their latent tendencies would be activated; public spectacles, especially executions; and above all the popular press.[58] While the dangers of reading novels were worrisome, it was the sensational accounts of crime in the popular press that drew the most sustained concern. According to criminologists, these staple columns of the new popular journalism inevitably spawned copycat acts, a thesis they saw confirmed in the formulaic structure and pronounced fashionability of particular criminal behaviors.[59] In its daily recapitulation of criminal stories, the press allegedly became "the fuse that ignited explosives accumulated here and there." Macé reported, for example, a case that became the archetypal anecdote animating discussions of crime and the press. In 1877 in the village of Carmaux, a young dressmaker had been seduced by a miner. When he refused to marry her although she was pregnant with his child, she blinded him with vitriol. At the criminal hearing, the presiding magistrate questioned: "Your imagination had undoubtedly been exalted by unhealthy reading. Did you read novels?" The defendant replied: "No, monsieur, I never read them; but I saw the story of a young woman who took vengeance in this way in a newspaper. It is that which gave me the idea to do as much."[60] Lest the message be lost, Macé commented that "imagination can have terrible consequences." Crime becomes here the product of imagination; they are causally linked through the medium of the press.

This recurring anxiety about the problem of contagion was fueled by the enormous growth of the reading public in the final decades of the century and the parallel expansion of the newspaper industry, which by 1880 produced 67 daily newspapers in Paris alone, with a circulation of slightly more than two million.[61] Between 1880 and 1914, the golden age of the popular press, criminal stories appeared not only in novels and specialized journals such as the *Gazette des Tribunaux*, but in the faits divers and romans feuilletons of hundreds of daily newspapers that sold for one sou apiece.[62] The fait divers had its origin in the *canards* of the first half of the century—broadsheets hawked by street venders who shouted out the latest details of extraordinary crimes or scandalous or curious events.[63] Successful *canardiers* began to collect several stories in one brochure, a format soon copied by owners of the daily and weekly press, who sought to replicate a winning formula. The earliest papers, *Faits divers* (1862) and *Le Journal illustré* (1863) provided the model for a rapidly expanding market. By the 1890s in Paris, both *Le Petit Journal* (with a readership between 300,000 and 500,000) and *Le Petit Parisien* published an illustrated Sunday supplement devoted to faits divers that were announced in multilined, sensational headlines and accompanied by colored illustrations designed to closely reproduce actual scenes.[64] Especially after 1870, these stories became both increasingly formulaic and bloodier: "A horrifying crime / six children assassinated / by their mother / and thrown in a cesspool"; "A crime without precedent!!! / a woman buried alive / by her children / horrible details"; "a terrifying crime!!! / a 60-year-old man cut in pieces . . . / horrible details!";[65] "A drama of madness / a mother who kills her child."[66] But stories less blatantly salacious also entertained because of their enigmatic and quirky juxtapositions of the expected and the unusual. Relying on paradox for its effect, the fait divers rejected the banal (a husband kills his unfaithful wife) in favor of a twist that made the story compelling: a husband murders his unfaithful wife while she prays in church.[67]

Serialized novels (romans feuilletons) addressed similar material on the bottom half of the page (the *rez-de-chaussée romanesque*) of these same newspapers.[68] Women typically read the installments aloud in the concierge's loge, and often removed the daily episodes from the newspaper and assembled them in homemade books they shared with neighbors and friends.[69] The fait divers and the roman feuilleton made use of similar rhetorical patterns; they depended on an element of surprise to achieve their effects, and addressed similar themes in a language they had made familiar, inflected by strings of adjectives and epithets. Both genres reduced the distance between the events of the story and the audience, mobilizing the reader's attention and participation through the deferred resolution of the plot. In fact, crimes reported in the faits divers often read like romans feuilletons, ending with the expected formula: "the sequel to follow in the next edition." Both the faits divers and the romans feuilletons worked through what Anne-Marie Thiesse has called a socially defined intertextuality in which everything referred to a prior set of references.[70] Readers were encouraged to experience the pleasure of reencountering the familiar under the apparent differences of the surface details of stories that were, in effect, *récits types*.[71] They intentionally blurred the line between real and fictional events, mixing elements of each so as to create a stock of characters and situations that emerged through well-understood, shared assumptions about motivation, causality, and outcome. Critics were not wrong in their perception of an emerging popular culture that appealed through its combination of the familiar and the shocking—an appeal that could become dangerously "contagious."

In the face of the disruptive potential of unsupervised interpretation—of placing pieces of cultural information in the public domain—one self-proclaimed arbiter argued for moving criminal matters behind closed doors, protecting "justice" from the contamination of the crowd as medicine had used antisepsis to prevent contagion:

[Unlike medicine], justice, which ought to be a social medicine, seems to take great pleasure in leaving wide open all its chambers where one ought to be curing the patient who is the criminal, so that the flood of human curiosity comes to disturb it, so that it is blown about by all the passions, and, finally, so that all the microbes of crime escape to poison the environment, thanks to the press who disclose and disseminate them like pollen—to fertilize other crimes throughout the world.[72]

The solution seemed to be the reporting of criminal activity in summary only, deleting all salacious detail. The press was asked repeatedly to censor itself. In an impassioned speech to the International Congress Against Immoral Literature and the Dangerous Publicity of Criminal Events, the physician Paul Aubry concluded with a heady image of the dismantling of feudalism in 1789: "Let us have our night of August 4; let us spontaneously renounce our *Gazette des Tribunaux* in its criminal sections, and you will see that your circulation . . . will not decline as you dedicate your talents to a more noble enterprise."[73]

These anxieties had not abated more than a decade later when the failure of self-censorship produced a more extreme effort to restrict the circulation of criminal stories. The Violette law, passed by the Chamber in 1910, established fines of 500 to 1000 francs for the publication of drawings or portraits related to crimes (against life, property, and public morality) that had occurred during the preceding ten years, or the reproduction of details about these crimes from the pretrial investigation, the judgment, or the sentencing. The same penalties applied to the reproduction in posters or leaflets distributed freely on public thoroughfares of similar but imagined crimes. At a meeting of the section on moral and criminal psychology of the Institut Général Psychologique, members voted unanimously to support the passage of this law, confirming the dangers of mental contagion for susceptible people in unsupervised or unhealthy milieus, and arguing that, in light of these grave conditions, it was "the duty of men who had, in their careers, acquired a special competence in these questions to publicly offer their disinterested opinion."[74]

While some criminologists argued that everyone was vulnerable to the power of morbid suggestion, that even "the most virtuous person has locked within himself a sleeping criminal," the more typical worry was that the wrong people were reading criminal stories.[75] Those with particular vulnerabilities to the "solicitation to imitation" were individuals "predisposed" to suggestion by either a hereditary or acquired susceptibility, "a particular semimorbid impressionability" in people with weakened capacities of resistance. In another version, those most likely to be driven to homicide by suggestion (or contagion) were sick individuals in whose illness "the instinctive, sentimental, passionate element was more significant than in a merely intellectual disorder."[76] The language here, while coded, is in fact transparent. Those individuals who succumbed irresistibly to criminal suggestion were not the ones who peopled the serene and severe halls of science, were not competent and capable (bourgeois, professional) men of probity and discernment. They were, rather, the worrisome groups—workers and especially women—who, according to standard, unquestioned presumptions of the period, were likely to lose control; to be erratic, overexcited; in whom instinctive responses predominated over intellectual ones; in whom the will had become feeble through faulty biology or moral lassitude or both; who were more likely to respond to "unhealthy incitements, antialtruistic and antisocial suggestions."

Commentators on female criminality typically discussed women's use of vitriol and the revolver in the 1880s and 1890s in terms of fads generated by women's reading. They also saw bourgeois sexual morality threatened by the unconventional, if not criminal behaviors allegedly sanctioned in novels whose audience was largely female:

There are women who are adulteresses in their dreams before becoming so in fact. The fall of the soul is a long one, with the exception of the pathological case of a Messalina: they pass through a slow period of preparation and of evolution, during which the novel has a more or less clear and explicit influence, often playing the role of the Devil as Tempter.[77]

George Sand in particular came under fire. Her novels were condemned for undermining traditional marriage and, even more, for "exalting . . . the poetry of ill-matched unions and for ennobling the love between coachmen and *grandes dames*, which has contributed to throwing young women into the arms of their subalterns."[78] In a celebrated legal case, Mlle Lemoine was accused of killing the baby that she had conceived with her coachman. At her trial she blamed literature, claiming that the novels of George Sand, especially *Valentine*, had disturbed her spirit. The novel in question turned on the relationship between a peasant and a countess who was persuaded by the peasant that "it would be beautiful and noble to elevate a humble person and to bring joy to a worm in love with a star."[79] Criminologists rushed to confirm the link between literature, moral lapses, and crime. In the words of a lawyer before the criminal court of Aix: "Modesty is like the thread that holds all the pearls of a necklace; cut the thread, and all the pearls fall."[80] I have found virtually no references to men being led into adultery by novelistic suggestion; the fall-by-suggestion was apparently a danger to which women were particularly, if not exclusively, vulnerable. b/c she didn't read men's cases

A discussion of popular culture that appeared in the *Revue des Deux Mondes* in 1903 provides a more direct expression of this anxiety about the subversive effects on the most vulnerable sections of the population of a specifically literary contagion. The author, Maurice Talmeyr, began by noting the ubiquitous presence of the cheap press. He imagined returning from a ball at six or seven in the morning, viewing workers as they began their day's activities, carters pulling their wagons, concierges opening their doors:

We encounter the dairymen and the women carrying bread. And what do we notice? Everybody is reading the newspaper. And what are they reading? The feuilleton! . . . The newspaper is the *leifmotif* of the street. What does the assistant butcher do as he is waiting for orders? He reads the newspaper. What does the coachman do while he waits for a fare? He sits on his seat and reads the newspaper. Open the basket of the maidservant and you will find a newspaper.[81]

For this flâneur, the roman feuilleton had become the daily manna of "the crowd," creating a repertoire of classic stories that were, in his words, "not merely repeated, but hereditary," passed from generation to generation, producing a set of values and a cast of characters that constituted the popular imagination. Talmeyr worried about what he saw as a *virus anarchiste*—manifested in disrespect for religious figures, sympathy accorded the unmarried mother, glamour surrounding the criminal. For him, these themes from mass culture constituted a series of images that seemed to be passed through a deforming set of "coloring lenses"—in short, the world turned upside down; workers had become heroes in their own lives, displacing altogether *hommes du monde*. He closed with a warning: "The roman feuilleton is able to create that frightening thing that is *une mentalité populaire*. . . . It is said that the life of a man ends always in resembling his dreams. Will the life of the people end in resembling its fictions?"

It is not a coincidence that Talmeyr expressed his worries about the handing on of stories that were "not merely repeated, but hereditary" in terms of a transmission among females—from the grandmother to the mother who nourished her (worker-)daughter on these tales—as if the vector of subversion had become not the popular press but mothers' milk.[82] "There is not one person who comes in contact with the people who has not noticed," wrote another critic, "that the roman feuilleton performs the same ravages in women's brains, perhaps does even graver damage, than does alcohol in the brains of men."[83] Experts spoke of women as "more readily penetrated by the influences of their environment than were men," more suggestible, more easily swept away by the fantasies produced by urban glitz and less resistant to the lures of urban vice, more corruptible by literature, theater, and leisure than were men.[84] Medical opinion confirmed such beliefs and contributed to their currency. In his study on the contagion of crime, Dr. Séverin Icard emphasized the "decisive influence" that reading exercised on woman's spirit, especially in the dangerous moments of her reproductive cycle, and claimed unequivocally that women (and children, the feeble, the degenerate) ceded to the power of suggestion more readily than did men.[85] His study uses only examples of women's crimes committed through contagion or "imitation" (except for a brief discussion of imitation among animals, where he notes, for example, that when one cow aborts, all the pregnant cows begin to abort!). Finally, in a move that brings together all the elements of the alleged syndrome, he tells the story of a woman he was treating who had baffled the most experienced physicians with the variability and incoherence of her symptoms. Icard eventually discovered that her various diagnosed illnesses occurred in alphabetical order: his patient had been reading a dictionary of popular medicine that appeared in installments; as soon as she read the descriptions, she fell ill with the symptoms that had been offered up to her.[86] He has managed in this account to link the unspecified social dangers of popular culture (including the vulgarization of scientific material) to women's reading and finally, in the context of his essay, to crime, condensing a set of assumptions that led prosecutors regularly to inquire about the reading habits of female defendants.

In this critique of the democratization of culture, the theater was also construed as an especially pernicious site in its capacity to produce both passion and knowledge among those who were alleged to be more suggestible and less discriminating. Félix Moreau, professor at the law faculty of Aix, expressed a common complaint when he wrote that

of all the means for promoting an idea, perhaps the most powerful of our times is the theater. . . . Our dramatists are well aware of the authority at their disposal, and they seem to have given themselves a more pragmatic goal, a mission more profoundly social than the analysis of character and the depiction of passions which, until our day, had been the purpose of theater. They do not hesitate to express their opinions, implicitly or explicitly, on every social problem. It would not be entirely outrageous if, one day, the government should decide to submit its proposed legislation to an advisory commission selected from among the masters of the theater rather than from the Council of State![87]

Citing the "distortion" of professional knowledge disseminated through this unfortunate mingling of law and drama, Moreau concluded that playwrights "ought not to interfere" in realms that they understood only incompletely: "*chacun son métier.*"[88] Not surprisingly, such claims for professional monopoly made no sense to more literary types. Balzac, Hugo, Dumas fils, and the Goncourt brothers all regularly visited (and commented on) the sessions of the Parisian criminal courts.[89]

It was the courtroom that in fact demonstrated most effectively the urgency of the problem of contagion in this period, because it was in the courtroom that the seepage of criminal stories into popular culture occurred most regularly, with the greatest visibility and élan. The Cour d'Assises had become flagrantly carnivalesque, its public benches filled by representatives of le grand monde, eating sandwiches, drinking champagne, and waiting for the drama to begin.[90] According to one commentator, the theater and the court generated similar expectations: the audience came to be entertained, to laugh, to weep, and to applaud. More and more, plays turning on amorous intrigues were performed in stage settings resembling the Cour d'Assises, while spectators in the criminal courtroom expected to be able to shout "Bravo!" at the end of the day.[91] The growing practice of correctionnalisation that sent cases to the lower courts, turning many crimes into misdemeanors and leaving the high court only the most "decorative crimes," seemed to confirm the entertainment function of the principal criminal court. One critic concluded that "France does not have, in reality, a criminal jurisdiction; what remains to her is a set, where, to the great benefit of judicial eloquence, several représentations de gala are played."[92] Noting the circuslike parade of witnesses and the lengthy oratorical duels, a commentator cynically observed that, as the twentieth century approached, for a case to become une belle affaire, it would have to have at least fifteen scenes in five acts.[93] To complete the image of dramas within dramas, we have only to listen to Maurice Garçon's description of a criminal court hearing:

Recently during a session of the Cour d'Assises, Alexander Dumas [fils] had taken a seat behind the Président to gravely watch the development of a crime of passion and to serve as a sort of sovereign arbiter; magistrates and jurors, desirous of being true Parisians, followed with great interest the signs of approval or disapproval that he was able to convey.[94]

It seemed that the justice of the Cour d'Assises had become "une justice théâtrale." Since the 1830s, popular theaters on the appropriately nicknamed Boulevard du Crime had made the criminal melodrama a standard genre, providing a well-established literary frame and set of references that participants brought with them to the courtroom. Criticizing judges who had become "literary psychologists," Garçon could claim with some validity that "the Parisian makes real the artist's fantasies."[95] In actual practice, the fashions of courtroom eloquence reinforced the elements of spectacle. During the July Monarchy, for example, hearings were formal and ceremonious, coldly solemn, characterized by a kind of grandiloquent prose punctuated with references to classical Greece. This style was gradually replaced by one clearly influenced by literary patterns drawn from Romanticism—including a reliance by the defense on the rhetorical gestures of interpellation, exclamation, and question and response, which foregrounded emotional effect at the expense of juridical analysis. This stylized presentation of a heated appeal on behalf of the client reached its most seductive articulation in the defense pleadings of Charles Lachaud, whose courtroom speech was recognized as the prototype of the widely imitated genre of "*l'éloquence criminelle*."[96] According to witnesses, Lachaud strove to establish an intimate communion with the jurors, holding them with his eyes, and working over with them, as if in collaboration on a common project, every resistance that they might have to his arguments until he believed that he had won their assent. An acknowledged master of psychology, he manipulated with considerable success the drama taking place in the courtroom itself, even as he addressed the dramatic developments that had brought his client and his audience together.

The trial of Marie Bière in 1880 provided a particularly vivid example of theatrical justice, demonstrating not only the performance standards of the courtroom, but the heightened emotional transactions among all the scripted and unscripted characters—court personnel, witnesses, and an audience that included Alexander Dumas (fils) along with several members of the aristocracy.[97] Marie Bière, a young lyric singer and actress, had been seduced by Robert Gentien, a wealthy *homme galant* who had fathered her child. He broke off their affair after the child's birth, refusing paternity, refusing even to look at the child, and, in an ultimate disavowal following the child's death, refusing to attend her funeral. Several months later Marie Bière exacted her vengeance; she shot Gentien twice in the back as he walked in the street with his new mistress. The case had more than enough elements to make it the stuff of popular melodrama: Bière had been chaste before her liaison with Gentien, uncharacteristically resisting the bohemian life of the theater; Gentien had urged her to have an abortion, but her maternal instincts had prevailed; a cache of passionate love correspondence survived and became part of the court record; before her vengeful attack, Bière had attempted suicide at her lover's feet; and, finally, Charles Lachaud would plead for the defense, bringing all of his rhetorical passion to Marie Bière's assistance.

Not surprisingly, the conclusion faithfully followed the melodramatic script. Marie Bière was acquitted of attempted homicide; Gentien was forced to flee town in disgrace, amid vague threats of extradition. For our purposes, the most interesting aspects of the courtroom hearing emerge in the way judgments were made and opinions registered. The prosecutor opened with an argument in which he outlined the informal codes that permitted men to take and discard mistresses at will. His speech drew noisy disapproval from the audience, not only, or even especially, because of the particular morals of the *monde galant* that he invoked, but because his presentation had been so tasteless, so lacking in style or talent—"an attack always cold, dry and systematic"—in effect, nothing but a harangue.[98] Even more significant was the press's ultimate condemnation, not of Marie Bière, nor of Gentien, but of the prosecutor who had had the arrogance to pursue a conviction that was so far out of touch with public opinion. *La Lanterne* reported, for example, that "the jury, in acquitting Mlle Bière, had performed a useful service. . . . In contrast, the conduct of the prosecutor . . . as is merited, will be sharply condemned by all men of sensibility [*gens de cœur*]. This magistrate rested all his honor on obtaining the conviction of an unfortunate woman who had won such complete sympathy from the public."[99] According to witnesses, the verdict was read by sobbing jurors in the midst of general pandemonium, leading a more cynical spirit to suggest that the victorious defendant be canonized as Sainte Marie, patron saint of gunsmiths, to whom abandoned women might make pilgrimages to have their revolvers blessed.[100] This ironic voice notwithstanding, Marie Bière had won in the courtroom the celebrity that she had sought, unsuccessfully, in the theater; she had become "the heroine of Paris." A crowd estimated at three thousand people waited in the street for the verdict; they nearly overturned her carriage as she was carried in triumph to her home where she held an audience for journalists from all the major Paris newspapers.

The case of Marie Bière brings into focus the dual implications of the problem of female criminality in the fin-de-siècle—highlighting contested domestic issues and shifting standards in private life on the one hand, and the newly powerful effects of popular opinion on practices and institutions in the public sphere on the other. In providing a glimpse of sexual and social transgressions (embroidered by romantic poetry and private correspondence), it offered both compelling entertainment and an opening for discussions of codes of sexual morality and social relations between men and women. In its confrontation between the dramatic Lachaud and the phlegmatic prosecutor (appropriately witnessed by Dumas), the case confirmed the link between literary conventions and the unfolding drama of the courtroom. And as the criminal drama of the courtroom-as-theater played out the drama of the crime, fundamental values and practices were placed before the court of public opinion. Most important, Marie Bière's diary, which had been transcribed by judicial officials and incorporated into the trial record, had become the authoritative source that shaped accounts of the crime and won popular opinion to her side. By granting her perceptions and emotional responses such extraordinary public exposure, the defense had, perhaps inadvertently, called into question the exclusive rights of jurists to tell their own story.

In the triumphant acquittal that vindicated the attempted homicide, the Bière case ultimately raised the issue of authority: Who should interpret the criminal act? What was the effect of Marie Bière's positioning of herself as a romantic heroine, or of her own voice becoming the source of the story's popular appeal? What was the relation between institutional justice and popular opinion? Did popular opinion reflect a consciousness that was essentially literary? Who would be the heroes and heroines in the emerging social order? And what would be the consequences of affirming Marie Bière's right to vengeance? In commenting on the increase of crime in relation to cases such as Bière's, one legal scholar addressed these issues directly, claiming that it was the court's failure to punish offenders and not literary suggestion that caused crime; he argued that the crisis was not generated by romantic literature but by the failure of authority.[101] We might insist that the authority in question was both institutional and literary, involving not only the formal power to punish or excuse, but also the emerging ability of popular opinion to establish meaning—a power that could make Marie Bière a heroine.

Bourgeois authorities were clearly worried about their ability to preserve a domain of professional authority immune to the contamination of public opinion. Ironically, however, while professionals saw their expertise compromised by popular accounts spread about indiscriminately through a literary and social contagion, they were in part responsible both for the seepage of this material into popular culture and for the slippage between popular and scientific writing. A striking example of this slippage is evident in the special genre of memoirs written by former chiefs of police. Although Goron described his reminiscences as "*photographies sociales*," "true stories, without retouching," they were produced and packaged precisely like Eugène Sue's serialized novel *Les Mystères de Paris*, with the four massive volumes originally appearing in 10-centime illustrated-pamphlet installments. Similarly, even as Macé simulated scientific authenticity, collecting in his *musée criminel* the *actual* gun fired, the *actual* hanging cords that figured in various causes célèbres, his critics lamented the literary pretensions that led him to "mix the personalities of the roman feuilleton with the sad figures, all too real, whom he had interrogated, imagining a theatrical setting for these stories" and creating, not the unadorned, mundane world inhabited by common criminals, but rather the thousand-and-one Parisian nights or "les Mystères de Paris naturalistes."[102]

Seemingly oblivious to the paradox, criminological studies endlessly repeated the sordid details of sensational cases even as they ritually condemned prurient interest in crime, soon producing a stock of familiar criminal lore and a long list of infamous causes célèbres that were so well known as to become reference points in both high and low cultural forms. In what Peter Stallybrass and Allon White have described as a characteristic ambivalence toward "the low" that pervades nineteenth-century reformist literature—an ambivalence that pushed reformers to make central the socially marginal—criminologists fused fear and desire.[103] This literature of social science conveyed simultaneously a repugnance and a fascination that inflected discussions of fearful Others—the slum dweller, the domestic servant, the prostitute, the criminal—who inhabited bourgeois imaginations as much as they populated bourgeois urban spaces. Criminologists themselves seemed only vaguely or intermittently aware of the ambiguities of their project. Despite Sighele's denial of "vulgar curiosity" and references to the "severe and serene halls of science," professional discussions of "the self [*le moi*]" in its criminal form teetered dangerously on the edge of voyeurism. Police chief Goron described his own memoirs as an effort to "raise the roofs of the houses of the capital" so as to permit a view (or a peek?) at the "human perversity" inside,[104] while a skeptic wondered rhetorically if one could attribute Macé's revelations, "his desire to see all and to know all," to something other than professional duty.[105] In ironic self-recognition, Macé dedicated one of his many publications, framed as nocturnal walks through the hidden sites of Parisian debauchery, to "the most spiritual of Prefects of Police of the Third Republic."[106] Describing somewhat more explicitly the fantasmatic component of this investigatory enterprise, Sighele wrote:

We want to savor the psychological convulsions, the agonies and the tortures, the surrenderings and the treacheries of the soul of the guilty; and we find in the summaries in newspapers, in books that rummage in the most secret abysses of the lives of criminals with the cold and lucid impassibility of a scalpel, not only the satisfaction of our curiosity, but a strange emotion that is at once egoist and feline.[107]

Another prison investigator expressed a similar compulsion, but revealed rather more explicitly some of his own ambivalence as he yielded to curiosity:

There is a sort of complex and mysterious attraction, arising at once from the overwhelming taste that we all have to a greater or lesser extent for the horrible, the abnormal, and the monstrous, from the morbid pustule which leads us to scratch and rub away at badly healed wounds and to find in this strange habit I don't know what sort of treacherous pleasure, and finally from the confused belief in the enormous social importance of a problem that would perhaps be immediately dangerous to leave unresolved.[108]

Reassuring themselves with a sense of the urgency of their tasks and pushing aside the "confusion" about the nature of their own engagement, the new social scientists who sought to extend their authority were, then, both victims and perpetrators of this unsettling mixing of genres that blurred distinctions between the stories produced by and for a mass audience and the more specialized knowledges of the professions.

Criminological and more literary or popular texts existed in a kind of symbiosis, each reinforcing the conclusions of the other with little regard to differences between the "truths" of science and the creations of art. Stendhal in *Le Rouge et le Noir*, Flaubert in *Madame Bovary*, and Zola in *La Bête humaine* fictionalized stories they had found in faits divers.[109] Confusing the territory further, convicted criminals such as Mme Lafarge and Lacenaire wrote memoirs that became best-sellers. But this sliding between fact and fiction in literary works is perhaps less telling than the erasing of distinctions that regularly characterized "empirical" criminological studies. In fact, the credo articulated by Zola in explaining the naturalist novel could as readily have been the protocol for professional criminologists:

The novelist starts out in search of a truth . . . he starts from known facts; then he makes his experiment, and exposes [the character] to a series of trials, placing him amid certain surroundings in order to exhibit how the complicated machinery of his person works. . . . The problem is to know what such passion acting in such a surrounding and under such circumstances would produce from the point of view of an individual and of society. . . . Finally you possess knowledge of the man, scientific knowledge of him, in both his individual and his social relations.[110]

Scientific experts wrote of vengeful women and unnatural mothers as Medeas, sexually suspicious women as modern Messalinas, finding in these ancient prototypes models that explained the "complicated machinery" of contemporary deviants. In Sighele's study of morbid psychology, he explored the dependencies that led two people to enact a crime by calling upon literary precursors—Iago and Othello, Heloise and Abelard—and he invoked Balzac and Hugo to confirm his empirical findings.

It is useful here to look more closely at Sighele's text to see how this particular kind of elision worked. He began with a lesson from Balzac: "The humanity of the courtesan," says Balzac, "consists of splendors that lift her to the angels." Sighele glossed this truth: "In effect, some of the most noble sentiments, that of motherhood, for example, sometimes are manifest in the prostitute in their most sublime form." He concluded by citing Parent-Duchatelet's scientific study of prostitution: "In tears, a prostitute told me [reports Parent-Duchatelet] that it was the dignity of motherhood that revealed to her the abjection into which she had fallen."[111] In the structure of this story, Sighele has inserted himself between literary and social-scientific truths.

In this search for verification, the expert could also move in the opposite direction—that is, from social science to literature. This directional shift is evident, for example, in Sighele's acount of a case reported by Macé. A pimp was arrested in 1885 for beating his prostitute and was sent to jail for six months. Macé noted that during this period the prostitute continued to help the pimp in every way that she could and was waiting for him on his release. The explanation that Sighele offered for this story—alleged confirmation of the empirical evidence—came first from the Goncourts and then from George Sand. He concluded that prostitutes prove the aphorism of the Goncourts that "women experience in love a passionate desire to grovel," or, in Sand's terms, "love is a state of voluntary servitude to which women aspire by nature."[112] Literary evidence and empirical "fact" merged, in this analysis, to produce the knowledge of the expert. The references to literature provided the language that confirmed older stereotypes, bringing them into discussions of more modern perils where, once invoked, they simultaneously attested to professional competence while undercutting the exclusive authority of the professional.

In the end, the search for truth that began with "known facts" and sought to establish the "complicated machinery of the person"—a search pursued by both naturalist novelists and empirical scientists—did produce a knowledge of character "types" who moved in familiar ways through conventional scenarios. But at the same time, the popularization of criminal stories raised new issues that destabilized the conclusions of science and produced unexpected ambiguities. Episodes such as the trial of Marie Bière brought home with particular force the subversive possibilities of criminal stories that had become more accessible through their literary allusions and more familiar by their diffusion in the popular press. Not only actual criminal cases (reported in professional and more popular formats) but also faits divers and serialized novels featured new kinds of social actors who challenged both customary assumptions and legal practices.

In 1882, for example, a fait divers entitled "L'Eau forte" (Vitriol) raised issues that could not be readily resolved by the knowledge of experts.[113] This was the story of Julie and Benjamin, who had lived together for four years. According to the narrator, when Julie gave birth to their daughter, she was forced to register the birth with the sad inscription "father unknown." Although Julie begged Benjamin to honor the promise of marriage that he had "so ardently made" before the pregnancy, he abandoned her and moved to another city. Julie brought a successful suit against him in civil court and was awarded 1,000 francs in damages. The court acknowledged that "her conduct had been unimpeachable except for the seduction of which she was the victim," that "she continued to be held in high esteem in her region," and that the promise of marriage had been valid. From the narrator's perspective, Julie's credentials were in order. She brought forth letters addressed to her father in which Benjamin promised marriage and referred to her as "his dear wife." According to the court, its decision to protect the honor of the victim and support the interests of the child was "a charitable act of justice and morality." Forcing the plot forward, Benjamin continued to flee. When Julie found him in Paris and asked him either to marry her or give her money, he responded that she could go walk the streets (*faire le trottoir*). Finding herself without recourse, Julie attacked Benjamin with vitriol as he left his workshop, wounding him slightly. Julie was arrested; Benjamin brought a civil suit for damages. He was awarded 100 francs by the civil court, and Julie was condemned by the criminal court to eight months in prison.

Condensed in this fait divers are a set of issues that refer to social codes and their violation—to women's disadvantages in both custom and law, and to the inability of traditional institutions to regulate domestic life, ensure public order, or render justice. It presents a liminal world without stable standards or effective authority, indirectly evoking the unsettled

conditions of contemporary culture. Like Marie Bière's case, it implicitly pointed to unclear rights in domestic conflicts between men and
women at the same time that it presented a challenge to formal and customary authority, enacted by new social actors (often represented as violent women) and supported by shifting popular beliefs. In reflecting on
stories like this one, professional experts and cultural critics wondered
along with Talmeyr whether the life of the people would end in resembling its fictions; whether traditional authorities could resist the subversive
effects of a wide-ranging, free-wheeling popular culture; and even
whether women were being forced, under contemporary circumstances,
to exact private justice.

Talmeyr's critique of the roman feuilleton suggested that "the people" had become "the living repository of all sanctities, of all genius, of all
sublimity." But what Talmeyr anxiously assumed as a fact or outcome
was, I am arguing, an issue that remained unresolved; more important
than the specific effects of individual stories about ordinary or dangerous characters was the space opened for a discussion of contemporary
culture. Criminal stories pointed to problems—people who did not fit,
values that seemed dangerous, behaviors that threatened conventional
standards, conflicts (invisible and unacknowledged) between groups, institutions that perhaps were not working. How would these problems be
addressed in a mass society? Criminal stories had become the lightning
rod that gathered the social and cultural tensions of the period. They implicitly asked questions about the relation between classes and sexes. They
brought to public attention the problems of unmarried mothers and seduced and abandoned working women. They provided a vehicle for a
discussion of adultery, of the rights of women in marriage, of unregulated sexuality, of cross-class alliances; they raised the question of how
public authorities could contain the passions that threatened social peace.
But they did not offer solutions. Rather than moving toward resolution
or closure, criminal stories advanced a negotiation centering on the tension between formal authority and customary practices. The slippage between fact and fiction in criminal stories and the rehearsal of these stories
in popular and scientific formats signal shifts in accepted understandings
of social and cultural codes, as well as efforts within diverse communities
to reimagine social relations, to retrieve an elusive stability, and to set
new standards.

In contrast to the worried responses of late-nineteenth-century critics like Talmeyr, more recent studies of popular genres have tended to

see them as essentially conservative. Michelle Perrot, for example, has dubbed the proliferation of sensational stories in the popular press "the colonization of the popular imaginary."[114] From this point of view, criminal stories may be understood as essentially strategic—part of an attempted solution to both the problem of crime and the crisis in authority that worked to draw the popular classes into mainstream culture. Emphasizing this conservative function, Perrot notes that in place of the decentralized and serendipitous publication of stories by *canardiers* who wrote and rewrote their accounts in response to their street audiences in the first half of the century, these same stories were later written by journalists employed by mass-circulation newspapers. In this milieu such stories allegedly became implicated in a broader campaign to attach the popular classes to the republican order; they became propaganda vehicles to form the republican citizen.[115] The *rez-de-chaussée romanesque* (the bottom half of the page devoted to stories) served, then, as one component of the larger integrative functions of the daily press. According to this analysis, the very act of cordoning off the abnormal, of locating crime at once on the margins of the society and within specific entertainment columns of the press, would define ever more clearly the province of the normal. And the satisfaction of symbolically breaching the constraints of ordinary life, of entering imaginatively into the realm of the deviant and the defiant, might confirm the very order that was temporarily and fictively undermined—vicarious experience called in to substitute for the real thing.

Critics who emphasize the conservative impact of popular genres also note that the structure of these popular stories encouraged conventional ways of social seeing. Such stories sought to evoke emotional effects through an appeal to universal truths, eternal values, stable and permanent meanings, and normative assumptions about cause and effect—that which goes without saying—that was largely insulated from a particular historical context. Roland Barthes has made this point in describing the fait divers as a closed structure that refers to nothing outside of itself. He compares this self-contained story to a report of an assassination that he designates, conversely, as *news*—that is, political—because "it fits into an extensive situation outside of itself, previous to and around it, . . . the manifest term of an implicit structure which exists before it. . . . Like the fragment of a novel, it is partial information."[116] In contrast, he argues, the fait divers, more like the short story, is complete. This very pretension to closure releases the story from its historical moment and allows the fiction to operate in a space that it claims as neutral or eternal, certainly not political—producing sociological categories and psychological types stretched out in a dehistoricized space. This closure and self-containment serves to obscure the immediate context and the possibility of multiple or contradictory interpretations.

Although it is possible to imagine such essentially conservative effects, I am arguing that it is more likely that the impact of popular criminal stories was multivalent, neither conservative in the ways described by Perrot and Barthes nor directly subversive as critics at the time imagined. Studies in mass culture have demonstrated that popular groups can make use of ritualized and literary opportunities for transgression to articulate alternative meanings, challenges to cultural authorities and practices.[117] And recent work in literary criticism has shown how inevitably unreliable ideological appeals to the imagination are; how meaning that is created through an interaction between readers and texts can be monitored neither by ideology nor authorial intention.[118] We cannot assume that the invocation of eternal truths and fixed character types reflected the beliefs of readers; I must argue quite the opposite possibility. The very structure of these texts, relying as they did on surprise and a certain disruption of expectations about causality, surely encouraged imaginative license. Thus, while these formulaic stories did attempt to promote conventional ways of social seeing in a format that implicitly confirmed the norm, they also were responsible for more ambiguous cultural outcomes—opening a space not only for alternative readings but, more important, for an extended negotiation around new and pressing tensions within the culture. Even as the faits divers and romans feuilletons presumed a neutral context, detached from and unencumbered by the political, readers of these stories clearly inhabited imaginative and material universes informed by both politics and culture.

In sum, late-nineteenth-century efforts to cure the contagion of crime were responses to a *question mal posée*. In the end, the various forms of criminal stories neither guaranteed bourgeois values nor undermined bourgeois society.[119] Criminologists and other professionals hoped to claim interpretive authority as they used these stories to construct and consolidate their expertise. But accounts told by scientific experts did not remain finally authoritative, immune from popular revision and appropriation and insulated from literary and journalistic tampering. The popular/literary and scientific versions of criminal stories were, finally, overlapping and inseparable, producing not any particular truth about crime or criminals but rather engaging a wide audience in ongoing negotiations over a set of implicit questions posed by the fact of crime.

The literature on contagion explicitly made the connection between the problem of cultural authority and female criminality. On the one hand, criminologists connected women's crimes to their suggestible predispositions and to their reading, linking female nature to cultural and social anarchy and symbolizing the danger of the lower classes in the eruption of sensational acts by women who copied each other's criminal behavior. Women's crime seemed to represent the most worrisome consequences of mass literacy and democracy, in which traditional patterns were fatally compromised by a kind of *virus anarchiste* spread through the organs of mass culture. If women were the mirrors in which society could recognize itself, then the contagion of women's crime and all that it represented could not be ignored. Because of its dramatic character, its symbolic valences, and the wide press coverage that made women like Marie Bière and Mme Grille national figures, female criminality became the material and discursive site where bourgeois authorities could attempt to address the problem of mass culture as they sought to secure their professional authority and cure the syndrome of modernity.

On a second level, female crime and the stories it generated pointed to specific problems that were moving from the realm of private domestic life into explicitly public arenas. Jacques Kayser has aptly described the effect of the popular press on fin-de-siècle culture as "the fait diversification of the political sphere,"[120] a process that turned politics into stories and engaged a mass audience in discussions of public questions that were rendered immediate and intensely personal by their representation through familiar rhetorical codes and melodramatic plots. It seems evident that the press could as readily turn stories into politics. Women who pursued their seducers and demanded retribution from the fathers of their children suggested both women's economic vulnerabilities and the inadequacies in the legal codes and practices that regulated women's rights in domestic and public life. Women charged with infanticide and abortion in effect produced a discourse that paralleled and promoted public discussions of depopulation and its links to laws that prohibited women from initiating paternity suits. Women who shoplifted in department stores raised questions about female autonomy, economic dependency, and the uses of new public spaces. Female violence that turned on adultery and betrayal generated and reflected growing dissatisfaction among reformers with the provisions in the civil code that regulated marriage. In the domestic dramas recounted in women's crimes, the female offender documented shifting popular opinions about such issues as the responsibilities of paternity, standards (double ones) for judging adultery, and the social codes that governed heterosexual relations. These criminal dramas mobilized popular sentiment around issues of private life that were beginning to attract more public attention.

As a double anomaly—someone who had violated both the legal and gender codes—and as the quintessential symbol of the problems presented by a new popular culture, the criminal woman was a titillating figure, positioned dangerously on the cusp of cultural change. Female criminals—as objects of investigation, as subjects of literature and the popular press, and as defendants passing through the criminal justice system— drew public attention to instabilities and uncertainties in contemporary life. Like the hysteric, the female criminal posed the enigma of herself. And like the hysteric, she dramatized for popular and expert audiences a range of issues that pointed not only to questions about women's nature but to issues that would animate the contemporary public arena. The criminal woman was identified as a problem, then, not because of increasing rates of crime, nor even because she was scarier or more disturbing than her male counterpart, but because she was positioned at the center of transitions that would define the character and culture of Third Republic France.

TELLING CRIMINAL STORIES

There is in female murderers in general a thoroughly delightful
mixture of poetry and arsenic, of sentimentalism and rat poison.
Restif de la Bretonne, *Les Gynographes*, 1777

The French word *histoires* translates, with felicitous ambiguity, as histories,
stories, tales, idle stories, falsehoods, sexual affairs, trifles. *Faire des histoires*—literally, "to make stories" (or even "to make histories")—means,
more idiomatically, "to make a fuss." Embracing the conceptual latitude
opened by this intriguing set of possibilities, I want to examine more
closely some of the stories told about female crime in the context of different modes of telling, "making a fuss" in order to explore the relationship between the telling, the story, and the meanings thereby derived.
This chapter is essentially about translation—the processes that interpreted behavior and conveyed the meaning of written and oral texts—and
about the move, rhetorical and social, from trifles and sexual affairs
through falsehoods, idle stories, and tales to the writing of a history, to
making sense of experience.

As we have seen, criminal stories were told within a cultural frame
informed by diverse social values and expectations; they were inflected by
literary images drawn from high and low culture and by the writing of
bourgeois professionals (criminologists, magistrates, lawyers, forensic psychiatrists). In the construction of the official accounts of crimes presented
in the courtroom, the stories were ultimately orchestrated by the structures of the penal process itself (the pretrial investigations, the formal
documents of the judicial dossier, the hearing). These stories, presented to
juries and popularized through the press, were received by diverse audiences who understood them within particular conditions that gave the
stories their credibility. We have, then, not only different kinds of interpreters but different tellings that were produced in different contexts.

If we examine the various representations of the female criminal, we
can begin to fill in the details of a process through which gender stereotypes were constructed, confirmed, and deployed, invoking and build-

ing upon what Michèle Ouerd has called "the persistent fantasies and formulaic nightmares" that inform discourses about the deviant woman.[1] Although sometimes perceptive and occasionally subtle, these writings made sense largely because they represented reality through stereotyped literary and cultural conventions that had wide currency.[2] They reinvigorated myths about women that set the narrative frame for the official courtroom tellings of criminal stories. It is not coincidental that bills of indictment and popular retellings of crimes were so formulaic—strikingly similar in their presentation of motivation and their plot development.

But stories, including those broadly credible within the culture, always exist in tension with other stories.[3] Even within the dominant classes the discourse about criminal women was not homogeneous; most important, female defendants themselves told stories that contradicted the official versions constructed through the judicial process. While some accused women read their scripts perfectly, repeating in their self-presentation the familiar conventions that organized perceptions of women's criminal acts, they did not always do so. Defendants sometimes told defiantly oppositional stories—accounts that specifically called into question the assumptions and conclusions of their accusers; others merely refused to assent to the official version of the crime. Interrogations collected in the judicial dossiers, accounts presented at the hearings of the Cour d'Assises, and their reproduction in the press speak to the coexistence of a multiplicity of stories, attesting to the impossibility of a unified, coherent, or finally authoritative version. The history of the telling of criminal stories must then be the history of stories-in-tension.

With a new attention to the effects of narrative, legal scholars have recently begun to explore "the perceptual fault lines" that inform criminal stories and to expose, in the deeply patterned activity of legal storytelling, the ways that the ideology of dominant groups passes for neutrality.[4] For some, the cure for the intrusions of ideology is to invoke counterhegemonic narratives that expose the assumptions embedded in and produced through the legal process itself. I am arguing, in contrast, that it is too simple to decontextualize the negotiation between accused and accusers, too simple to frame the negotiation as between two opposing interpretive communities. In fact, boundaries between communities are inevitably culturally porous. The dominant culture is neither fixed and static nor impervious to influences from below; or, put in reverse terms, more marginal groups are neither colonized by nor immune to the messages circulating within the dominant culture. It is more useful, then, to think about culture as an arena of exchange and about story-telling in particular as an interactive process among differently positioned people, while acknowledging the inequalities that structure the reception and diffusion of particular narratives. The production of criminal stories through the judicial process provides an unusually vivid site for an examination of this kind of cultural intersection.

It is my intention here to bring together the cultural myths, official accounts, and alternative/oppositional stories that were joined to produce narratives of women's crime in order to examine what Arlette Farge has called the "multiple inflections of history":[5] the production of cultural meanings, the circulation of stories within different constituencies, and the circumstances and institutional practices that made particular stories authoritative, effective in social and cultural terms. We need to look not only at the way stories were produced but also at the way different kinds of stories achieved or failed to achieve cultural weightiness. In this way, we will be able to see something of the cultural field that endowed particular stories with credibility and to suggest the necessary conditions that enabled alternative or contradictory stories to be voiced and heard.

In her perceptive study of eighteenth-century crime, Farge has warned of the seduction of the judicial archive, of its ability to generate illusion. Through its recovery of the forgotten or neglected details of ordinary life, of "the exceptional normal" made visible in criminal behaviors, we are led, she argues, to give both too much and too little weight to these "pieces of the real." In the end, Farge concludes, we must see the voices of the archives as speaking within a system of power relations that governs the production of discourse, revealing not any specific truth about their subjects but rather the imbrication of private and official worlds in a way that produces these particular conversations.[6] Following Farge's insight, I am arguing that the criminal story emerged through a kind of enforced collaboration between accused and accusers. The defendant passed through police interrogations, which were followed over a period of months by extensive questioning by the *juge d'instruction*, the prosecuting lawyer charged with compiling the state's case; finally, she appeared in court where she was interrogated by the presiding magistrate, the *président de la cour*. In each of these settings, the different modes of examining elicited different kinds of responses and different types of information. At each level, different (and sometimes random) principles governed the inclusion or withholding of pieces of the story. And at each level, contradictions might be resolved, ignored, or suppressed. There was not, then, a single or even a linear story for any individual case. The dossiers are themselves anarchic, presenting not only the interactions between defendant and interrogators but also the depositions of numerous collateral parties that were equally contradictory and inconclusive. What we can examine, then, are the processes that produced an official version of the crime and the disparate voices that contributed to this account.

The judicial dossiers of the Cour d'Assises included: reconstructed accounts of the initial police interrogations of the accused and all witnesses; transcribed accounts of three interrogations of the defendant by the prosecutor preparing the state's case; the depositions of witnesses, including family, neighbors, and employers; medical and forensic reports; and all responses (by mayors, local police, justices of the peace) to official queries about the moral history of the defendant and her family. The prosecution's case was summarized in two final official documents, the *requisitoire définitif* (final charges) and the *acte d'accusation* (indictment). The indictment was more than a formal statement of charges. By selection, omission, and emphasis, it announced the state's conclusions. In theory, the bringing of a case to court meant that there was sufficient cause to believe that the accused might have committed a crime. But in practice, and in contrast to the Anglo-Saxon system, the presumption of guilt was even greater. The recommendation of an indictment by the preliminary investigation carried with it the assumption that the defendant was guilty until proven otherwise.[7]

It was, in fact, the language and plot presented in these official narratives that situated a particular crime within a credible system of meaning. In compiling the pretrial investigation, the prosecutor built his case by choosing the details, elaborating "hierarchies of relevance and centrality," that framed the story and identified the behavior and motivation as criminal.[8] Because the indictment was read in the courtroom, it was extremely influential in shaping responses to the case. By invoking conventional narrative and social codes, it not only interpreted criminal acts and situated behavior in contexts that were familiar, but also promoted particular story lines that conveyed the desired social judgments most effectively. According to one critic who noted the already interpreted information of the indictment, "It is a summary that the law wanted; it is a novel that was substituted."[9]

Indictments typically began with a capsule assessment of the character of the defendant, based especially on a summary review of past behavior. Women were either *honnête* (respectable, honorable, with no sexual history to report) or characterized by *une légèreté de moeurs* (disreputable). Setting the context for an analysis of her character, the indictment charging Marie Arnoult with attempted murder began, for example, with reference to a damaging moral lapse: "Following an intrigue in her home town, her mother sent her to Paris." The next sentence consolidated this judgment, reporting that several months later, Marie Arnoult became the mistress of a man whom she met in the Tuileries gardens. There can be little doubt that Arnoult's questionable morals were meant to be an issue in the trial, especially because her lover was a married bourgeois.[10] With similar effect, the indictment of Marie Charrier opened with a description of the defendant that represented the investigator's conclusion that Charrier's character was an important factor contributing to developments that led to the crime: "The sordid avarice of the accused, her slovenly demeanor, and her unjustified jealousy alienated her husband."[11] Nowhere did the official documents record Marie Charrier's counter-charges of neglect, infidelity, and cruelty.

The case of Marie Charrier suggests with particular clarity the close links between the indictment's assessment of character and its presentation of plot. According to the official documents, in the midst of their last argument and following an exchange of insults, Marie hurled a bowl of cleaning fluid at her husband's face—in fact, vitriol—which seriously wounded him. In their respective depositions, he maintained that she had bought the vitriol to use against him, a charge seconded by neighbors. Marie, who claimed that she had been washing pots in the kitchen at the time of the argument, insisted that it was entirely coincidental that she happened to be washing with vitriol (sulfuric acid), and that she had thrown the liquid at him impulsively, without thinking. Convicted and sentenced to three years in prison for her attack, Marie Charrier had been constructed in the prosecutor's dossier in terms that identified her as a *femme criminelle*.[12] The indictment codified the prosecutor's conclusion that Marie was jealous, mean-spirited, and excessively stingy—so stingy that she did not prepare sufficient food for her husband, who began to believe that she might poison him, causing him to take his meals elsewhere. (Charrier apparently on two occasions consulted a doctor, who found nothing to indicate that he had consumed anything poisonous.) Quoting almost directly from the husband's deposition, the indictment described Marie as ill-kempt, slovenly in her person as well as with her household, a woman determined to embarrass her husband by becoming an object of gossip.

Although it is impossible to unravel all the charges and countercharges presented in this case, it does seem that the thread that pulled all the details together, that linked all the stories to form a consistent narrative, was Marie Charrier's character, evident in her decidedly undomestic behavior and her willingness to embarrass her husband publicly. Included among the stories contained in the dossier, and especially telling for the prosecutor, was an account of the Charriers' wedding, when she allegedly took away a cigar that he had lighted, *in front of everyone*, and later embarrassed him by spying on him in the street (a situation that he found particularly embarrassing, he said, because he was a uniformed officer [sous brigadier de gardiens de la paix]). She was also said to dress in a way that brought him shame. The indictment thus gathered various stories suggested by different witnesses to convey the image of a difficult, if not unnatural woman who would be capable of a vicious attack like the one of which she was accused.

In building a case, indictments might omit evidence (as in the case of Marie Charrier's alternative version of events), and might come to conclusions that directly contradicted information that had been preserved through every stage of the investigation up until the writing of the summary documents. In the case of Rose Méhu, for example, a laundress accused of burning her former lover, Paul Lelong, with vitriol (aggravated assault), the indictment concluded by stating, "The accused claimed that she wanted to avenge herself for the desertion of her lover. But he claims that he did not dream of ending their common life and never told his mistress of such an intention."[13] In fact, the summary of the investigation states that Méhu learned that Lelong had renewed relations with a former mistress; that when Méhu asked him not to abandon her (because she was pregnant with his child), he taunted her in response; that without informing Méhu, Lelong went to take another apartment after their landlord had given them notice.[14] These omissions are especially noteworthy because they effectively deny Méhu the sympathy that was becoming more readily available in the courts to young pregnant women, seduced and abandoned.

Similarly, in the case of Rose Chervey,[15] a former barmaid who had maintained a longstanding liaison with a middle-class entrepreneur, Paul Parquet, the indictment carefully selected the details that would establish the context in which the disruptions surrounding the termination of this relationship would be understood: "This liaison had, for the two lovers, only an ephemeral character, and it was never a question of their becoming a couple." From the beginning, it is to be understood, Chervey could not have expected anything other than the separation that did occur. The prosecutor told Chervey, for example, that her situation did not compare to that of other women: "Here it is not a question of betrayed promises, nor of seduction, nor of a shameful abandonment, nor of disavowed paternity." Chervey's case could not be assimilated to categories that might legitimate her action. He continued:

You knew perfectly well that this liaison would end. . . . When a woman wants to be protected against an abandonment, she finds a means in marriage; but if you had wanted to marry, you would have been obliged to marry a man of your station and to work for your living. Instead you preferred to take the risk of a free union with a rich man.

Although Chervey agreed that she did not expect marriage, she had indicated in her depositions that Parquet had told her "one hundred times" that they must have a baby in order to win his mother's consent to their marriage. In the end, however, it is Parquet's right to leave her that discounts any other testimony. The prosecutor reminded Chervey that, even if Parquet did not conduct himself well, "you are guilty because he has only exercised his right in seeking to extricate himself from an irregular situation that was distressing to his family." In so reinforcing Chervey's marginal social status, the indictment invoked the class differences between Chervey and Parquet, providing an interpretive filter that would necessarily marginalize Chervey's grief, erase her (perhaps contradictory) expectations, and finally undermine her explanation of the attack.

The stylized format of the prosecutor's questioning further worked to confirm the assumptions that underpinned the state's case. The three formal interrogations of the accused proceeded with "questions" from the prosecutor that actually outlined his tentative conclusions in the form of declarative statements to which the accused was invited to assent. The questions were not open-ended and did not seek to explain so much as to confirm the "facts" unearthed in the earlier police investigation. Rarely did accused women respond with more than a single sentence; rather, they replied with a "yes" or "no" to the interpretations they were offered. In Marie Charrier's case, she refused to sign her depositions.

Victorine Lelong's dossier demonstrates the ways in which the social transactions of the interview itself reinforced the prosecutor's story.[16] Lelong was charged with the murder of Constant Langlois, at whom she had hurled a bowl of vitriol (a charge later reduced to aggravated assault causing death), and was sentenced to five years imprisonment. Lelong and Langlois had lived together for seven years; at the time of the attack, they had been separated for four years, although he continued to visit her and to send her some money to support their child, a detail that appeared prominently at the very beginning of the indictment. The most important aspect of the prosecution's case against Lelong, however, was the large amount of vitriol that she had purchased (two liters) and her apparent vehemence during the attack. She emerges in these documents as exceedingly vicious, a monster.

When the prosecutor insisted that she must have intended to kill Langlois (stating, for example, "If you had only wanted to wound him, you would not have bought two liters of vitriol"), Lelong explained that she did not bring all of the vitriol to Langlois's house. She claimed that, after making the first purchase, she became frightened and spilled most of it into the toilet, noting that the police commissioner had in fact found a mostly empty bottle at her house. The next day, she bought another bottle, and, according to her testimony, the police found the second bottle still almost full after the attack. To this response, the prosecutor asked, as if she had not spoken, why she had armed herself with two bottles of vitriol. Lelong did not reply to this question. The prosecutor continued with a discussion of the kind of bowl that she had used, concluding that she had chosen it in order to have a more accurate aim. Lelong remained silent. Finally, he asked, "Do you persist in your claim that you did not intend to kill Langlois?" Lelong replied "Yes." He continued, "We have a different opinion." In the end, like Marie Charrier but unlike most defendants, Lelong withheld her signature from the transcript, no doubt unsure about whether her story had been recorded in any way that made sense to her. In an ironic coda to this set of interactions, the presiding magistrate at her court hearing lectured Lelong on the inappropriateness of her silences: "Instead of closing yourself up in your silence and in your pride, you would perhaps do better to ask the pardon of the jury."[17]

In contrast to the kind of narrative closure produced in the official interrogations of the accused by the investigating magistrate, it was possible for the accused woman to tell her own story in her initial interview with a local police officer at the time of her arrest. In keeping with their more open-ended style of questioning, Marie Charrier, for example, was asked by her police interrogator, "Why did you do this [throw vitriol]?" This was the only time, in all of her interviews, that her motive was not assumed, not already incorporated into the developing story. In response to this question, Charrier explained her domestic situation in terms that at least called into question the image of the defiant and powerful figure drawn by the indictment. Instead she spoke of the sexual and emotional disappointments of her marriage, of her fears of abandonment:

My husband made me unhappy, not because he beat me, but because he considered me as a stranger and he had mistresses. Last Sunday, he had arranged a meeting with another woman; I followed him; he noticed me and insulted me. I am always haunted by the idea that my husband no longer loves me; this morning at eleven o'clock, he was sweeping the house which he never does. I pointed this out to him and he said that I was ugly [*mal faite*], that I had unsightly teeth; we insulted each other. My husband finally said that he would end his days with one of his mistresses. Exasperated, I threw the bowl in my hand at him.[18]

In a letter written from prison to the police commissioner, Marie Charrier again invoked her painful frustration, asking the commissioner to intervene on her behalf and promising ultimately to leave her husband, as he had wanted, if the court would shorten her prison sentence. She explained that she feared Charrier had married her for her money, but had hoped that, with patience, she could win him over. In spite of every effort, she believed that "absolutely everything that she did turned out badly. . . . Everything was useless; he entreated me constantly to leave him." In one of his depositions, Charrier actually confirmed his wife's understanding of the tensions in their marriage; he reported that she refused to contribute to the household expenses, claiming that she did not want to be merely his unpaid maid. Marie's stories did not emerge in any of the official accounts of the case. And, in fact, they do not shed any light on whether or not her violent act was premeditated or spontaneous; but they do offer a somewhat different explanation from that presented in the official documents—documents that described Marie Charrier as a powerful woman whose arrogant public refusals had shamed her husband—a figure readily recognizable in contemporary repertoires that chronicled female deviancy, but not necessarily more accurate or relevant to the case than the suppressed story told by the defendant.

The interpretive authority of the judicial investigation was reinforced by the practices of the hearing itself. Nowhere was the editorial power of court officials more visible than in the courtroom interrogation of the defendant by the presiding magistrate. Although his role was supposed to be impartial and supervisory, in practice he exercised enormous authority that could determine the outcome of a case. Before 1881, following the presentations by the prosecution and the defense, the presiding magistrate made a lengthy summation to the jury, a practice that had drawn considerable criticism because, in effect, the impartial arbiter had become too influential, interpreting the case for the jury without the possibility of a rebuttal by the defense. In 1881, this summation was abandoned, only to be replaced by an informal practice that, ironically, enhanced rather than reduced the presiding magistrate's impact on the case. Instead of a summation, he engaged in an extensive interrogation of the defendant immediately after the reading of the indictment and before the first witness was called. Because this practice was essentially extralegal, it followed no prescribed rules; the magistrate might refer at will to material from the dossier not included in the official case, leaving the defendant no way to deal with damaging allusions.[19] Or he might confront the defendant, at the very outset of the trial, with his unofficial verdict. When the presiding magistrate interrogated Victorine Lelong, for example, he noted that "Langlois died after horrible suffering. It was a great misfortune for him to have met a woman like you."[20]

Typically, the presiding magistrate reiterated the claims of the indictment, restating the state's case in the precise terms presented by the investigation. In the courtroom interrogation of Melanie Lerondeau, accused of poisoning her husband, we can see clearly how the performative aspects of the courtroom underscored the conclusions reached by the prosecutor. The summary documents of the dossier provided the following story: The Lerondeaus had married in 1859; he was a master mason with some considerable savings and was fifteen years her senior. The indictment claimed that the Lerondeau household had become, in the words of their neighbors, "a veritable hell" in recent years. She did not prepare his meals, left his clothing in a shameful state of disrepair, forced him to sleep in the barn, even in winter, insulted him publicly, and occasionally hit him. In the presence of neighbors, she asserted that she detested him because he "was not a man as he ought to be." She complained that he would not make the necessary repairs on their home after the destruction caused by the violent events of the Commune; in retaliation, she hid his money from him, forcing him to borrow from his workers. His friends urged him to leave her, but he refused for the sake of their one child. During the preceding two years, he had complained of stomach pains and told friends that he suspected that his wife wanted to poison him. One Monday, she served him a bouillon that she did not

Female defendants in the Cour d'Assises.

share and later chased him from their house, hurling stones after him. That afternoon, he was overcome by an attack of cramps and vomiting and died. When her husband's body was returned to his home, Melanie did not register any grief, did not shed a tear. Following an autopsy, medical experts concluded that Lerondeau had died from poisoning by oxalic acid.

In the conclusion to his investigation, the prosecutor framed an explanation of Melanie's motives that would shape the presentation of the state's case: "Your vanity, your avarice, and above all, your wantonness led you to hate your husband; your hatred, becoming more inflamed each day, finally led you to crime." We can hear the force of this perspective in the Président's questioning, which effectively reproduced the prosecution's conclusion, representing Melanie Lerondeau as an unnatural woman:

Q: Your household became a hell for him.
A: I loved him very much, even too much.
Q: You insulted him; you hit him.
A: Never.
Q: You threw stones to chase him away.
A: Oh! . . .
Q: You sent him at midnight to the barn.
A: That is a falsehood.
Q: He was very poorly clothed.
A: That I agree with. I did not maintain his clothes well enough.
Q: He was forced to eat here and there.
A: Because he worked here and there in the countryside . . .
Q: You said: "Ce c— -là, it is more than three months since he has touched me."
A: No. That is an invention of neighbors . . .
Q: Your hatred seemed to grow. . . . Your husband feared you, feared that he would be poisoned.
A: I cannot believe that . . .
Q: You were violent and out of control [on the morning of the death].
A: That's true, I agree. I am a little quick-tempered, I shout . . .
Q: Everyone in your district accused you of killing him.
A: From jealousy. . . . In small villages, those who succeed a bit are envied.[21]

The jury deliberated for ten minutes and found Melanie Lerondeau guilty, with extenuating circumstances, of poisoning her husband. She was condemned to twenty years of forced labor.

This kind of courtroom interrogation suggests both the conceptual limits of a believable story—what could be heard and understood—and the way that the criminal narrative became a form of social transaction, shaped by the social relations between teller and audience in the particular context of the telling. The presiding magistrate organized the story that the court would hear and lectured broadly on the social codes and customs—not the laws—that were relevant to the case, providing both the language for interpreting criminal behavior and the assumptions that gave this language meaning. A direct example of such informal intervention is evident in the case of Marie Sivadon, who had shot her husband's mistress. The presiding magistrate used the occasion of the hearing to shift attention from the accused to her victims, unequivocally reprimanding both the errant husband and his mistress for their complicity in the violent episode:

[To Mme Millet, the mistress:] You claim . . . that when Sivadon took you as his mistress, you were several months pregnant. . . . We have already seen that [behavior] in the history of the Roman emperors. It is disgusting!

[To the husband:] You had an honorable and excellent wife and, if she is here today, you are the cause. You left her to go with this other woman . . . it is always the same . . . you have destroyed your honor yourself. . . . You knew that she [Mme Millet] was pregnant and that did not prevent you from taking her as a mistress? Well![22]

The presiding magistrate's interactions with Marie Sivadon were equally pointed. A visible display of repentance was often an expected aspect of the courtroom drama (female defendants frequently carried small statues of the Virgin, for example); but when such contrition was not immediately forthcoming, symbolically or verbally, it was more directly elicited by the presiding magistrate. When he asked Marie Sivadon if she regretted what she had done, the defendant responded, according to the *Gazette des Tribunaux*, in a whisper: "Oui Monsieur." He next asked if she had intended to kill Mme Millet (and her husband, whom she had pursued without success). Without hesitation, Marie Sivadon admitted, apparently in a more normal voice, that that had been her desire. While the journalist, in commenting on the defendant's tone of voice, was producing his own narrative of the crime, the presiding magistrate also accomplished several objectives with his interrogation. He had at least elicited the obligatory expression of regret and created a context for identifying the conduct of husband and mistress as finally more offensive than the shooting. The *Gazette des Tribunaux* announced the case in a headline that urged an interpretation: "A woman deceived by her husband. Attempted murder." The jury brought in an acquittal.

★

While the interpretive authority of the prosecutor and presiding magistrate was undeniable, it was the response of the jury that ultimately established the viability of particular stories while discrediting others. The
jury's role was officially interpretive: to determine whether the defendant was guilty of a crime, not whether the act itself had been committed by the accused.[23] In order to establish culpability, the jury considered
the question of aggravating or extenuating circumstances, various formal
excuses established in law, and the issue of discernment. In light of a progressive increase in the number of acquittals for crimes against persons
in the period 1860–90,[24] critics argued that juries were entering more
and more the realm of metaphysics, responding to the particular social
and psychological circumstances of the accused individual rather than to
the dictates of law or the general interests of society—a refocusing on
the criminal rather than the crime that Foucault has discussed in reference
to the new discipline of criminology.[25] Nevertheless, even given the
court's alleged interest in the specific motivation and particular condition of the defendant, formulaic courtroom narratives persisted, peopled
by stock characters caught in familiar situations who responded in predictable ways. The purported commitment of juries to the "individualization of penalties" did not mean, then, as contemporaries feared, that
juries sacrificed the general welfare in the service of individualism, but
rather that they tended to define the general good in terms of a set of
assumptions about character and motivation that were, in practice, fairly
uniform and broadly shared.

It was a combination of institutional and discursive practices on the
one hand and recognized social codes and familiar stories on the other
that shaped the accounts of crime produced in the Cour d'Assises. The
narrative conventions that organized stories of women's crimes at once
derived from and contributed to the consolidation of cultural stereotypes.
In the cases of Marie Charrier and Melanie Lerondeau, the defendant's
character was the source of her difficulties with her husband and within
her neighborhood. The bourgeois men of the court and the working-
class people of the *quartier* found common ground in the broad outlines of
the charges brought against each woman. Each was sharp-tongued, publicly critical of her husband, and engaged in an ongoing struggle that was
expressed through a variety of public refusals: the refusal to cook, clean,
darn; the refusal to keep up public appearances; the refusal to defer. These
behaviors were recounted in the indictments, and ultimately in the courtroom, in a formulaic way that identified a woman who was dangerous

particularly because, refusing deference and domestic responsibilities, she was out of place—or perhaps without a place. Detached from an acceptable female social location, she could be assimilated to more mythical figures of dangerous women.

This focus on character, and especially on inappropriate female behavior, echoed in cases that were very different both in the ambiguities raised by the factual situation and in the judicial outcomes. Anastasie Schlegel, for example, was condemned to forced labor for life for allegedly setting fire to her husband's bed as he lay, drunk, sleeping.[26] The story told in the summary of the pretrial investigation established the context for judging her act, rehearsing familiar and damning vignettes: he was patient (*patient*), she was evil (*méchante*); he returned from work and his meals were not prepared; he sometimes went to bed without dinner, and developed drunken habits in response to his unhappy household; she quarreled with him, reproached him for not earning enough money, and hit him in the street in front of others. When neighbors came to his aid following the fire, "she remained impassive in the midst of the general commotion. She remained inside and did not concern herself with the condition of her husband, apparently indifferent to what was happening around her." When she was informed by the hospital that her husband had died, she did not cry.

The case of Clara (Lolote) Nodin, who stabbed her husband to death, repeats some of the same rhetorical conventions but this time in the idiom and context of a slightly lower social stratum.[27] According to the dossier, Lolote was clearly "unnatural" on many counts: she was eight years older than her husband, married him when he was eighteen (although he had been her lover since he was fifteen), earned most of the income for the household, often refused to give her husband money, and was known for her gross language and violent character, fighting with men as well as women. Neighbors, who were very much privy to the workings of the Nodin household, reported that both drank and that arguments were constant, often because the children refused to obey him or because she refused him money, or, from her side, because he did not work enough. The most often repeated gossip recited Lolote's assaults on his manhood: she called him a "*fausse couche*" (miscarriage), treating him as *déculotté* (unmanned), telling everyone that "he had nothing between his legs." In their last, fatal fight, Lolote had refused him his usual three francs on a Sunday. He pushed her down, took her wallet, and went to a cabaret, where she followed him and, with a baby in her arms, stabbed him in the stomach. In a final act of defiance, Lolote refused to give her carriage to take him to the hospital.

By the end of the century a fairly consistent portrait of the criminal woman was regularly produced in the courtroom by which contemporaries across the social spectrum might recognize a deviant or dangerous woman, someone predisposed to commit a violent crime. She was likely to be sharp-tongued, insufficiently deferential, and publicly critical of her husband; she might invert appropriate female behavior by refusing domestic responsibilities or by engaging in questionable sexual behaviors; she was prone to slip into excess, unable to contain or control the emotions generated by her reproductive system; or she might be moved by a much-discussed, particularly vicious, particularly female vengeance. The criminal stories recounted in the Cour d'Assises participated in this work of cultural myth-making and responded to well-established and enduring assumptions. We need to turn here to look at the way that notions about deviant women—both older, nearly archetypal ones and more contemporary images—were invoked, rewritten, and brought up to date in the judicial process.

In their efforts to establish their scientific credentials, criminologists in the fin-de-siècle were preoccupied with classification, with providing a consistent set of personality traits that could be relied upon to identify specific criminal types. Not surprisingly, sexual difference was a primary criterion of categorization; like many nineteenth-century discourses of the social sciences, criminological taxonomy participated in the discursive construction and consolidation of sexual identities. Because "woman" was believed to be an inert, unchanging category, criminological writing found its references in classical literature, asserting a historical trajectory of "natural" female qualities that were allegedly as evident in ancient civilizations as they were in the present. So powerful were these essentialist convictions that they inevitably led to rather bizarre turns in the logic of "scientific" proof. Listen to the argument of Raymond de Ryckère as he describes the temptation to steal among female servants:

Often thrown from the country into the cities, into the homes of the rich (or simply the comfortable, but who always seem to them as millionaires), poorly paid, and with the opportunity to handle money for the daily household purchases . . . they find awakening in them the innate avarice of women.[28]

"The innate avarice of women": the opening sociological and economic explanations are abruptly folded into a biological model that posits the

Lolote Nodin and her husband.

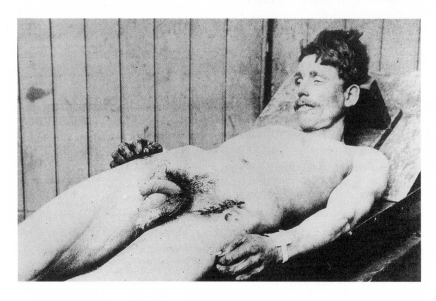

atavistic awakening of natural and inevitable character traits. Theft becomes, in this analysis, the product of "this weak organic repulsion" that
makes the normal woman less respectful of property, more responsive to
temptation, and more willing to deceive herself about the seriousness of
the theft she has committed than a man.[29]

De Ryckère seconded Lombrosian conclusions about the born criminal, so his repeated return to "female nature" as explanation is not surprising. More telling is the fact that the same underlying assumptions
regularly reappeared in the writings of experts representing quite different schools of criminological thought, including those opposed to Lombrosian determinism. With the same abrupt jump in logic that interrupts
de Ryckère's explanation—the same kind of unsettling shift in the text—
the jurist Louis Proal could write:

What atrocious vengeance is that of Medea! To kill her own children in order to
make their father suffer cruelly! . . . There is something of the character of Medea
in all women. To torture the father in order to make the husband suffer is an
essentially feminine kind of vengeance. Men less often exercise this form of atrocious vengeance. Several months ago, however, a man named Deblonder took
vengeance on his wife who wanted to divorce him in order to marry another by
murdering his two small daughters in order to torture their mother.[30]

The behavior remained indisputedly "feminine" in Proal's mind, making it possible for him to not even pause over his contradictory example. What men might do in exceptional cases, he assumes, women did
from their nature.

Most criminological writing described the female criminal in the
same terms used to discuss women more generally. The criminal woman
was like all women, only more so: she was suggestible, weak in the face of
temptation, deceitful, prone to excess, intellectually limited, and morally
stunted. But she could also be described, like all women, as moved by
love and devotion.[31] Such diverging images of the female criminal typically appeared together in the same text, which represented women as
both better and worse than men, careening between myth and misog-
yny. To some extent, invocations of the transhistorical mystery of femaleness could be used to authorize this imaginative license; the mystery could be "solved" as essential feminine qualities were identified, and
could remain forever mysterious, enhancing the power of unexamined
contradictions. The usefulness of this particular perspective is evident in
one expert's effort to represent criminal women as defined by an "excess of lying" and "an excess of truthfulness":

The deceitful [*dissumulatrices*] habits that are innate in woman, the intellectual insensitiveness, the absence of logic, the rapid fading of their memories of the crime, all of these make the female criminal a liar to the point of absurdity. But the need to gossip and to reveal secrets, the jealousy, calculation, and love [of woman] often cause her to admit her crimes without restraint. Woman, honorable or criminal, is always a being of contradiction.[32]

The contradictory assertions of this text point to deception as the discursive hallmark of criminological writings on women: the author's sense of being thrown off balance by women's contradictory nature, and the rhetorical/sexual tension captured by the juxtaposition of concealment and revelation. Women's habitual lying meant, quite simply, that men could be tricked. One criminologist noted that women were more likely to feign illness in prison; hysteria offered them *tout naturellement* a genre of dissimulation that they freely made use of for their own purposes. In this analysis, "woman" is both ill and cunning—a hysteric by nature who could pretend to be a hysteric—in the service of deception.[33] He continues by explaining that it was very difficult to do a psychological analysis of a woman because just "when one believes that she has been sincere and open, she dissimulates once again and hides from us all, or a part of, the truth. It is that which gives her a manifest superiority over men."[34] This skillful and persistent lying also suggested that female defendants might be able to manipulate inexperienced judges and juries—a talent, one author notes, that was especially developed in attractive women.[35] This observation was voiced as a plea for professional expertise, for the presence in the courtroom of "those who thoroughly know the biology and the psychology of criminal women." But what is inescapable in this comment, as in all of the discussion of deception, is the sexual subtext that threads itself throughout.

It is the predicament of being a man that seems most in evidence here. As male commentators encountered the female criminal, they seemed to encounter their own fears of being duped—as judges, jurors, and inevitably as lovers and husbands. They described women's propensity to lie as a matter of instinct, a natural defense arising out of female characteristics such as their weakness; their modesty, which forced them to hide certain organic functions, especially menstruation, from men; the sexual conflict that obliged women to conceal physical and moral defects from men (age, illness, the financial condition of their families), as well as their superior qualities (mind, talent, generosity) that men did not want to see; maternal responsibilities, which obliged women to conceal sexual matters from children; and, finally, their suggestibility, which encouraged them to believe their own inventions and made lying a nearly normal condition for all women.[36] Again, the elision between criminal women and all women is quite automatic. But even more interesting in this text is the repeated return to the multiple fronts of the battle of the sexes—separate battles, but all circling about the problem of deception and the possibility that men, in spite of their superior logic, might be disadvantaged in ways they could neither control nor overcome.

Nor is it clear in these writings that full disclosure was the desired goal; rather, it seems that the fear of being duped was only matched by the fear of knowing. To prove women's consistent lying, Ferrero cited Stendhal's comment that "for women to be frank would be as if they went out without clothing."[37] If women gave up deceit, would men have to confront their nakedness? The above list of reasons why women lie refers obliquely to the complexities of the position of men: what they might want to know (woman's physical and moral defects); what they did not want to know (her superior attributes); what they could not, and might not want, to know (the hiddenness of her sexuality; and, unspoken but implicit, whether their wives were faithful, whether their children were really theirs, whether they had been secretly humiliated by women's verbal or sexual betrayal). The same literature that spoke of women's natural duplicitousness referred to typical female crimes as "perverse" (adultery, prostitution, infanticide, murder), "hidden" (shoplifting, abortion), and "cunning" or "invisible" (poisoning). We can read in this language the importance of *female* in female criminality as woman's crime seemed to be at least in part her sex. And we can read as well the uneasy tensions around the male expert's desire to know, his fear of being tricked, and his unresolved anxiety about knowing.

Such efforts by criminologists to discover and document the essential, often perverse qualities that marked the female criminal are important especially because these conclusions were not only incorporated into popular and literary accounts of crime but emerged as well, if somewhat less directly, in the assumptions that underpinned the formal documents of a judicial investigation. For example, the rhetoric about female deception was regularly invoked in cases where women made paternity allegations, especially when a working-class woman accused a middle-class man.[38] The case of Eugénie Belligand is intriguing in this regard.[39] Belligand was convicted in 1887 of aggravated assault leading to the victim's death and condemned to forced labor for life. The case is noteworthy, even striking, because of the unusually harsh sentence at a time when most female crime received light punishments or relatively short prison terms and when acquittals for murder were commonplace. Belligand, a widow who had become a midwife after her husband's death, had had a six-month affair with an architect, Courty. When he decided to marry, Courty broke with Belligand, a break followed by Belligand's apparent harrassment of both Courty and his wife, encounters that often required police intervention. Finally, Belligand ambushed Courty as he walked with a friend in the street, hurling a vial of vitriol at him; he died ten days later from his wounds. Belligand claimed that she had attacked Courty because he had refused to legally recognize the child that she had given birth to one month earlier.

In spite of an extraordinarily large dossier with testimony about every aspect of the relationship between Belligand and Courty, the details of the case remain murky. The prosecutor claimed that there was nothing to indicate Courty's paternity, emphasizing Belligand's loose morals and the fact that, if the baby had been carried to full term, Courty would have been absent for military service during the time when the child was conceived. He asserted that Belligand had engaged in previous attempts to extract money from Courty for alleged abuse when in reality she had fallen and injured herself, and suggested that she had bribed witnesses to say that they had heard Courty promise to recognize the child. The summary of the case states that "the facts prove that the widow Belligand only invented this paternity in order to bring her former lover again under her domination and to extort money from him." In sum, she is depicted as immoral, manipulative, unscrupulous, and, above all, deceitful in a quintessentially feminine way.

Most of the voluminous testimony collected in the dossier represents the prosecutor's efforts to guard against the possibility that Belligand might effectively deceive the court. The summary documents presented to the court report speculation that Belligand had not been pregnant at all, that the baby was not hers, but rather one that she had secured in her capacity as a midwife. They include testimony that Belligand refused a medical examination and instead asked a midwife to declare the birth of the child at the town hall; there is considerable discussion among witnesses of the weight and color of the baby in order to assess the validity of Belligand's claim that the birth was premature (hence that Courty was not away at the time of conception). The report of the medical expert had concluded, in fact, that it was highly likely that Belligand had recently given birth: her breasts were enlarged, pressure could elicit several drops of a milky fluid, and the skin of her abdomen was covered with well-defined stretch marks. But in this case, the doctor's testimony was entirely discounted; it could not outweigh or overturn the prosecutor's story, which gained its authority by narrating a recognizably female pattern of deception. In the midst of all this testimony—the quantity of which attests to an enormous amount of energy brought to bear by the prosecution to tease out the truth of each individual charge—it is possible to forget that Belligand was tried for the crime of assault leading to Courty's death, and not for an attempt to perpetrate a false claim of paternity.

It is, of course, impossible to reconstruct a definitive explanation for the severity of the sentence in this case, but it does seem consistent with the material collected in the dossier to suggest that Belligand was found guilty of more than one violation; murder was made more horrible by its contemporary resonance with specific anxieties about the broader vulnerabilities of men at the hands of lying women. As concerns about high infant mortality, especially among poor illegitimate children, intensified toward the end of the century, reformers increasingly urged a change in policy that would permit unmarried mothers to seek support for their children. In the context of heated controversy about the potential abuses that might arise from a law allowing paternity suits, cases such as Belligand's carried these preoccupations into the judicial process, where conflicting opinions and their implications could be played out in quite specific terms. In effect, then, accounts of the crimes that women committed not only worked to produce and reproduce gender definitions but also were interpreted in a particular historical context that gave them added cultural weight—in this case, at a moment of intense concern about women's right to initiate paternity suits and the dangers this posed for bourgeois men and the bourgeois family. Older, formulaic assumptions about a specific kind of female perversity thus gained a contemporary twist in the new criminological literature and in the courtroom, making available a set of meanings that could be mobilized to produce a unified, familiar, and apparently conclusive story from among a mass of contradictory and ambiguous details.

Perhaps more than any other offense, the crime of poisoning focused all of the themes circulating around descriptions of the essential criminal woman. In looking at discussions of poisoning as well as at actual criminal cases, we can see in sharp outline the intersections of cultural myth-making and social practice. From the middle of the nineteenth century, the number of suspected poisonings decreased continuously, and by the period between 1886 and 1900 there were only about eight prosecuted cases per year in all of France; of this number, slightly more than half of the defendants were women.[40] Nevertheless, the symbolic importance of poisoning persisted and anxieties about the possibility of being poisoned remained high. According to one commentator in 1894, "suddenly poison is on the scene again, spreading horror everywhere, multiplying suspicions, and creating *stories that are more terrifying than the truth itself.*"[41] This unusual formation—linking poison not to death but to stories and to escalating anxieties—seems to cry out for clarification. In what way was "poison on the scene again"? What was the relation between "stories more terrifying than the truth itself" and actual poisonings? And if there was a disparity between terrifying stories and reality, who was telling these stories and what (and how) did they mean in the culture of that moment? Did these horrifying stories convey something that was as important as the more elusive "truth itself"?

The answers to these questions could only refer to the activities of women. Contemporaries universally identified poisoning as *the* female crime *par excellence.* If women were to be criminals, poison would be their weapon of choice. In his study of female criminality, the jurist Louis Proal reported the continuing decline in the number of poisonings (about nine in 1887), but followed this fact with an account of the trial of an herbalist in Bouches-du-Rhone who had opened a boutique to sell poisons to women who wanted to murder their husbands "in order to give themselves over more freely to libertinage." He was allegedly discovered because, in a parallel sloughing-off of men, a woman in the same business wished to rid herself of the competition.[42] Thus, even as he recorded the small number of poisonings, Proal contributed to the mythmaking that put poison "on the scene again" in his presentation of a kind of chic Murder Incorporated for ladies (the new ready-made product substituting for the cruder homemade variety), plagued, as any ordinary business, by all of the underhanded dealings that affect enterprises operating in a competitive market.

Accounts of poisoning as a woman's crime dating from the eighteenth century focused on the moral and physical weakness of women that led them to murder in this particular way, a presumption that was confirmed at the end of the nineteenth century in the concept of *les empoisonneuses*

Quinzième année. — N° 777.   Huit pages : CINQ centimes   Dimanche 27 Décembre 1903.

Le Petit Parisien

SUPPLÉMENT LITTÉRAIRE ILLUSTRÉ

TOUS LES JOURS
Le Petit Parisien
CINQ centimes

CHAQUE SEMAINE
LE SUPPLÉMENT LITTÉRAIRE
5 centimes

DIRECTION: 18, rue d'Enghien (10e), PARIS

ABONNEMENTS
PARIS ET DÉPARTEMENTS
12 mois, 4 fr. 50. 6 mois, 2 fr. 25
UNION POSTALE
12 mois, 5 fr. 50. 6 mois, 3 fr

L'EMPOISONNEUSE DE MARSEILLE
Mme Massot à la prison des Présentines

"L'Empoisonneuse de Marseilles."

nées—"born (female) poisoners"—a category for which there was no male equivalent.[43] The persistence of well-established conventions for talking about a poisoning is suggested by a late-nineteenth-century description of an eighteenth-century poisoning committed by a man, Desrues. Two prominent criminologists explained Desrues's act by documenting his "female" nature. They noted that Desrues had been raised in his early childhood as a girl and seemed psychologically and physiologically feminine as an adult, even called in his neighborhood "*commère*," a (female) gossip. Described specifically as someone afflicted with "moral anasthesia" and possessing the "power of dissimulation," Desrues was, according to the accounts of his contemporaries, given to fantasizing, lying, vanity, perversity, and mythomania—all recognizably female traits. The report concluded, not surprisingly, with the observation that "even when it is a man's act, the crime remains feminine."[44] And, as if the feminine coding of the crime of poisoning needed any further clarification, Dr. Charpentier's thesis for a medical degree in 1906 completed the composite representation of *l'empoisonneuse* by emphasizing the fact that contemporary poisons had become so subtle, so disguised, that even the medical expert could be tricked.[45]

Criminologists wrote of the odiousness of what was, in essence, domestic treason, committed by the person one trusted the most. In the terms of this discourse, poisoning became the crime of hypocrites and those capable of pretense, "requiring a certain kind of affective perversity" that allowed the perpetrator "to slowly torture the person with whom one lived, with whom one shared meals, whose confidences one heard, while watching the slow agony of the victim that could last for hours, for days, or sometimes for weeks."[46] The judicial dossiers reveal that many men who lived with considerable domestic conflict repeatedly visited doctors to determine whether their stomach upsets were provoked by their wives' attempts to poison them, while others anxiously checked the pallor of their skin and confided their suspicions to friends. It is especially important to emphasize here the metaphoric valences associated with poison, because in ordinary practice during the nineteenth century several substances (mercury, arsenic, laudanum, for example) circulated relatively freely as both medicine and poison, making the fear of poisoning both more real and more ambiguous.[47]

Stories of the *grandes empoisonneuses*, such as Marie Lafarge, Jeanne Daniloff, and Hélène Jegado, provided the concrete details that gave the myth of l'empoisonneuse its contemporary character by establishing a set of widely recognized cultural references. The case of Jeanne Daniloff (Mme Weiss) is especially revealing. At the end of the century, Daniloff's crime became a cause célèbre that produced a rehearsal in popular and professional literature of the female qualities that made poisoning so unmistakably a woman's crime. Thirty reporters were sent to Algeria from Paris to cover the trial and crowds gathered hours in advance to fight for places in the courtroom. Daniloff's attempted poisoning earned her a place among the Great Female Sinners (who, according to the defense lawyer, Henri Robert, included Mary Magdalene, Sappho, and Mme Récamier).[48]

In May 1891, Jeanne Daniloff was arrested for attempting to poison her husband; her lover, Roques, who had allegedly provided her with the poison, was also arrested and immediately took his own life. In establishing the background for this case, commentators emphasized details that rendered Daniloff's story both poignant and perverse: an illegitimate child of a Russian nihilist mother, she had been raised in questionable circles in the south of France by her grandmother. Although she was no longer a virgin at the time of her meeting Weiss, he forgave her past and left his career as an officer in the military in order to marry her against his family's wishes. The marriage was apparently a happy one, producing two children, until Mme Weiss became infatuated with Roques. Over a period of months, she continued to pour *liqueur de Fowler*, a derivative of arsenic, into the medicine Weiss had been taking for a stomach ailment, until a friend, suspecting foul play, intercepted correspondence between Mme Weiss and Roques and exposed the plot. She was tried and condemned to twenty years of forced labor.

The story had all the elements to bring it instant notoriety. The defense argued that Mme Weiss had become a love slave to Roques, losing her will and her ability to resist his demands, obeying his orders. In her prison notebooks, fragments of which appeared in the popular and professional press, she wrote of passion and madness: "I was no longer in control of my actions. M. R . . . had made me into a woman of whom I was unaware, a woman violently passionate, passively submissive; not only did he turn my life inside out, but he turned inside out my entire essence."[49] The emotional charge of this melodramatic scenario was heightened by defense depictions of Mme Weiss as a devoted mother whose previous behavior had been irreproachable, by the presence in the courtroom of the wronged husband, by Mme Weiss's expressions of profound regret, and, in the final coup de grâce, by her dramatic suicide on the night of the verdict. A funeral cortège carrying the open coffin moved slowly through the town, inviting viewers to speculate on the wages of sin.

This image of the dishonored mother–repentant wife–punished adulteress was a compelling one; it circulated widely in contemporary fiction as well as in more journalistic and scientific accounts. I want to emphasize here not the morality tale but the way in which this case reinscribed all of the stereotypes around the crime of poisoning and revitalized the figure of the "poisonness" at a time when the actual number of cases of criminal poisoning was rapidly declining. The *Gazette des Tribunaux* introduced its report on Jeanne Daniloff's case in the following terms:

Of all crimes, poisoning is perhaps the one that at times denotes the greatest perversity and the most determined perseverance in evil. The guilty person watches day by day the progressive worsening caused by his detestable acts; he is present for the slow agony of his victim while no moment of remorse arrives to awaken his conscience and inhibit the hand that is preparing death.[50]

Although the pronoun was masculine, the familiar formula referred to a crime that was unquestionably feminine. The repetition of this formula opened the way to a discussion of what was believed to be a distinctly female form of perversity and persistence in evil.

While the most sensational crimes produced a set of associations that endowed certain criminal types and behaviors with larger-than-life proportions, in more ordinary cases the judicial process became a site where professional knowledge and cultural myths intersected. In constructing the case against Pauline Druaux, accused of murdering her husband and brother, the prosecution drew directly on contemporary lore about *l'empoisonneuse*.[51] She emerges in the dossier as a woman of suspect morals and violent character—so violent that she threw bottles and wooden shoes at her husband when they quarreled. The climax to their conflicts came when her husband discovered her with a lover. Several days after this scene, Druaux and his brother-in-law were found dead. Medical experts concluded that their deaths had been caused by ingestion of toxic substances, but neither the autopsies nor the chemical analysis of body organs retrieved any poison. Local public opinion held unanimously that Pauline had caused their deaths—a conclusion reinforced within the neighborhood by Pauline's silence and passivity following the discovery of the bodies. And, in a detail that invoked older discourses on the deviant woman, neighbors testified that Pauline often visited a sorcerer, Leborgne, a fishmonger (*marchand de poissons*, that is, a seller of fish) who had a reputation for causing cattle to die and provoking abortions—for being, that is, a *marchand de poison*, a seller of poison.[52] Pauline maintained her innocence throughout and insisted that she visited Leborgne only to buy fish. She was condemned to forced labor for life.

This conviction was overturned, although not until eight years later, in response to a bizarre series of accidental deaths met by succeeding tenants of the Druaux's house. In the end, medical experts found that all the deaths, including those of Druaux and his brother-in-law, had been caused by noxious emanations from a furnace on contiguous property. Pauline's unforgivable sangfroid in the face of her husband's death was belatedly explained as the result of partial asphyxiation. The initial readiness to convict, even in the absence of conclusive physical evidence, and the severity of the conviction seem related, then, to the meanings suggested by a poisoning, associations that became explicit in the Druaux case with its evocation of sorcery and witchcraft, linking the *empoisonneuse* to the archetypal denatured woman.

In the 1880s, vitriol began to acquire the symbolic associations traditionally linked to poison; *l'empoisonneuse* was joined by a new rhetorical (and actual) figure, the *vitrioleuse*, while the French language incorporated a new verb, *vitrioler*, to burn by means of vitriol. Like a poisoning, an attack with vitriol was considered to be a woman's crime. *Le Petit Parisien* reported an assault in September 1880 in the following terms: "Always it is vitriol! The sad series of revenge by sulfuric acid continues. This time, however, the roles are changed; it is a man who has had recourse to this terrible liquid to avenge himself for the desertion of his mistress." The man in question, who had, it seems, taken on a female criminal style, was described as "small and nervous," a man who "took excessive care with his appearance," marking with these details the essentially feminine nature of his crime. In delineating the characteristics of the female criminal type in 1899, Louis Puibaraud could write that "the female character is revealed in its essential traits [in two styles of criminal activity]: sometimes with a deceitfulness, a patience from which nothing diverts her (*l'empoisonneuse*), and sometimes with a tumult, theatrically (*la vitrioleuse*)."[53] So obvious were these all-encompassing images of female deviance that the criminologist Camille Granier believed that "aside from the usual methods of vitriol and arsenic, the classification of female criminals according to their weapon of choice offered little of scientific interest."[54] The use of poison and vitriol—behaviors that *did* produce "scientific" stories—came, then, to identify the quintessential criminal woman. In a telling linkage, Granier described a category of "sexual criminality," that is, when "the unfaithful wife offers arsenic to her husband, [or] the unfaithful (male) lover is inundated with sulfuric acid."[55] According to Granier, the legal status of the victim, husband or lover, determined whether he received the fatal substance internally or externally. But more to the point, it seems that it was often the repeated juxtaposition of female domestic duties with poison and vitriol—the suggested inversion of appropriate female behavior—that signaled the potential danger of women.

Presiding judges typically questioned female defendants about their familiarity with the properties of vitriol, emphasizing the link between women's domestic expertise and their characteristic criminal style: "You know the consequences of vitriol? It is used in your trade. You cannot be ignorant of the consequences of your action."[56] Grocers and hardware dealers who most often sold the vitriol reinforced this connection in their reports that women had undoubtedly requested the acid for cleaning purposes. In an interesting refusal of this association, Alexandrine Breton claimed that she had never used vitriol for household cleaning and had bought it expressly to throw in the face of her husband's mistress. She asserted, moreover, that no one had asked for what purpose she wanted the vitriol.[57] In practice, it seems that few merchants paid any special attention to the sale of vitriol; it was both cheap and readily available. The fact that women could openly purchase such a dangerous substance under the cover of their ordinary household activities made real the more mythic images of aggrieved or abandoned women as especially ferocious and vengeful. We can get some sense of the worrisome juxtaposition of domesticity and revenge in a rather trivial piece that appeared in *Le Petit Journal* in 1892, entitled "While They Cook":

What can I tell you, my friend? My hands are red and bloody. During all the long day, I subdued, I pressed, I massacred thousands of victims while the blood ran in streams into deep vases. I did this with an infernal smile on my lips and with fury in my heart. Then, in my rapture, I gathered all this horrible debris, all the hideous parts, and I repressed, remassacred them so that not a drop of the red liquor escaped my effort. Oh shame! And the bright sunshine illuminated this work of darkness which left me exhausted, annihilated, but satisfied.[58]

The story is, of course, about making jam, and, while we cannot make too much out of what was meant to be humorous and ironic, the references are so close to the stories told in the criminological literature as to

VENGEANCE AU VITRIOL

"Vengeance by vitriol."

warrant more serious notice. Women who were dangerous through their very domesticity—who transformed the ordinary and the womanly into the menacing—underscored not only female duplicity but male dependencies and vulnerabilities. And, in fact, the damage produced by vitriol attacks was often extensive and irreparable, involving lengthy and painful convalescences, blindness, serious disfigurement, and often death.

Not only, then, was the *vitrioleuse* the most recent incarnation of the homemaking woman gone awry, but the macabre quality of the crime itself inspired a new level of fear that vulnerable women were not reluctant to exploit. The husband of Amélie Sanglé claimed, for example, that after an argument, his jealous wife took some vitriol that she had bought and threw it in the street, sending an unmistakable warning. With similar effect, in the course of the dissolution of the liaison between the domestic Louise Charot and her lover, Dr. Gromolard, Charot threatened him with a revolver (in fact, one that was not loaded) and followed him in the streets carrying a vial that "he and others supposed to be filled with vitriol," although Charot claimed that it only contained warm water.[59] Another domestic in the household also reported that she often saw Charot carrying a vial of a liquid with which she burned her fingers and the hem of her dress. Charot stated in her pretrial interrogations that she hoped that by threatening scandal she could prevent Gromolard from sending her away. But was he not also meant to be held anxiously in a state of alert? It appears that the link between jealousy and vitriol had become part of the commonsense perceptions of the period, alleging its own transparent logic. When Rose Chervey was confronted by an emissary from her lover who informed her that the relationship must end, he warned her, as if to forestall the inevitable, "Above all, no scandal; no vitriol."[60] While attacks with a revolver were consistently likely to draw an acquittal, this was not necessarily the case with the more worrisome crime of *vitriolage*. Vitriol, the new (female) menace, seemed to represent the menace of the new female—the woman who refused to be a victim, who could generate fear in her antagonists, and whose retaliation could be effected readily, with grim if not lethal consequences.

It seems clear that cultural myths such as those of the *empoisonneuse* and the *vitrioleuse*—produced and mobilized by criminologists and court personnel and diffused by the popular press—had considerable power in setting the terms for interpreting women's crimes. In effect, there was a latent discourse about the unnatural woman that provided the vocabulary and the connecting assumptions from which the judicial documents drew, in part, their substance and form. And, as we have seen, institutional practices further reinforced the (re)production of culturally meaningful stories. But it is equally clear that these cultural constructions did not go entirely unchallenged, either in the courtroom or in more popular versions of criminal stories. Even as cultural myths were deployed in familiar ways to identify criminal types and produce stable definitions, they were qualified, rewritten, and reinterpreted through the judicial process as different people tried to make sense of the circumstances surrounding women's crimes.

We need to return to the case of Mélanie Lerondeau to witness the kind of disruption of the formulaic narrative that I am describing. A year and a half after her conviction for murder in the criminal court at Versailles, Mélanie Lerondeau was retried in the Paris court because of a procedural irregularity in her initial trial. This time, the jury deliberated for three minutes before announcing an acquittal. The depositions and transcripts make it clear that Mélanie Lerondeau was, according to the judgment of her neighbors, dangerously perverse. She reversed accepted gender roles and became the aggressor in the face of her husband's passivity; she refused ordinary domestic responsibilities, implicitly calling their inevitability into question; and she openly expressed her sexual frustrations, publicly shaming her husband. These behaviors were sufficient to cause the entire neighborhood to believe in Mélanie's latent criminality, permitting them to fill in the gaps in the narrative so as to "prove" a poisoning. For example, witnesses stated that because Lerondeau asked for milk instead of wine to ease his stomach pains, they *knew* that he had been poisoned, while most witnesses connected Lerondeau's taking his dinner in cafés to the likelihood, if not the probability, that his wife would poison him. Clearly the community sought to punish, and in fact to exorcize, this disruptive woman, a perspective that Melanie apparently understood well, as she commented, ironically, to her interrogators that her household was not "impossible," was perhaps ordinary, but that she, presumably unlike her neighbors, didn't care whether her windows were open or closed.[61]

The indictment states that Mélanie reproached Lerondeau for his "coldness and his negligence in giving her the sums that were her due," linking perhaps unconsciously the financial and sexual conflicts of the Lerondeau household. These links were drawn more explicitly in an 1897 commentary on the case: "Lerondeau . . . was in the autumn of life; she

was in the heat of summer. From that, arguments, daily scenes. Mme
Lerondeau taunted her husband for being as prodigal with his pennies as
he was miserly with his tenderness."[62] The pretrial investigation arranged
these assumptions so as to make the causal links clear and unambiguous.
Women who were aggressive, sexually assertive, outspoken, who refused
the community's behavior codes, who "refused to provide sufficient
nourishment" for their spouses or to cry, could be readily understood as
deviant and probably criminal—the contemporary version of the archetypal *empoisonneuse*. Local medical experts who performed the autopsy
found some lesions and traces of oxalic acid in Lerondeau's stomach and
concluded with certainty that he had succumbed to a violent death provoked by poisoning.

Mélanie Lerondeau did attempt to interrupt the logic of the case
against her. The interruption could be quite literal, as at the end of her
interrogations. Her examiner concluded: "The investigation proceeds
from the certainty that Lerondeau's death was due to poison." Melanie
responded: "No, sir, the death certificate states that my husband died
from pulmonary congestion caused by a stroke [*apoplexie du cerveau*]."
Undeterred, her examiner noted that it was possible that, before the autopsy, stroke might have been identified as the cause of death, but as a
result of the autopsy, a poisoning had been recognized. Melanie persisted,
however, stating that it was, in fact, *after* the autopsy that the doctor provided the death certificate.[63]

But even with less direct confrontations, her responses complicated
the neat story that was being written by the investigating magistrate. In
the course of her various testimonies, Mélanie attempted to paint a different picture of her marriage, one more complex, reflecting a couple
locked, but also bonded, in conflict that was expressed through subsidiary
battles, including sexual ones, each partner seeking a kind of parity in
their respective refusals. When questioned about her unwillingness to
cook for her husband or repair his clothes, Melanie indicated that she
had told him, "since you do not do your duty, I will not do mine," insisting throughout that although she did not moderate her words, she did
not hate her husband. And it was she who tried to point out the reci-
procity, albeit a negative one, that bound them together and that may
even have kept him from leaving. Undoubtedly she realized that she had
embarrassed Lerondeau in making his sexuality a public topic; but she
also described her anger about their unrepaired house in terms of the
shame that such a decrepit home brought to the wife of an entrepreneur.

It seems evident that both Melanie and her husband understood that these two issues were connected, even though they could find no way out of their stand-off. When Melanie's examiner asked her about Lerondeau's "failure to fulfill his conjugal duty," Melanie responded that her husband "did not have the temperament that led him to women, and that [she] would have let it pass if he had given her what she wanted for her interior."[64] There can be no clearer example of the implicit interchangeability between sex and home improvements. When Melanie was confronted with reports that Lerondeau cried out that she wanted to make him die of grief, she noted that this was an expression that they used (and presumably felt) reciprocally.

It was not, however, the more nuanced story, fragments of which lay embedded in the contradictory accounts of the judicial dossier, that produced the stunning reversal of Melanie's conviction. With the transfer of the case from Versailles to Paris, a new set of medical experts examined the toxicology and autopsy reports that had buttressed the prosecutor's case in the first trial. This group, composed of some of the most prestigious names in forensic medicine (Vulpian, Bergeron, Wurtz), concluded that it was physically impossible for Lerondeau to have died from poisoning by oxalic acid: the delay of several hours between ingestion of the bouillon and the time of death was impossible if oxalic acid were the presumed toxic substance; Lerondeau could not physically have consumed enough oxalic acid to cause his death without realizing it, the taste was too bitter; lesions such as those found in Lerondeau's stomach were not typical of a poisoning by oxalic acid; and, finally, Lerondeau was plagued by the same internal ailments that had killed his father and brother, and probably died, as had they, from a cerebral hemorrhage.[65] Testimony by these experts led the prosecuting attorney to dismiss further witnesses and withdraw the charges, while the presiding magistrate decided to forgo his summation, sending the case to the jury with a recommendation for an acquittal. The newspapers reported that when the verdict was announced Melanie Lerondeau did not cry.[66]

In the words of her defense attorney, Charles Lachaud, Melanie Lerondeau owed her salvation "not to the doubts raised by insufficient proof, but to the brilliant demonstrations of science."[67] Melanie's contestation of the official story did not find its way into the courtroom in any meaningful way and was not likely in any event to shift the weight of the presumptions against her. There seem to have been two different interpretive frames that affected the outcome of this case: the first involved

no: Chateaufort

the relationship of the Lerondeaus to each other and to their neighbors; and the second juxtaposed the local community (Versailles) and its representatives on the one hand against prestigious Parisian scientific authorities on the other. In the first hearing, the cultural myth of *l'empoisonneuse*, given particularity by the values of the community, was confirmed by the nearly unanimous opinion of the people among whom the Lerondeaus lived. In the second, Melanie's story and those of the 51 witnesses who had been deposed became secondary to a separate struggle that positioned the codes of a local community against the knowledge and status of Parisian experts. The myth that explained Melanie's nature and propensities may have been equally present, but had to accommodate, this time, a different cultural myth, that of the power-to-tell-the-truth of the scientific expert. Scientific expertise did not necessarily prevail in resolving contested issues (for example, medical testimony about the probable pregnancy of Eugénie Belligand was ultimately discounted); but it might shift the terms of the debate, as it did in the Lerondeau case. The stories that experts told about women did not, then, simply work in and on the culture, but existed in a dynamic tension with other stories and other kinds of imperatives as the courtroom provided the arena for the expression of diverse interpretive positions—for contests of interpretive authority not only between professionals and defendants but between different professional communities as well.

My point here is to emphasize the multiple venues of the writers of criminal stories and their audiences. The collective voices of the neighborhood could make themselves felt in the courtroom, as they clearly did in shaping the cases against Pauline Druaux and Melanie Lerondeau, women identified by their neighbors as likely perpetrators of heinous crimes. But the voices of the *quartier* could also vindicate criminal behavior, providing extralegal justifications of crimes that drew upon a shared code that superseded legal definitions. In an exemplary case in 1885, the husband whom Marie Couffin attacked with vitriol had left her six days after the delivery of their fifth child to go off to Algeria with a mistress. When he returned to his home, nearly five hundred people had assembled to harrass him. The numerous neighbors who were deposed by the prosecutor collectively articulated a judgment that rendered Marie's attack on her husband and his mistress as less revolting than her husband's behavior. Although the prosecutor's line of questioning led to the reproduction of a more formulaic story (he led Marie through a series of statements that concluded with his suggestion that Marie still loved

her husband, finally offering her the scripted motive: "So, it was a sentiment of jealousy that moved you?"), it seems evident that the stories of
the husband's abuse, betrayal, and irresponsibility recounted by neighbors, even more than the jealousy/vengeance motif, became part of the
record that resulted in an acquittal.[68]

Jurists also noted the persistence of local, extralegal definitions of
theft. A young domestic who had climbed a tree to break into the room
of a lover who had left her, taking 380 francs and a handkerchief that she
claimed to have left there, insisted that her object was not theft, but rather
to avenge herself for his abandonment. To make this message clear, she
left behind a glove that would unmistakably identify her as the author of
the act.[69] And cooks and kitchen servants regularly participated, along
with local merchants, in a system of kickbacks and overcharging that had
become merely common practice. According to de Ryckère, in the eyes
of a servant, "to steal was uniquely to take money from the pocket of
her mistress, to hide a valuable piece of jewelry or silver in order to sell
it"; all other "indelicate acts" were not theft in the dishonorable sense
of the word:

This cook does not ever steal 50 centimes that her mistress has forgotten on the
corner of the fireplace. For her, this would be a theft and she is an honest girl.
She raises the price of the meat that she buys for the household, in complicity
with the butcher. She believes herself to be, very sincerely and in good faith, in
accord with the rules. She does not see herself as doing anything that is not legitimate or permissible.[70]

In like manner, doctors suggested that abortions and infanticides had become so much a part of social custom among certain sectors of the population that they no longer could be thought of as crimes.[71] These common understandings, derived from the habits of ordinary people and represented in depositions as well as in the imaginations of ordinary jurors,
could, then, become an integral part of the judicial process.

In her study of the lives of working-class women in twentieth-century
Britain, Carolyn Kay Steedman has written compellingly about the problem of accounting for lives "lived out on the borderlands, lives for which
the central interpretive devices of the culture don't quite work."[72] She
has sought to address the difficulties of people who need to tell themselves stories about how they got to the place they currently inhabit, even
as they recognize, on some level, that their stories are in deep conflict
with the familiar interpretive devices of the dominant culture. Such cul-

M. Couffin and his mistress, victim of an attack with vitriol.

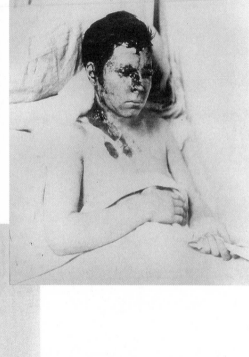

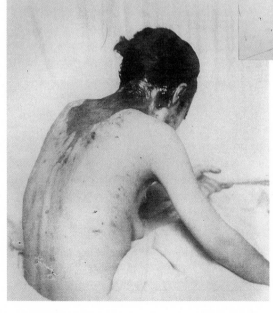

not unique to women at all

tural dissonance was clearly a part of the experience of the criminal investigation for the women we have been looking at. Many of them, nevertheless, tried to place their own accounts on the public record. It was not uncommon for women who committed violent acts during this period to immediately turn themselves in to the local police commissioner. At this initial interrogation, it is especially striking that these women tended *not* to discuss the crime itself, but rather to rehearse a litany of longstanding grievances captured in a selected sequence of events that were meant to account for the crime in some much broader sense than the immediate provocation. By means of these narratives, women identified the particular moments that, in their minds, gave coherence and legitimacy to their lives, even when the logic of the story was quite different from the versions that were ultimately constructed through the judicial process.

The stories told by female defendants, even those entirely suppressed in the official documents, did not, however, stand starkly apart from the kinds of interpretations either imposed by the structure of the criminal investigation or inflected by the broadly recognized cultural references that informed the narratives throughout. Some women modeled their defense, for example, in the precise terms offered by their accusers, merging their voices with those of their interrogators in ways that produced contradictions and ambiguities that elude final resolution. This would usually require that their own narrative include an admission of being *surexcitée*, out-of-control, or mad—even as they described other motives—followed by profound expressions of regret. Such stories incorporated personal needs, community values, the expectations of the court, models of criminal stories readily available in popular cultural forms, and, no doubt, some measure of calculation. As Natalie Davis has suggested in her discussion of sixteenth-century pardon tales, women traditionally have had a problematic relation to their own violence and incorporate this ambiguous positioning into their self-presentation as perpetrators of crime.[73] In many cases, in earlier periods as well as in the nineteenth century, women made use of received story lines, and explained their motivation and behavior in terms of well-understood plots that fulfilled the expectations of their accusers. Because these expectations were also, inevitably, at least partially internalized, the repetition of recognizable plots must have been both intentional and unconscious. To separate the cultural from the personal, the calculated from the unconscious, is, of course, neither desirable nor possible.

What we can look at are the ways in which different codes and interpretations competed for authority in the judicial process. Women who believed their stories to be constrained by the formalities of the prosecutor's interrogations often found ways to include quite different written accounts in their dossiers: through sending along old correspondence, by writing out the stories that were not heard or fully articulated in the interrogation, or even by telling the medical expert a different version of the events that led to the crime. For example, nine days after what Victorine Lelong believed to be an unsatisfactory interview with the prosecutor, she sent him a lengthy letter from prison, stating that she had not yet been able to speak as she wished and wanted the opportunity to explain more fully the circumstances surrounding her crime. Lelong took her story back in time, beginning with the period of unhappiness that was, for her, the source (and explanation) of her violent act. The story Lelong told was one of suffering and deprivation. She identified in specific terms her claim to the sympathy of her listener, assuming the moral high ground in comparison to the shoddiness of her lover Langlois and, while never justifying her act, rehearsed her experience of profound grievance at Langlois's hands. Her story began with the serious illness of her daughter, during which Langlois "never spoke a kind word nor offered to spend the night with me, even though it was his child as well as mine." Following the child's funeral, Langlois left to visit his mother for eight days. Lelong seems to have felt especially deserted in her grief. She then moved on to what appears to be the center of her story. During that summer of 1870, in the midst of war, Langlois was unemployed. Lelong reported: "We had only my wages; I worked day and night and he never lacked for anything even though he was not working." In the difficult winter of that year, according to Lelong, although she was two months pregnant, she gave Langlois her portion of meat as well as a small bit of wine provided by a generous benefactor "because he was so delicate and in such poor health." With the outbreak of violence during the Commune, she helped him to flee Paris so as to escape harm.

Lelong continued by describing a time when both she and her second child were ill, a time in which she appealed to Langlois for assistance, which he gave, but in a fairly restricted and grudging way; following her ability to resume work, she once again paid for her own meals so as not to be a burden. At this time, Langlois no longer lived with Lelong, but she continued to do his laundry, which he regularly brought to her. Her account describes her increasing need for Langlois's help and his growing distance from her, culminating in his advice to give up the child to public assistance. When the child died, Langlois refused to pay for the burial. Lelong found herself alone, deprived of her two children and abandoned by her lover, who had taken another mistress. In her despair, Lelong reported, she began to think that if Langlois were disfigured, he would return to her, knowing of her abiding devotion. Shaken by the sight of Langlois and his mistress, "seeing her enjoying the happiness that I deserved," she hurled a pot of vitriol at Langlois as he mounted the stairs to his home.

The details that Lelong provides in this letter place her crime in a context that attempts to establish a set of principles by which to evaluate her deadly act. Her emphasis on the ways that she cared for Langlois and her belief that he owed her loyalty and support in return mark a way of understanding the world that Lelong expects will be cogent, if not compelling, for her listener. The story itself is self-serving; more interesting is Lelong's mobilization of a set of assumptions about maternal devotion and domestic responsibilities that she sets against the story of female jealousy and vengeance. She appeals to the prosecutor by means of conventions that describe an ideal domestic manager whose consistently honorable behavior was thwarted by a man who had broken the codes that entitled her to his financial and emotional support.

Like Lelong, Rose Chervey wrote to the prosecutor in order to tell her story outside the format of the interrogatory. Again like Lelong, she began with an extended history of domestic patterns and expectations that she believed had to be set in place in order to understand her (failed) attack on her former lover, Paul Parquet.[74] She wrote: "I kept his house, cooked for him, even shined his shoes, and took care of him when he was sick." She explained her "*petites économies*" (cooking ragouts instead of chicken), and how she had pawned her possessions to support their ménage because Parquet gambled away his money. She noted especially that she had been as devoted to him as any legitimate wife, caring for him when he had a "shameful disease" (one that she eventually contracted), consenting "to wash his linen in order to spare him certain humiliations." Instead of the reciprocal loyalty that she believed she deserved, she found herself abandoned in a particularly humiliating manner—that is, via an emissary "who showed her little respect."

The accounts told by Lelong and Chervey reveal precise social codes that structured each woman's perception of her situation and provided the criteria that allowed each to identify a set of relevant details different from those produced in the official documents of the investigation. In Chervey's case, for example, the indictment presented a picture of a kept woman whose lover took care of all her needs, "who lacked for nothing," omitting all references to either his gambling debts or to her contributions to their domestic economy, details carefully restored in Chervey's letter. The narratives recorded by Lelong and Chervey established motivation and gave meaning to their acts in ways that made use of assumptions about gender-appropriate behaviors readily recognizable within the culture. While both women were most likely familiar with the canonical stories of jealousy and vengeance circulating in the popular press, it seems clear that this perspective did not encompass fully their own sense of identity nor did it exactly coincide with their own ways of understanding their social experience. Both women contradicted the assumptions embedded in the indictments, and also began to put in place alternative explanations referring implicitly to personal hopes and desires and emerging from their sense that the only real justice available to them was personal, not formal. In generating their own defense, they explicitly made use of expectations about appropriate gender roles—elevating in particular the good domestic manager—that were authorized by the culture and could be invoked to counter the more sensational popular stories about eruptions of vengeful jealousy. In fact, women quite regularly substituted explanations that drew upon current understandings of domestic responsibility and family order, pushing criminal stories toward a social meaning.

These alternative stories could not, however, simply displace the court's accounts, which remained for the most part strikingly formulaic. To be sure, some defendants, as we have seen, did attempt to tell stories quite different from the ones produced by the prosecutor, while others denied the validity of official accounts and persisted in refusing the language and style that was expected of them—insisting finally in the courtroom that they regretted only that their attacks had not fully succeeded. The implications of Marie Sivadon's whispered regret were drawn more explicitly by others who neither disavowed their intentions nor begged forgiveness. Instead, they persisted in their claims that the wrongs to which they had been subjected outweighed their crimes, or maintained to the end that the story needed to be told in a context and time frame that rendered their acts reasonable. On occasion, defendants attempted to forestall the direct interventions of the prosecutor and their courtroom interrogators. With unusual fortitude, Célestine Béal interrupted the pre-

[handwritten margin note at top: →as if the reality or the stories of the lower classes are unknowable]

siding magistrate to remark that "it is not worth the trouble of questioning me if you are already sure [of my guilt] and if you do not want to believe me."[75] But this breach in deference was rare in an environment that was both formal and austere, filled with symbolic reminders of the authority and power of the state and its representatives. And it is not at all clear that defiantly oppositional stories produced any immediate effects. Often these stories were entirely omitted from all official accounts or so reinterpreted by court personnel and by the press as to be unrecognizable. Most important, many, perhaps most, female defendants were acquitted, often on the grounds of their mental incapacity, an outcome that enabled the court to discount their alternative stories and to assume their repentance even when it could not be publicly elicited.

[handwritten margin notes: not; contradicts p. 134; ?]

More usual than direct confrontations were the awkward non sequiturs, the discordant patterns of question and response and the silences that appear again and again in so many transcripts. This nondialogue signals an ongoing contest over meaning that attests to cultural divides, exacerbated by class and gender differences, between accused and accusers. Such narrative disjunctions did not necessarily affect the outcome of individual cases or disturb the larger balance of power of which they were emblematic. Rather, through them one can glimpse the intersections between the stories produced by the prosecutor's investigation and those of individuals who did not necessarily share in the culture's dominant values, who interpreted the codes differently, or who were motivated by interests and desires that moved them to repudiate the narratives of the dominant culture.

On occasion, female defendants chose to remain silent when they found themselves unable to speak through the interference of already emplotted narratives. When the disjunction between the official story and the personal interpretation became too extreme, or when the rituals of the court became too intimidating, any speech at all may have seemed irrelevant or impossible. In her study of women's prison writings in recent times, Elissa Gelfand has noted that female criminals have often been silenced by their inability to speak through the rigidly dichotomous representations of deviant women preserved in the culture: feminine/virile; maternal/sadistic; hysterical/cunning; responsible/irresponsible.[76] It is this inability to find the appropriate cultural information that may explain the vacant places in women's stories—silences that were often realized in actual physical muteness.

The suggestive but ultimately opaque case of Cecille Breton in 1880 seems to reflect the interpretive difficulties—then and now—raised by Steedman's discussion of lives for which there are no available stories.[77] The fifteen-year-old defendant had set fire on three occasions to the attic and the bedroom of the building in which she lived with her mother, stepfather, and sister. The documents of the judicial dossier present deeply contradictory characterizations of Cecille Breton. According to her mother, Cecille was lazy, undisciplined, and wicked, given to lying and theft. Several of her employers testified, however, that she was "gentle, hardworking, and obedient"; one stated that she had raised her wages every week and would have kept her on if the mother had not spoken so badly about her; and another noted that the girl, sweet and hardworking, seemed unhappy and brutalized. Initially, Cecille remained mute through her interrogations, nodding only to admit that she had set the fires. Her silence suggested to the prosecutor that she might be mentally incompetent. He ordered a medical exam that found her slow, mentally defective, and incapable of monitoring her own behavior. The medical experts recommended that she be placed in a correctional institution for minors and, ultimately, the jury followed this line of thinking. Cecille Breton was judged guilty of setting the fires, but of having acted without discernment; she was confined to a correctional institution until she reached the age of twenty.

But we can be sure of neither her mental capacity nor her character. Nor can we know whether Cecille's silences were motivated by "inattention" or "lack of frankness" as her doctors suggested or by a self-censorship produced by the impossibility of the story that she would tell. When Cecille did finally speak, she told of parental neglect and abuse. She specifically denied that she did not want to work, but claimed, instead, that she wanted to be a dressmaker, although her mother refused to hear of it because of the long apprenticeship it would require, and continued to place her as a laundress, that is, at the most menial level of work. Above all, she accused her stepfather of attempting sexual contacts with her, in the attic and in the bedroom, when her mother was away. The fires, she claimed, were to take revenge.

During her court appearance, Cecille Breton was asked by jurors who had difficulty hearing her responses to move to the center of the room— a young girl, small for her age, having the stature and demeanor, according to medical reports, of an eleven- or twelve-year-old, moved to stand alone in the grand *salle d'audience*. We are led to wonder just how difficult it was for her to tell her particular story. What did Cecille's muteness mean in her circumstances? Was she ambitious, but in a situation in which inchoate ideas about a better life had little meaning? Did she lack even a language to give such ideas meaning? Or was she only lazy? Or, if lazy and defiant, what might have been the cause? When she claimed that she set the fires in order to get away from her mother and stepfather, exactly what was she fleeing? This case is especially interesting because the prosecutor did seem to want to hear Cecille's story, although the final summary documents of his investigation called most of it into question. Departing dramatically from the typical format, he spoke at length in the privacy of his office both to Cecille and to her mother, lecturing the mother finally about her own inability to listen to Cecille and her apparent disregard of Cecille's feelings and needs:

There has been a complete transformation in your child. At the beginning, she presented a complete mutism so that one could not get a word out of her. One wondered if she were an idiot, hence the medical exam. But since the conversations with Dr. Blanche, your daughter has changed her demeanor. She responds when she is spoken to and her language is very sensitive. Hence she has explained today before you the bad feelings that led her to set the fires. She explained equally why she was returned from the houses where you had placed her. . . . It is evident that no one has been responsive to her interests and that with another kind of influence, this child would not have fallen to where she is.

Once again we must defer to Farge's insistence that the dossiers cannot be more than "fragments of the real," leaving us finally uncertain about the knowledge that we think we see revealed and even uncertain about the ways that these nineteenth-century people might have interpreted their own experiences. It does seem, however, as in the case of Cecille Breton, that there was neither the language nor the social space for certain stories to be told and heard.

In seeking to find a way to write of her own working-class childhood, Carolyn Steedman has objected to an "extraordinary attribution of sameness" in the literature that narrates working-class lives. She found that most cultural criticism produced an "absence of psychological individuality . . . the refusal of a complicated psychology to those living in conditions of material distress."[78] Analyzing the stories of working-class lives generated in the judicial process, we do not find the particularity that Steedman is searching for, and are more likely to be struck by the "sameness" of the accounts. But neither do we find a unified, unchallenged official story. Rather, what emerges are the intersections through which conflicting cultural expectations, existing social relations, and institutional practices produced various and differently nuanced stories of women's crime. Penal procedures pushed these stories toward homogeneity, toward accounts that largely reinscribed cultural norms, while flattening out the fantasies and hopes and suppressing the specificities of needs and desires that inflected women's accounts of their own lives. And the class and gender divides that separated female narrators from their listeners—that is, the disparity of power between the parties—further promoted the cultural weightiness of some stories over others. Yet the official stories could neither control the meanings women's behavior would have for the larger society nor monitor the ways in which they were appropriated by different groups in different contexts.

Public fascination with the female criminal "type" and the proliferation of stories "more terrifying than the truth itself" provided a broad audience for accounts of women's crime. The production of a unified and formulaic story in the judicial investigation was often undercut by the women who had immediately turned themselves in to police commissioners in order, above all, to explain themselves. Although the prosecutor's accounts often disregarded and distorted women's voices, the prosecutors themselves, and sometimes the jurors as well, were listening, over and over again, to descriptions of the emotional and material circumstances of women's lives, to women's own ways of understanding their criminal acts, and to their sense of unacknowledged but valid entitlements. Female criminality and its varied and contradictory representations reveal, then, moments of cultural construction and cultural dissonance. Without the broader contemporary debate about women's place in French society, the stories told by criminal women might have remained entirely marginal, without cultural weight. In the context of the social ferment of the fin-de-siècle, stories of women in all their diversity became part of contested cultural territory. The meaning of women's criminal acts remained an open question as the judicial system provided an arena for the expression of stories-in-tension as well as a site from which these conflicting stories would circulate more broadly.

DISORDERED BODIES, DISORDERLY ACTS

Medical Discourse and the Female Criminal

> Each culture has its risks and its specific problems. It attributes a power to some image or another of the body, according to the situation of which the body is a mirror.
>
> Mary Douglas, *Purity and Danger*, 1966

Nineteenth-century physicians were preoccupied with the relationship between women as reproductive bodies and questions of female deviance. Witness the following exemplary moments:

Henriette Cornier was orphaned in infancy and was raised alternately by an aunt and, from the age of twelve years, by a tutor who treated her harshly. At nineteen, she married, but left her husband after four months, traveled to Paris, and worked as a seamstress and as a domestic. She became more somber, more taciturn, and, according to contemporary reports, gave up religion and lost her morals, living with several men in succession and producing two children whom she later abandoned. In November 1825, at the age of twenty-seven, she invited her neighbors' nineteen-month-old daughter into her room and murdered the child, severing the head from the trunk and throwing the head out of the window and into the street. According to witnesses, Cornier showed no emotion (and no remorse) following this act, while Cornier herself claimed that the murder had been premeditated and that she had wanted to kill the child. At her trial, the prominent alienist, Ch.-C.H. Marc, argued that Cornier had been overcome by an irresistible homicidal impulse deriving from a "profound lesion of the will" that had destroyed her moral freedom. Marc concluded his medical testimony with the previously unrevealed evidence, introduced to explain the pathological loss of will, that at the time of the murder, Henriette Cornier was in the midst of her menstrual period. Rejecting Marc's diagnosis, the judge found Cornier mentally competent, hence responsible; she was condemned to forced labor for life. (1826)[1]

Mme R had been married for one year, but the marriage was not a happy one. Her husband developed chronic bronchitis and worked for only four months. Mme R had to abandon her trade of waistcoat maker in order to attend to her housework and care for her ailing spouse. She was pursued unrelentingly by demanding creditors. She no longer ate or slept properly, became anemic, and her menstrual periods ceased. She developed sensations of congestion in her head, irritability, bizarre forgetfulness, and "poorly restrained compulsions." During this time, Mme R stole 1,500 francs. Medical experts argued that the cessation of her periods produced a condition of physical and moral debility that attenuated her criminal responsibility. The court decided not to prosecute Mme R. (1868)[2]

A woman whose psychic difficulties began with puberty committed a crime under the sway of her mental condition; she was condemned to forced labor for life. Her madness became evident and she was confined to an asylum. She spent twenty years there, and having reached menopause was suddenly cured. It was only by the suppression of her periods in menopause that she was able to be cured. (1880)[3]

The historian Catherine Fouquet has pointedly wondered if the history of women must necessarily pass through women's bodies, if the story of the female body is, for contemporary historians, *un détour obligé*.[4] With a similar sense of frustration, and even exasperation, Simone de Beauvoir wrote in *The Second Sex* that "the subject [woman] is irritating, especially for women, and it is not new."[5] Implied in both statements is the concern that a rehearsal of the terms by which women have been enclosed in their sexed bodies recapitulates the conceptual categories of the past—or at least leaves them unrevised. Fouquet notes that the history of the body as it has been written in the past twenty years has primarily been a history of women: that is, even as women's bodies have been given a history, the bodies of powerful men have remained outside of and irrelevant to historical accounts, which have only intermittently taken note of male bodies belonging to the poor and powerless—the peasant, soldier, or worker. The new histories of women's bodies, she argues, escape in some ways older masculinist assumptions but, inadvertently perhaps, echo others that have linked women more closely to nature and generated a narrative peopled largely by embodied women and disembodied men.

Yet Fouquet concludes, I think rightly, that the story of the female body, the unavoidable detour, is necessary in order to demystify the ways that assumptions about sexed bodies have operated historically. This seems particularly true for historians of the nineteenth century when preoccupations with the essential feminine—the biological female, the woman fully and definitively comprehended by her sex—attained, in Fouquet's terms, the status of "an emotional paroxysm." According to Thomas Laqueur, this preoccupation took shape in the late eighteenth century, a period that witnessed a reinterpretation of the female body in relation to the male. In his recent study *Making Sex*, Laqueur argues that En-

lightenment thinkers of all sorts replaced a centuries-old paradigm that
described a single-sex model of the human body, in which the female
was in effect an imperfect male, with a new model of radical dimor-
phism.[6] Where earlier discourse had construed female genitals as the interior version of a single male model—that is, as structures similar to
male genitals but tucked up inside the body—late-eighteenth-century
writers saw difference; male and female bodies that had been understood
as possessing similar structures on the same (male) continuum came to
be interpreted as incommensurable. Beginning in the Enlightenment,
biology became the ground for a new conception of *opposite* sexes.

In both social theory and medical science, writers produced new evidence that attested to the primacy of difference. In Laqueur's words,
"women's bodies in their corporeal, scientifically accessible concreteness,
in the very nature of their bones, nerves, and, most important, reproductive organs, came to bear an enormous new weight of meaning."[7]
The work of the nineteenth-century historian Jules Michelet is exemplary of the kinds of literature that reconfigured women as their sex.
Seeking ostensibly to challenge what he saw as medieval superstitions
about female impurity and depravity and to break the silence surrounding female bodies, Michelet created a scandal at midcentury by publishing *L'Amour*, which included such taboo topics as women's sexual pleasure, sexual hygiene, and menstruation. Michelet's goal was to rewrite
the imagery of female biology, rehabilitating "woman" so that her potential role as republican mother could be realized. Invoking recent dis-
coveries in ovariology and embryology in order to link women scientifically to the advance of civilization, he associated menstrual blood with
the beneficent functions of reproduction and motherhood. In thus spir-
itualizing and purifying *la crise périodique*, Michelet created what Thérèse
Moreau has called the sacred cult of the bleeding womb.[8] In this sancti-
fication of reproduction, however, Michelet most dramatically collapsed
woman into her womb, rendering her a being apart whose essential life
experiences and possibilities were dictated by biology. Her natural role
may have been transcendent, but her natural condition left her imprisoned in her body:

She is generally unwell one week of four. The week that precedes the crisis is already troubled. And in the eight or ten days that follow this painful week there
is a prolonged languor, a weakness, that could not be defined. But we now understand it. It is the healing of an internal wound which, at bottom, is the source
of the whole drama. So that in reality, fifteen or twenty days out of twenty-eight
(one might say nearly always) the woman is not merely sick, but wounded.[9]

Michelet was one among many writers in diverse fields who searched for, and thus found, evidence to support Rousseau's dictum that "the male is only a male now and again, the female is at all times a female."[10] This consolidation and intensification of ideas about gender difference grounded in biology became the basis not only for the ways in which men and women lived in their bodies but also for their socially prescribed ways of occupying public and private spaces.

As social discourse became increasingly committed to enumerating the concrete implications of biological difference, doctors specializing in women's illnesses—that is, gynecologists, obstetricians, and (especially as the century wore on) alienists, specialists in the new discipline of mental medicine—began to stake out their claims to scientific authority. Because medical speculation about the relationship between mind and body raised fundamental questions about the nature and limits of free will and the meaning of human agency, these same issues preoccupied philosophers, theologians, social scientists, and politicians as well as lawyers and criminologists. All were engaged in efforts to sort out the social consequences of urban life, to assess the potential danger of the psychopathology of crowds, discover the sites and sources of antisocial behaviors, and separate the mad from the bad. Doctors were thus but one constituency struggling to understand the nature and limits of human willfulness and the relative impact on human behavior of environmental and biological conditions.

The pursuit of *"une gynaecologie militante"* was, however, one of the means by which doctors could separate themselves from the many experts and amateurs who produced the new vision of sexual difference. In generating scientific knowledge that asserted the primacy of the natural body—making the natural body "the gold standard of social discourse"— doctors created the ground for their own authority. In the process, they became participants in a secular discourse that worked especially to preempt clerical authority on matters of morals and culture.[11] The female body was constituted in their writings as an animal body, stripped of religious superstition and metaphysics and assimilated to the larger natural world. To prove this perspective was to displace their professional competitors. Doctors analyzed menstrual blood to demonstrate its absolute identity with other kinds of blood; they studied the precise physiology of menstrual functioning, drawing the analogy between menstruation and animal rut; they described ovulation so as to underscore the natural, mechanical, autonomous nature of female fertility, removing it from the more sentimental context of human affect.[12] This was a preeminently naturalized, secular body whose secrets would be revealed by men of science.

In the context of this epistemological shift and in the service of their professional aspirations, alienists sought to insert themselves into the criminal justice system as the most qualified arbiters of the meaning of behavior. They were concerned with underwriting the attributes of femaleness (and, more derivatively, of maleness) while offering simultaneously a conceptual grid for separating the normal-natural-healthy from the abnormal-unnatural-pathological. Beginning in the 1830s and continuing through the century, they challenged assumptions about the transparency of madness, calling into question customary understandings of mental health as well as the ability of a lay person to recognize the subtle manifestations of disease. They claimed that, in assessing criminal responsibility, only specialized clinicians could separate illness from moral weakness, irresistible impulse from unresisted impulse. As a privileged (that is, scientific) interpreter of female behavior—as the professional best able to attest to the relationship between a woman's mind and her body, between her will and her emotions—the medical expert began to establish an institutional anchor for his professional authority in the judicial process.

The cases that introduce this chapter mark out, chronologically and discursively, a period in which new standards of criminal responsibility emerged in tandem with new medico-legal understandings of women's reproductive biology, sexuality, and madness. In the years between the unsuccessful medical defense of Henriette Cornier—the first attempt to invoke this particular kind of menstrual incapacity as a defense—and the release of Mme R, a new medical discourse that linked female reproductive biology to intermittent or partial insanity emerged to support pleas for attenuated responsibility. In the clinic, in the asylum, and in the courtroom, alienists described female deviant behavior in terms of mental disease produced by disordered biology. Marc's novel and somewhat quirky defense, unconvincing in 1826, moved quickly from the periphery to the center of a medical discourse that increasingly drew tight conceptual links between female criminality and reproductive functioning. Acquittals or mandatory confinements of women on the basis of actions perceived as biologically driven had become commonplace by the middle decades of the century and persisted well into the twentieth century, even as understandings of disease etiology were transformed. Femaleness became in itself a mitigating factor in the penal process as women, saturated by their sex, were seen as essentially and inevitably responding to forces beyond their control.

In producing their expert knowledge, alienists situated Woman, defined in terms of biology, at the crossroads of several intersecting cultural developments. This symbolic female was placed at the juncture of nineteenth-century efforts to redraw the boundaries between men and women, between reason and madness, between the criminal and the sick, between law and medicine. Each of these efforts was independent *and* linked to the others; none was focused exclusively on the reproductive female. But by linking disorderly acts with disordered female bodies, physicians who claimed to be experts on motivation and self-control created a space in the judicial system from which they urged a medicalized understanding of female biology. It is the purpose of this chapter to explore the articulation of this discourse and the effects of medico-legal expertise in the criminal courts.

It was in establishing the new specialty of forensic medicine that doctors most directly participated in larger debates about individual pathologies and social danger. While the penal code of 1810 was predicated on the doctrine of free will and personal accountability, beginning in the 1830s doctors of mental medicine began to speak of mental disease in terms that blurred the line between sanity and insanity, making it considerably more difficult to determine the parameters of individual responsibility, and making expert consultation all the more necessary.[13] According to an 1824 law, judges were empowered to reduce penalties in cases that had been affected by extenuating circumstances; under the terms of this statute, the mental condition of the accused became a primary criterion in justifying a plea for leniency, providing an opening for alienists to secure their specialty both professionally and institutionally. In defining their areas of competence, alienists focused more and more on the factors that compromised human self-control, producing a model of a human actor whose rational choices were undermined by overwhelming neurophysiological impulses. In the case of women, they marshaled data about the female reproductive cycle and feminine nervous irritability to account for behavior that, they alleged, was beyond personal volition.

The diagnosis of monomania, which emerged to chart a space between reason and madness, was instrumental in opening procedures in the criminal justice system to medical intervention.[14] First elaborated by J. E. D. Esquirol, one of the early alienists, and formally admitted into the French language by the Académie Française in 1835, "monomania" referred to behavior characterized by a "profound perversity" that could not be explained in terms of complete mental alienation.[15] Alienists described "a delirium more silent and more restricted" than the burning, generalized delirium of the maniac—a partial mental impairment among people who, absent the interpretive skills of the specialist, might pass for sane. Monomania could manifest itself as a single pathology of the intellect, characterized by an idée fixe in an otherwise sound mind, described by alienists as *folie lucide, manie avec conscience* (lucid madness, insanity with consciousness).[16] This definition could not, however, encompass the full range of behaviors that seemed to fall within the umbrella classification of partial insanity. For example, in cases such as the homicide committed by Henriette Cornier, what was especially noteworthy was the profound passivity of the accused. Cornier's crime did not appear to emerge from either a single compelling idea or from an emotional excess. Doctors explained such cases as instances of *monomanie instinctive*, a pathological disturbance of the will in which the accused was propelled into action by an irresistible impulse. When neither the intellect nor the will appeared to be the source of the abnormal behavior, alienists described further a *monomanie raisonnante*, or a *folie morale* (reasoning madness, moral madness), characterized by a perversion of the inclinations and emotions.

These syndromes presented a model of madness in which the essential pathology was temporary but recurring, if not explicitly periodic—*folies partielles, transitoires, passagères*. When applied to female behavior, the monomania diagnosis was strikingly apt as a means to connect mental illness that could be intermittent and limited (even passing or migrating) to organic functioning. The reproductive life cycle of women—punctuated by puberty, childbearing, and menopause—offered convincing material ground from which to account for partial mental derangement. In cataloguing the range of psychic disorders that could arise from disturbances in the reproductive cycle, alienists charted a direct path from symptoms to mental disease. Each of the variable symptoms could, according to medical theory, readily deteriorate into its characteristic form of madness: melancholia became suicidal monomania; excitability became erotic monomania or homicidal monomania; irritability became religious monomania; and so on. And each form of monomania had its characteristic place in the female life cycle, which was understood as inevitably and immutably defined by the workings of biology.

Alienists claimed, on the basis of both medical theory and clinical practice, that the female reproductive cycle was itself a kind of pathology that placed women chronically at risk. According to medical texts, a woman's life divided into three phases—before, during, and after reproductive functioning—a cycle that left her in a permanent state of physical, mental, and spiritual disequilibrium in which she fluctuated between reason and unreason. Woman could, at any point, cross this unstable boundary in the throes of "menstrual psychosis," "puerperal insanity," or "menopausal mania." Paraphrasing Mme de Stael's remark that love, merely an episode in the life of a man, is the entire life of a woman, Dr. Aimé Schwob explained that woman's reproductive cycle *was* her life *en tout*.[17] In a major treatise on menstrual neuroses, the alienist Dr. Pierre Berthier laid out the terrain:

In effect, from birth to death, a woman who experiences the full range of her obligations finds herself, each day, in submission to a multitude of impressions and mishaps. From one side, the nervous temperament that is her fate predisposes her to reactions from the brain to the uterus; from the other side, she is compelled to obey the operations of the uterus on the brain. . . . During the period of her fecundity, a woman must be regulated because her organism is the theater of a general and local inflammation that disturbs the harmony of her economy.[18]

Here, then, was the "natural" female—the female as animal body—fully realized.

Medical language unequivocally conveyed alarm, speaking equally of puberty, menopause, pregnancy, and ordinary menstruation in terms of "attacks," "eruptions," "crises," "outbreaks," "critical moments," and "abnormal states." Citing ancient texts that claimed that it was enough simply to walk a menstruating woman through a garden to prevent flowers from growing and to kill all the insects, nineteenth-century doctors claimed that, although menstrual blood had proved to be chemically innocuous, classical beliefs had gained credibility because the ancients had rightly perceived that menstruation was essentially fearsome, and could, in fact, "annihilate reason."[19] In Berthier's terms, every hemorrhage produced a heightened nervous susceptibility that approached illness.[20] Menstruation thus allegedly exercised dominion over the woman, who inevitably succumbed to its hold on her reason: "*l'empire de la menstruation sur le délire*."[21] A. A. Tardieu summarized the medical consensus: "It is certain that the menstrual cycle, when it involves the suppression of the period, when the flow is moderate, even when it presents nothing out of the ordinary, plays a large role in the production of neuroses and madness."[22]

What is striking in the medical literature is the extraordinary flexibility of the theory that linked menstruation to mental illness. For example, because Berthier claimed that "the menstrual anomaly does not impart the character of the nervous disorder that it produces"—that is, that there was no obvious relation between symptom and its biological source—he was able to list no fewer than seventy varieties of disease deriving from problems of menstruation, including twenty-nine forms of madness.[23] Nor was there any systematic attempt to explain exactly which kinds of menstrual difficulties led to nervous disorder or the exact physiology that produced the "pathogenic action of the uterus on the brain." Berthier speculated that the most vulnerable women—those with the greatest loss of blood and hence the most heightened nervous sensitivities—were either women living in hot climates or those who had given themselves over to sensual pleasures or licentious reading.[24] With little regard to coherence or consistency, doctors speaking from clinical experience reported that menstruating women were prone to extreme lethargy and indifference and to hyperactivity and overexcitement—in Berthier's words, "a maniacal overexcitement approaching incoherence, as much as a melancholic depression capable of descending into stupor."[25]

More to the point, following Tardieu's lead, alienists identified all experiences of menstruation as inherently pathological, as a departure from or a disturbance of a never-identified normal condition; the unspecified state of health against which aberrant functioning was measured became a vanishing point that receded into the infinite distance. In this context, the underlying assumption seems to be that in normal states biology is silent, missing; pathology becomes, then, the condition in which biological functions are visible.[26] The menstrual anomaly was, quite simply, menstruation itself. The early arrival of puberty, as well as its late appearance, were construed equally as warning signs of immanent mental illness; a light menstrual flow and a heavy flow were both dangerous; the beginning of puberty was likely to fatefully disequilibrate the young woman, but the suppression of periods was even more likely to throw her into a state of unreason; menopause could either produce madness or cure it. The following brief case reports convey something of the character of this literature:

Onset of menstrual period cures illness

A Parisian woman had experienced the suppression of her menstrual periods for the preceding three months, which caused her continuous headaches and threw her into a permanent state of melancholy; she decided to commit suicide by throwing herself into the Seine. She was about to exercise this plan when her periods returned. Her ideas immediately changed; she renounced her project and returned, cured, to her home.[27]

A twenty-nine-year-old woman, predisposed by heredity, experienced violent attacks of jealousy after her marriage; her periods stopped and she became insane. One day, her periods reappeared; the flow was abundant on Tuesday. From that day forward, all her ideas became reasonable, her accusations dissipated, her hallucinations ended, and after a month, the sick woman was in a condition to return to her family.[28]

Suppression of menstrual period cures illness

Mme L, who was sixteen years old when she began her menstrual periods, soon suffered the most violent hysterical crisis: marriage was advised. With her first pregnancy, the attacks ceased; with the return of her period, the attacks resumed. With her second pregnancy, the attacks were again suspended, but reappeared from the moment that menstrual periods resumed.[29]

Rather than disabling the authority of medical discourse, these contradictions, by rendering the theory infinitely malleable, constituted a large part of its power. Writing in 1880, Dr. Benjamin Ball could claim with authority that "disturbances of the uterus are today among the best recognized causes of mental illness . . . and *la folie utérine* has been established beyond dispute."[30]

In this enumeration of the pathological possibilities of the female reproductive cycle, some alienists described a gradual process by which the illness became fixed. According to Dr. Dauby, for example, "It is ordinarily by a slow, progressive process, by a more or less long succession of pathological events, that menstrual troubles lead to madness."[31] Others described a recurrent danger of "autointoxication" in which "the woman is effectively poisoned" as her blood is alternately retained and expelled.[32] But whatever the specific argument, the dominant mode of explanation saw each menstrual period as an episode of generalized systemic disturbance producing temporary mental imbalance. According to the physiological assumptions of the time, a periodically unstable, disequilibrated system was always a predisposing factor in the advent of disease in *les déséquilibrés*, the mentally ill. In cataloguing the ordinary physical and psychological changes of the female reproductive cycle, alienists had turned symptoms into disease entities.

It was but a short jump from the ordered symptoms—the illness—to the assumption that biology was the *cause* of behavior. The relation of behavior to body functions was assumed to be direct, unmediated, and determinative; menstrual functioning (or malfunctioning) produced moral lapse. The case of Mme R's theft, with which we began this chapter, is exemplary. At her first interrogation, Mme R offered a complete confession; however, the story shifted a bit over time. Although there is no conclusive evidence that Mme R was influenced by the medical experts who examined her, it is at least suggestive that the medical report notes that, while "today she still maintains this story [her original confession], she adds that if she had not been in a weakened physical and moral condition, she would have been able to resist the suggestions of poverty." The report concludes with the observation that "Mme R found herself in a state of physical and moral disturbance, produced by the cessation of her periods, which considerably attenuated her criminal responsibility and merits the court's indulgence."[33] What we see here, then, is the interpretive filter that medical expertise provided. Of all the possible ways of explaining or understanding this theft, the one that resonated most deeply, that seemed to link all the circumstances most logically, that proved most convincing for all parties, was the medical explanation that grounded women's behavior definitively in their bodies.

The argument had come full circle: female reproductive biology was construed as recurrently morbid; biological symptoms were codified as diseases that were manifested in temporary, partial loss of reason; and unreasonable or problematic behavior confirmed the presence of disease. By pathologizing behavior that did not conform to a hypothetical normal state, medical discourse ignored all the possible mediations that intervene between biology and action. The label of mental disease effectively obscured the personal meaning of behavior and drained it of social content. Murder, theft, despair, and eroticism all became equally, unproblematically, products of biology and manifestations of disease. By constructing an interpretive frame for explaining women's behavior in relation to their bodies, medical discourse laid out "scientific" definitions of femaleness that were brought into the courtroom, where their connection to sensational crimes introduced them to a popular audience.

At the time of the French Revolution, the criminal code had stipulated that a woman accused of a crime carrying the death penalty could not be tried unless it was first ascertained that she was not pregnant at the time of the trial, on the presumption that pregnancy deprived her of the mental acuity necessary for her defense.[34] These medical concerns were gradually extended to include every aspect of female reproductive biology. Nearly half a century after Michelet had described the disabled reproductive female, his pronouncements could be heard echoing in the statements of a prominent alienist who cautioned against allowing menstruating women to testify in court. He noted that, through most of the month, women had no recollection of their behavior during their menstrual periods, while, in the midst of their periods, they could not remember what had occurred on intermenstrual days.[35] One might say, as had Michelet, that women were "nearly always" in a state of relative incapacity.

Alienists argued that in all criminal cases the medical expert ought to provide a complete menstrual history. With the spectre of Henriette Cornier continuing to haunt both medical theory and legal opinion, experts increasingly attributed crimes of murder (homicidal monomania) to a mental imbalance generated by reproductive functioning:

A young woman of St-Germain-en-Laye was brought, in 1829, to the hospital Beaujon; it was evident that she was afflicted by a profound melancholia. . . . In response to the pressing questions that were addressed to her, she responded, in tears, that she was tormented by a violent desire to kill someone. This young woman was married and a mother. When these attacks overcame her, it was especially her husband and children who became the focus of her deadly inclination. . . . Antecedents for this illness were investigated carefully; she had never experienced a tragedy, she had never been ill. Her character had never been irregular; at no time had she had a melancholic disposition. She loved her husband and children. This murderous instinct had taken her suddenly; it coincided with a disturbance in her menstrual periods, which had become irregular. Every time that these attacks recurred, she experienced a violent headache; they occurred especially at the time of her menstrual period. . . . Medication was ordered to regularize her menses. The treatment was successful and she left the hospital completely tranquil.[36]

[Dagonet reports] the case of his patient who, with each monthly period, was taken with homicidal impulses and who, under this influence, had killed her three children.[37]

On April 16, 1874, Héloise Désirée, widow, age thirty-one years, went out in the evening accompanied by her two children. Having arrived at a pond, she took the little girl, age five, under her arm, and gripping her little boy, age eight, tightly by the hand, she jumped violently into the pond, dragging her children with her. She was pulled out, but her two children drowned. [Legrand du Saulle . . . stated in his report] that the widow D was in the second day of her menstrual period at the time of her crisis and that she evidenced migraine [*cephalalgie*] and temporary aberrations of reason with each menstrual period.[38]

DRAME DE LA FOLIE

UNE MÈRE QUI TUE SON ENFANT

"A drama of madness: a mother who kills her child."

Similarly, by midcentury, Dr. Brierre de Boismont claimed authoritatively that theft (*monomanie du vol*) doubled in intensity during menstrual periods.[39] In the case of Mme Ch, for example, who, "under the sway of physical excitations" (anomalies of menstruation), stole several articles of small value, the consulting doctor maintained that the accused suffered from *monomanie du vol*.[40] He claimed that her impulsive acts were surrounded by mental and physical disturbances that clearly revealed a condition of mental illness. While the initial trial resulted in a condemnation to thirteen months in prison, a second court pronounced her acquittal. The report of the medical expert concluded with the confirming observation that, with the return of regular menstrual periods, Mme Ch was restored to health—and, we may presume, to moral probity as well.[41]

In the 1880s, alienists attested to a growing "epidemic" of kleptomania. The definition of the disease itself—the criteria that separated criminal acts from those provoked by illness—spoke specifically to the problem of apparently unmotivated behavior driven by desires that were out of control. These discussions were fueled by the advent of department stores. With their proliferation of elegantly displayed merchandise, and with the emergence of the new leisure activity of "just looking," they generated increasing concern about shoplifting and, more generally, about women's behavior in newly opened public spaces. Alienists characterized kleptomania as the act of well-brought-up women from good families, belonging to a respectable social stratum, who had never gone astray, lived in essentially comfortable, even luxurious conditions, and yet were found stealing items of small value for which they had no particular need.[42] The case histories of kleptomaniacs typically included representations of a woman "whose husband had never refused her any necessity,"[43] or, for example, women like the marquises, comtesses, baronesses, and other *grandes dames* arrested in the Bon Marché department store on a single day during the Exposition of 1889, all apparently overcome by an "excess of temptation."[44] The diagnosis of kleptomania accounted for behavior that did not conform either to experts' beliefs about the bourgeoisie or to their assumptions about criminal theft. As Patricia O'Brien has argued, by focusing on bad heredity and psycho/physiological disturbances, alienists confirmed that bourgeois women who stole what they did not need were sick.[45]

In an apocryphal but exemplary anecdote, one husband reported that he was required to keep his wife locked in a closet once a month in order to control her instinctive impulsion to steal.[46] Medical opinion endowed this *histoire* with interpretive power as psychiatrists accumulated evidence of a clear causal connection between such thefts and female reproductive biology. Case histories described moments of physical weakness, confusion, vertiginous sensations, hot flashes, and headaches that preceded the impulsive act, all pointing to its source in some form of "genital or ovarian debility." The alienist Tardieu reported, for example, the case of a woman who "had matured late, without regular periods, which sometimes were missed for three or four months; she had been subject to headaches, to sensations of suffocation, to cramps that doubled in intensity with her periods; it was after a miscarriage that she performed her first larceny. Is it not evident," Tardieu asks, "that the instinctive impulsion, as well as the convulsive state, emerged under the sway of menstruation?"[47] From Tardieu's perspective, the logic that ordered his selection and assessment of the "evidence" was beyond question.

This connection was drawn more formally as a result of several discussions by the Société de Médecine Légale in 1881. The alienist Henri Legrand de Saulle reported his analysis of data collected by the Paris Prefecture of Police between 1868 and 1881. In 104 cases of women accused of theft, but whose behavior was specifically considered sick rather than criminal, he found 24 to be "pathological" thefts, that is, committed by imbeciles, insane hysterics, epileptics, and those afflicted with senile dementia. In the remaining 80 cases, he alleged, 35 were women in the midst of their menstrual period, 10 were in a state of "grave debility" due to menopause, 5 were pregnant, and 30 were women with more or less hysterical symptoms, only 6 of whom did not have their period.[48] It was possible, then, to explain nearly all of these cases in terms of reproductive functioning. The women who were arrested for theft confirmed the story of a compulsion they could not resist and, at the same time, suggested other motives: their lack of personal money; their desire to buy things (including presents for lovers) without their husbands' knowledge; their wish to *possess* the objects spread out so temptingly before them; their decision, in effect, to strike the ultimate bargain in the new consumer economy.[49] These explanations tended, however, to be obscured in medical discussions that focused more insistently on biological determinants.

This linking of female biology and madness was not, of course, entirely new in the nineteenth century. Ideas about women's psychic vulnerability and the ways in which women were seen to live in permanent, intimate connection to uterine rhythms had long histories that remained surprisingly consistent over the centuries. The history of the disease of hysteria brings together with particular vividness the intersections of longstanding mythical associations around women's bodies, their reproductivity, and their sexuality, on the one hand, with medical understandings that shifted over time on the other. In the mid-nineteenth century, for example, hysteria was considered to be a specific disorder of the reproductive organs, an illness that was, in its enigmatic and mysterious aspects, self-evidently female. This perception represents what Gladys Swain has called a persistent, traditional *imaginaire* focused on the uterus—a mythical/physiological system that revealed the alleged truth of the female body.[50] In actual practice, throughout nearly all of the century, those suffering from hysteria sought out doctors who specialized in "women's illnesses" (gynecologists), and medical literature routinely referred to hysteria in connection to menstruation.[51] These associations are especially interesting because they attest to the persistence of assumptions about uterine disorders at exactly the moment in the final third of the century when medical discourse shifted the site of investigation of hysteria from the womb to the nervous system.

Swain argues that the explosion of the problem of hysteria in the 1880s marked the last episode of a very old story and the opening moments of a new one.[52] Beginning with Jean-Martin Charcot and culminating in the work of Freud, hysteria came to be seen as a sign of psychic rather than bodily disturbance; the fractured subject would lose, after Freud, its corporeal reference, replaced by a notion of divided consciousness. In the period we are looking at here, however, these distinctions existed only in the loosest sense. Rather, gynecologists and alienists typically preserved the aura of disordered biology suggested by hysteria's links to the uterus, referring vaguely (and sometimes specifically) to problems in organic functioning, while the connections between women's reproductive apparatus and nervous disease remained apparently valid but imprecisely rendered. Charcot's work was transforming medical understandings of the relationship between mind and body but without important practical effects, as gynecologists and alienists as well as the general population continued to describe a particularly female neurosis whose origins lay in women's bodies.

In the 1880s, the most significant effort to provide a precise description of the disease of hysteria occurred in the lecture halls and photographic ateliers of Salpêtrière, an asylum for indigent and insane women, where Charcot, the famed *Napoléon des névroses*, produced a map that charted an exact symptomology for his newly defined stages of hysterical illness. Under the influence of Charcot's powerful personality, and in response to explicit and subliminal clues from Charcot and his assistants, the hysterics of Salpêtrière enacted the master's formulations. In his flamboyant "Tuesday lectures" and in his photographic laboratory, Charcot educated patients and doctors alike in the appropriate behavioral and gestural manifestations of a disease that had become by this period nearly epidemic.[53] In front of a packed hall of journalists, authors, actors, actresses, demimondaines, and medical students, Charcot's hypnotized patients gave spectacular hysterical performances. At the same time, the photographic laboratory of Salpêtrière generated an unparalleled visual repertoire of hysterical characteristics, poses, and attitudes—enhanced by sets and theatrical lighting and peopled by an increasingly familiar cast of patients-cum-models—that traveled quickly from the institution into popular culture.

The effects of Charcot's codification were, however, somewhat ambiguous. His "scientific" data ultimately coexisted with older ways of explaining hysterical illness, as medical discourse continued to describe a symptomology of hysteria that, in effect, defined the outlines of femininity: emotivity, suggestibility, volatility or emotional mercuriality, irritability. It was the excessive quality of these characteristics—hyperemotivity, hypersuggestibility—that turned ordinary femaleness into disease. And it was the medical expert who claimed authority to make that distinction. So although Charcot had demonstrated the existence of male hysteria, it remained, as Elaine Showalter has argued, in both its medical and popular incarnations, a quintessentially female malady. Even as physicians sought to give greater precision to their descriptions of symptoms, medico-legal experts relied as much on the general qualities that linked hysteria to femininity as they did on a more technical discourse; science and myth coexisted in an easy symbiosis. Thus physicians familiar with the specific symptoms catalogued at Salpêtrière checked female defendants for the presence (or absence) of a hysterical syndrome or crisis: the *boule qui remonte*, constriction of the throat and a sense of suffocation; loss of consciousness; loss of sensation on one side of the body; reduced auditory or visual acuity; ability to be easily hypnotized; and the contortions and poses that identified different phases of the hysterical attack. But more characteristically, they searched their subjects' medical histories for early experiences of loosely defined "nervous crises," menstrual difficulties, and evidence of personalities that were *exaltées* and *surexcitées*, prone to the *accidents nerveux* that attested to the essential instability (*mobilité de caractère*) that announced the hysteric.

The medico-legal report on Rose Chervey, prepared in 1882 by Dr. Paul Brouardel of the Paris Faculty of Medicine, is particularly interesting in this regard.[54] Chervey had fired several shots at her former lover, who had ended their irregular liaison in response to pressure from his parents; she was arrested and accused of attempted murder.[55] Brouardel's court-ordered report indicates that Chervey claimed to have experienced several "attacks of nerves" since her incarceration in Saint-Lazare prison. She reported a sensation of suffocation and of heat and pain in her head, but no members of the staff had witnessed these episodes. Brouardel himself observed a diminished cutaneous sensitivity to pain on her left side, although she responded normally to contact and heat. He concluded, "in sum, [she] is a hysteric. The symptoms that she notes . . . leave no doubt on this point." He indicated further that Chervey did not belong to the class of grand hysterics (convulsives), but that her hysterical condition could be confirmed in a variety of revealing behaviors. She evidenced, according to Brouardel, a telling "spontaneity," "a vivacity of affect" that suggested an inability to reflect on the implications of her actions, which, when the hysteria was not too pronounced, "gives the conversation of these women a piquant charm." Finally, Brouardel noted, "like all hysterics," she succeeded in presenting her story "artistically," making it difficult for the expert to discern in what measure she was lying.

Brouardel seems here to be caught up in his own ambivalence—to be charmed by the woman before him, yet anxious that he might be duped by the appeal that she exerted. He is, at the same time, clearly aware of some of the contradictions that her dossier presents. He states, for example, that she has behaved precipitously, the telltale *mobilité de caractère* being evident in her becoming her lover's mistress without much forethought; but, immediately following this statement, he notes that she has also shown a capacity for devotion and constancy by staying with her lover for several years through numerous privations. It is in the diagnosis of hysteria that Brouardel resolves the ambiguities of Chervey's case. With this diagnosis, he is at once able to accommodate unresolved contradictions, to connect his subject to a disturbing femininity, and to offer an authoritative medical report that comments on "all hysterics" (if not all women) as it simultaneously refines and blurs the characteristics of the disease of hysteria.[56] In the end, Brouardel asserts (as do nearly all medico-legal reports that reflect on the possible hysteria of female defendants) that the hysteric, whose reason is not disturbed, who is not subject to delirium or delusion, is responsible for her behavior, although this responsibility is necessarily attenuated by the emotivity associated with her condition. The hysteric, then, was not mentally ill, but neither was she competent. As exemplified in Brouardel's report, medico-legal opinion on hysteria confirmed a recognizable nineteenth-century disease while preserving the metaphorical resonance of older assumptions about emotionally disordered women. It is this potent combination of scientific observation and evocative inference that enabled medical discourse to authorize the disabling of the feminine—creating the terms in which femaleness would become a mark of limited capacity.

In his discussion of what he calls the eighteenth-century "humanitarian narrative," Thomas Laqueur has suggested a useful way of thinking about the effects of official documents such as the medico-legal report.[57] In looking at the autopsy, the parliamentary report, and the clinical case history, Laqueur argues that these documents built a "reality effect" based on minute observations and accumulations of detail whose increasingly formulaic expression "exposes the lineaments of causality and of human agency," constituting a "step-by-step account of the history of the body in relation to itself and to social conditions."[58] The repetition of these formulas, especially in a context endowed with institutional power, made them culturally available to a broad audience that was increasingly prepared to find in them a means of comprehending the behavior of others. In the late nineteenth century, the medico-legal report served this interpretive function, providing a scientific grammar that circulated widely within the culture. Like Laqueur's documents, the medico-legal report established its authority through the careful recitation of detail, based on clinical data and confirmed in a court of law. The ordered details—that is, the form of the narrative—became familiar, repeated in professional arenas as well as in the popular press, in realistic fiction, and in mundane genres such as the faits divers.

Medical reports of female defendants typically began with a discussion of the onset of menstruation followed by details of menstrual functioning (regularity, emotional responses, and so on) and, if appropriate, similar investigations of the physical "symptoms" generated by pregnancy, childbirth, or menopause. They recounted a possible history of "nervous crises" often dating back to childhood and confirmèd by a pattern of incorrigibility. They noted the nervous condition of the woman on the day or days immediately preceding the crime and the persistence (or termination) of nervous symptoms during the period of incarceration. They observed especially the volubility of the defendant and her emotional volatility (or withdrawal) during the medical interview, noting every occasion of crying and laughter. On the basis of these carefully arranged details, the medico-legal report drew conclusions that provided, finally, the causal connections that made the behavior understandable and invoked an appropriate social and institutional response—one that typically worked to acquit the defendant while delineating a particularly female incapacity.

The narrative strategies of the medico-legal report emerge in sharp outline in the case of Louise Charot.[59] Charot was accused of attempted murder in April 1885. She had worked as a domestic for Dr. Gromolard and had become his mistress. When, on his brother's insistence, he spoke of firing her and sending her away, she threatened him with both vitriol and a pistol. Finally, following her dismissal, Charot staged an elaborate ambush in her determination to take vengeance. She borrowed money from a friend and rented a small apartment; feigning illness, she asked a domestic to send for the doctor and then dismissed her for the evening; when Gromolard entered, she saluted him with gunshots and wounded him slightly. While the prosecution accused Charot of attempted murder, she countered by accusing Gromolard of performing an abortion on her in her early days of service, of knowingly giving her a venereal disease (syphilis), and of unconscionably sending her away before she was cured and could resume work elsewhere.

There is a striking discrepancy between the character of Charot that emerges in her interrogations by the investigating magistrate and the representation conveyed in the medico-legal report. Dr. Bouchereau of the St. Anne Asylum examined Charot for the court.[60] After surveying her family history, he found no record of poor mental health, yet concluded that her emotional responses to her conflicts with Gromolard suggested that she, in fact, had hysterical symptoms even without exhibiting the *grande attaque*. Bouchereau drew special attention to the fact that Charot seemed joyful in the days before the ambush and emphasized her repeated assertions that her only regret was to have misfired. He noted (presumably as evidence of impaired reasoning) that she continued to recount her assault on Gromolard with apparent pleasure, failing to realize that this would not help her case, and concluded, finally, that "there is an absence of equilibrium in her whole being; her lower faculties (those of animal existence) take precedence over her higher intellectual functions; everything is subordinated to her instincts, as in the case of all degenerates." In a final aside, Bouchereau observed that when dealing with people who are so naturally deceptive, the listener must remain skeptical of all that is said. His opinion was that Louise Charot exhibited a feeble intelligence and a moral insufficiency that left her unable to make appropriate judgments in everyday life, and that this rendered her only marginally responsible for her criminal act.

In an unusual turn, the attorney general (*procureur général*) found that this report did not provide an adequate assessment of Charot's responsibility (perhaps in light of the seriousness of her charges against Gromolard), and ordered a further examination by a panel of three eminent psychiatrists: Blanche, Motet, and again Bouchereau.[61] As a group, they confirmed all the findings of the earlier report in essentially the same terms, adding only several comments on Charot's "vanity" and "self-importance" that made her "inaccessible to the counsel of moderation" and immune to efforts to contradict or interrupt her story. In his courtroom testimony, Motet placed Charot in "the class of hysterics . . . the class of women for whom any exaggeration is possible," a woman incapable of resisting the pull of her instincts and appetites. Because she had carefully premeditated her crime, Motet concluded, she could not be declared completely without responsibility; but that her degree of responsibility was severely attenuated was beyond question.[62] In the end, Charot was acquitted.

The intellectual and moral inferiority attested to in the medico-legal testimony—the interpretive grid provided by the narrative of the hysteric—was far removed from Charot's self-presentation. She responded to questions directly and precisely, often qualifying with some care the exact terms of her grievances. At the very beginning of her testimony, she made a specific point of acknowledging that she was not a virgin when she met Gromolard and did not accuse the doctor of having seduced her. When the interrogator spoke of Gromolard's sending her away, Charot insisted that his offense was, more particularly, to send her away *while she was still sick*. In the same context, she informed her interrogator that Gromolard had paid her the 150 francs owed for her service; that is, she was accusing him of a particular offense and not others that might be more familiar to her audience. Throughout the questioning, she appears to be

My assessment: Charot was acquitted b/c she was really nuts

measuring her charges against the doctor according to a code of behavior that she deems reasonable and just.

The messiest and least resolved issues in this case involved Charot's charges that Gromolard had given her an abortion and infected her with syphilis, both of which he vehemently denied. It appears that Charot began to suspect, in spite of Gromolard's assurances, that the vaginal discharge she was experiencing could be a symptom of serious illness. (In a surprising moment in the midst of Gromolard's deposition, he noted that he found Charot reading his medical books.) She had observed that Gromolard gave himself drugs and injections and made her wash carefully after each episode of sexual intercourse. Finally, she consulted another doctor who confirmed her suspicions. Again, Charot made her precise accusation clear, commenting that she did not claim that Gromolard failed to care for her (he actually did treat her illness), but rather that he did not tell her that she had syphilis and lied about the severity of her illness. To support her allegations that Gromolard had performed an abortion, Charot requested an examination by a court-appointed physician. The subsequent medical exam refused to draw absolute conclusions that would implicate Gromolard, but did find that it was likely Charot had recently had a pregnancy of three or four months duration.

In sum, none of the testimony of the dossier, including Gromolard's, provides evidence to support the medical litany that rehearsed the terms of Charot's high-strung temperament and feeble intelligence. It seems more likely that the charged nature of this set of complaints and countercomplaints—ones that crossed class lines and threatened the reputation and career of a physician—set into play an already emplotted story. A medical narrative had become available that could organize the myriad details of the case, synthesizing the moral and physical evidence so as to produce a coherent and believable story.

While not always as sharply defined as in Charot's medical record, a list of "hysterical symptoms" figured prominently in many medico-legal reports. In an ironic commentary on the loose references that characterized the hysteria diagnosis, the mother of one defendant noted with some confusion that she "had never noticed that her daughter was a hysteric."[63] But perhaps even more revealing is the extent to which this particular medical narrative had become a part of popular culture. Working-class female defendants with menial occupations and sometimes limited ability to read and write could recount a history of nervous crises, especially on the days immediately preceding their criminal acts, that followed the ba-

— stung removed only down to Charot's deposition of 22 mai

sic outline of the medical report. And families hoping to gain an acquittal for their daughters supplied details of such nervous instability. In the case of Marie Cherrière, for example, an unmarried kitchenmaid accused of attempted infanticide, her parents sent the court documents attesting to several cases of insanity in the family and claimed that Marie had earlier experienced hallucinations and had been treated by several doctors.[64] (Cherrière rejected this line of defense, however, and insisted instead that, while she was living with her family, there was "nothing wrong with my head. I worked hard, we were poor and we didn't make very much, but we were not too unhappy. The doctor did not come for me, but for my sister.") In a similar case, this time of a young domestic, Justine Joseph, accused of setting fire to buildings belonging to her mistress, the letter from the mayor of the commune where Joseph was born testified to the respectability of the Joseph family and explained Justine's behavior as self-evidently a case of *monomanie du mal*, "a kind of insanity."[65]

My argument here is that the medico-legal report worked rhetorically to construct in scientific terms the disabilities and incapacities of the feminine. In actual practice, however, medical expertise did not secure for female defendants a judicial leniency that they did not already receive. The physicians who were listed as acceptable witnesses for the court did make extensive claims about professional expertise, and medical schools promoted professionalization with a range of special courses on medico-legal issues.[66] Nevertheless, medical testimony was not automatically authoritative. Jury verdicts often had no obvious connection to either formal legal principles or medical tests of responsibility. They reflected, rather, the jury's sense of whether or not the defendant was deserving of sympathy, that is, deserving of an acquittal based on extenuating circumstances emerging out of the defendant's character and social position and her readiness to express remorse. The jury was influenced in particular by the degree to which the defendant's situation corresponded to contemporary understandings of natural behavior. It seems likely that medical expertise may have been more important in the stories it told about female nature and women's bodies—stories that became part of popular culture and formed part of the imaginative repertoire of the men who sat on juries and of the women who appeared before them—than in the more specific, professional judgments that physicians offered.

The primacy of the symbolic and cultural effects of the discourses of forensic medicine may be seen especially in the persistence of particular narratives—specific explanatory models—within a context of changing medical paradigms. Medico-legal reports were, in effect, the product of conceptual layering in which theories and beliefs were not so much replaced as repositioned. Even as understandings of disease etiology shifted and old concepts became obsolete, the metaphorical and perceptual overlay of these earlier doctrines did not necessarily disappear; rather, they were incorporated into new diagnoses—given a diminished place, to be sure, but nevertheless retained.

By the 1880s, for example, the monomania diagnosis had largely fallen out of favor; monomaniacs disappeared from both the asylum and the courtroom.[67] Many alienists (especially Falret and Morel) had rejected from the beginning the possibility of so localized a mental illness.[68] They argued that monomania presumed too complete a separation among intellect, will, and emotions and failed to provide acceptable criteria for distinguishing between morbid passions and merely exaggerated ones. Because the monomania diagnosis had operated most effectively on the level of discourse, it could be discarded readily and without practical consequence. Similarly, rather than speak of specific diseases such as "menstrual psychosis" and "puerperal mania," medico-legal discourse in the closing decades of the century worried over: "unhealthy passions" arising in puberty;[69] the possibility of "bizarre disturbances of the intellect" that diminished moral freedom during pregnancy;[70] the likelihood that pregnant women "predisposed by their eminently nervous constitution" would develop mental illness;[71] and the ways in which the physical compulsions of pregnancy might produce secondarily an irresistible impulse that culminated in moral perversion and ultimately in crime.[72]

Echoing earlier pronouncements, the alienist Hélis Courtis insisted at the turn of the century that the medico-legal examination ordered for the defense take account of the "nervous excitability" of a woman during her menstrual period, "the abnormal reactive state" that diminishes psychic resistance to impulsions and "exposes women to recidivism with each menstrual period."[73] Similarly, Dr. Georges Morache, professor of legal medicine at the University of Bordeaux, argued in the 1890s that women could not be held to the same standards of responsibility as were men. He pointed to "troubles in various stages of genital life"—especially connected to accumulations and transformations of menstrual blood—that induced a condition of "autointoxication." Because of this "poisoning" that rendered her not insane, not sick, but "troubled in her psychic functioning," a woman could not be held fully responsible. In

Morache's words, "she feels differently [*autrement*], she thinks differently, she acts differently. In everything, she is *Other*, and the same principles of justice cannot be applied to her."[74]

The representation of the female life cycle as essentially pathological thus persisted, but with some significant differences. In a new medical climate, menstruation, pregnancy, and menopause were typically described less as the *cause* of mental disease and behavioral disorder than as triggers that released latent pathology. According to Dr. Icard, "menstruation is only the occasional cause; it is the drop that overflows the vase, the spark that ignites . . . but the seed has already been sown in fertile ground."[75] This shift was underpinned by the centrality accorded the disease of degeneration. Degeneration was a disease in which both symptoms and causes were believed to be simultaneously moral and physical. As a diagnosis it was especially compelling because it explained antisocial behavior in terms of tainted heredity—that is, the presence of a latent seed for pathology—that could be triggered equally by moral lapse or a depraved environment.[76] The concept of degeneracy allowed psychiatrists to have it both ways: the degenerate harbored a biologically compromised constitution (thus inviting specifically medical interventions); at the same time, appropriate moral fortitude and a hygienic environment could retard the eruption of inherited morbid tendencies (thereby engaging the medical community in broader issues of social explanation and social reform).

Within the framework of degeneration theory, it was the presence of morbid heredity that allegedly exacerbated the perturbations of the female life cycle, intensifying the forces of unreason and diminishing women's capacity for psychic resistance.[77] Psychiatrists maintained that what had been seen as partial insanities were more accurately the modalities through which degeneration revealed itself.[78] Women were thus increasingly seen to be vulnerable as a consequence of tainted heredity and/or because their most intimate environment, that is, their bodies, rendered them recurrently susceptible to instability, if not disease. Following larger currents in medical and social theory, alienists in the closing decades of the century were, then, more likely to connect mental disturbance to a hereditary defect, shifting, although not eliminating, the position of female reproductive biology in explanations of criminality.[79]

The medical interventions in the case of Joséphine Citoleux suggest with unusual clarity the way that the medicalization of the female reproductive system accommodated transformations in medical theory as the conceptual universe provided by degeneration theory superseded other explanatory models. Joséphine Citoleux was a twenty-two-year-old accused in 1878 of repeatedly harrassing the local parish priest, breaking and entering, and stealing from the rectory.[80] Because of her demeanor, her *surexcitation* (she disrobed down to her chemise in police custody), her gross language, and her continued insults to the priest, the mayor of the commune ordered a medical examination by a local doctor who reported that Citoleux was in the midst of an agitation caused by her "periodic flux" and diagnosed her as afflicted with *monomanie des persécutions*. His urgent recommendation was that she be sent to an asylum.[81]

Local authorities clearly had identified Citoleux as an incorrigible who resisted both parental and institutional authority. She had been implicated in numerous minor infractions that had sent her both to an asylum and to prison for short spells. Medical reports through the period 1870–78 characterized her as having a "feeble intelligence," and referred especially to her "perversity of instincts," "lack of emotions," "total absence of remorse," and propensity to lie. The same doctor who had been called to respond to the most recent episode in 1878 had observed six years earlier that Joséphine Citoleux had, at the onset of menstruation, "lost the use of her reason." "Later," he continued, "at the time of her menstrual periods, she carried out acts that proved the diseased condition of her brain. She is afflicted with nymphomania, which contributes to the exalted state of her nervous system in its episodes of temporary insanity."[82]

In response to her most recent offenses, the court ordered a medico-legal report prepared by two psychiatrists associated with the Paris Faculty of Medicine (Valéry Combes and Benjamin Laprée), who surveyed Citoleux's medical history and prior delinquencies, examined her, and finally pronounced on her condition. In their conclusions Combes and Laprée both separated themselves from earlier reports while confirming, in the more sophisticated language of current medical discourse, the essential (female) pathology of the young woman. Following their summary of Citoleux's dossier, they commented that "although they have some reservations with regard to the precision of earlier diagnoses" (this in response to a claim that Citoleux was in love with the priest and was driven by an obsessive jealousy as well as by *monomanie des persécutions*), they concurred with the general picture of the accused as a woman deprived of her full intellectual capacities, constantly under the sway of a neuropathological condition that became manifest in a variety of inap-

propriate behaviors, and, finally, subject to states of "cerebral overexcitement" when in the midst of her menstrual periods.[83] They recapitulated
her menstrual history and explored at length her most recent attempt to
escape from the asylum—a failed effort that, they emphasized, coincided
with the onset of her menstrual period and attested to a kind of insanity.
(Prior to this attempted escape, Citoleux had asked repeatedly to be transferred, insisting that she was not at all insane and did not belong in an
asylum.)

In a significant shift, however, Combes and Laprée then produced a
detailed description of Citoleux's physiognomy—in language most rem-
iniscent of the physical stigmata described in Lombrosian criminal anthropology—outlining especially malformations or irregularities of the
face (thick lips, crooked teeth) and neck (abnormal thyroid gland), and
the incomplete separation of two toes on her left foot, all of which they
attributed to defective development at the base of her skull. Linking
Citoleux's intellectual insufficiency, moral perversion, and physical ab-
normalities, they concluded that she was unmistakably a degenerate, the
only diagnosis that could adequately account for "the convergence of
multiple disorders [*altérations d'ordre divers*]."[84] The fact that Citoleux's father had been prone to alcoholic excess and had died of suicide, while a
cousin was at that very moment confined in an asylum, provided seemingly irrefutable support for the conclusion of morbid heredity, the hallmark of degeneracy. Specifically aligning themselves with their "theoretical masters"—the alienists Falret, Morel, Zabé, and Caspar—they argued that the pathological manifestations of degeneracy coincided with
"the arrival of puberty, the exaggeration of genital sensibility, and the
periodic phenomenon of menstruation," all producing morbid impulses
that pushed menstruating young women, *faibles d'esprit*, to set fires and
to commit thefts, murder, or suicide. Joséphine Citoleux emerged here as
a classic example of a familiar, immediately recognizable type.

The conceptual trajectory that led to the diagnosis of degeneracy both
drew upon and moved beyond older and more general diagnoses linking women's erratic behavior to their reproductive biology. Equally important, however, is the mingling of theoretical models that are presented
in this report as complementary and not contradictory, reflecting a kind
of ecumenical blending of ideas that implicitly denied the need to discriminate among them. The cataloguing of Citoleux's stigmata sits com-
fortably next to descriptions of various monomanias, even as the more
comprehensive diagnosis of degeneration embraces all of the others. And,

as if it were an afterthought, but one foreshadowed early in the document, Combes and Laprée returned emphatically at the end of their report to the fact that, of the eight offenses that Citoleux had committed in the preceding decade, six of these had been thefts. Without mentioning the word "monomania," but apparently welcoming the return of the repressed, they concluded that science had clearly established this "particularity," which invariably led weak-spirited individuals to crime (theft, murder, arson, suicide) but rarely produced more than one "tendency" in any single individual. The monomaniac, softened around the edges a bit, reappeared in a new guise that reordered the terms of a diagnosis that remained eclectic and inclusive, responsive to echoes that lingered just beyond conscious recognition. In the end, the medical experts found Joséphine Citoleux unredeemably degenerate, subject to irresistible impulses while in the throes of menstruation and hence deprived of free will, making her a chronic threat to society. She was judged not responsible and confined to an indefinite stay in an asylum.

Cases like Citoleux's invite us to examine medicine's immersion in contemporary culture. I have been arguing that changing medical theories did not automatically disrupt or transform the practical implications of medical expertise—that the symbolic effects of medical discourse on social theory were finally more important than its impact on criminal trials. What we need to take into account as well are the specific ways that doctors specializing in women's illnesses contributed to wider discussions of female nature and sexuality. Diseases like monomania, hysteria, and degeneration were especially culturally porous, capturing in a given moment a web of significations that expressed some of the most deeply held beliefs and pressing anxieties of the culture. Because these diseases described anomalies of character as well as a sick body, they enabled physicians to join with philosophers, moralists, social critics, politicians, and reformers in assessing individual and social pathologies. Both Jan Goldstein and Klaus Doerner have described the imaginative hold of monomania as a reflection of midcentury cultural anxieties about single-mindedness, one-sidedness, and irregularity that invited medical intervention to restore the equilibrium.[85] Doerner argues that

the concept of monomania supplies the formulas that make possible the identification of the "transgressors" of the norms psychologically as well as morally, politically, and legally. Monomania is the framework for the "excessive," hence offensive extent of, say, self-confidence, arrogance (megalomania), need for love (erotomania), . . . craving for alcohol (dipsomania), impulse to steal (kleptomania), incendiarism (pyromania), etc., but also for all kinds of compulsives, homosexuals and sexual "perverts," recidivists or habitual criminals.[86]

The discourse was less about madness than about mysterious aspects of human nature, presented as perversions of the feelings, inexplicable or unreasonable desires that seemed as much *"une maladie de la civilisation"* as the problem of a unique individual.[87]

In evidence here is what Ruth Harris has described as "an unusual degree of cultural interchange . . . between different levels of the social and intellectual world," in which medico-legal theorizing was linked to the day-to-day preoccupations of both high and popular culture—a world in which medical discourses were threaded through larger cultural debates.[88] In terms that were both interpretive and prescriptive, medico-legal experts spoke to a "problem" of female responsibility that extended well beyond questions of criminal responsibility. As challenges to assumptions about the immutability of gender differences began to emerge in the fin-de-siècle, as women began to threaten some of the practices and presumptions that had preserved a separation between public and private spheres, professionals sought and found scientific explanations of gender difference that might forestall these changes.

Medico-legal discussions of hysteria, for example, produced a discourse about the dangers of a disequilibrium particularly embodied in women. Because hysteria described a condition in which moral consciousness and reason were essentially unimpaired, the disease became a state of disequilibration and disinhibition in which disordered feelings impeded rational choice. Physicians who treated hysterical women patients spoke of an illness manifested especially in exaggerated emotional states. For example, in his classic study *Les Hystériques*, the alienist Henri Legrand du Saulle wrote of hysteria as a disturbance in the *harmony* of the moral sentiments, an affective perversion characterized by a confusion in the *orderliness* of feelings that compromised free will (which was not dead but sick, *malade*).[89] Dr. Emile Laurent argued similarly in 1891 that morbid love resulted from a "rupture in the equilibrium" that harmonized the physiological and psychological aspects of love.[90] And, according to Dr. Charles Féré, women in a pathological emotional state suffered from a "defective rapport between their emotions and their sensibility."[91] Doctors who aspired to become the arbiters of healthy and unhealthy passions attempted to distinguish between obsession and delusion, between exalted feelings and morbid ones.[92] In spite of the amount of ink spilled in this effort, however, no generally recognized criteria for separating exaggerated emotions from madness emerged. Instead, using the occasion provided by the hysteric, doctors pathologized imbalance as they struggled to find a ballast that would preserve the social order from the threat presented by emotional excess and the loss of self-control.

Catherine Clément, who has written intriguingly about the symbolic possibilities of femaleness, argues that women historically have been "allied with what is regular, according to the rules, since they are wives and mothers, and allied as well with those natural disturbances, their regular periods, which are the epitome of paradox, order and disorder. It is precisely in this natural periodicity that fear, terror, that which is offside in the symbolic system will lodge itself."[93] Women simultaneously represent, then, that which is orderly/balanced, the rule (*règle*) and the potential for disorder, periodic unruliness (*règles*).[94] In the fin-de-siècle, women's embodied paradox provided a symbolic vehicle for articulating fears of excess and disorder, especially fears related to the vagaries of human reasonableness, personal control, and sexuality.

The intense interest in hypnosis in the fin-de-siècle reveals some of the ways in which women's disordered emotions and problematical sexuality figured in broader cultural debates. By the 1880s, Charcot had made hypnosis a centerpiece of his theatrical lectures at Salpêtrière, demonstrating with his suggestible hysterics that conscious will could be so impaired as to permit hypnotized subjects to act in ways that violated their conscious principles. In a stunning spectacle, for example, one of Charcot's acolytes, Gilles de la Tourette, instructed Blanche W to poison Jules Claretie, the director of the Théâtre Français.[95] Smiling benignly, and following without hesitation the orders she had been given, Blanche W offered Claretie the poisoned drink. When he feigned illness, she became terrified of the part she had been led to play; but the point had been made. In the context of this commentary on anesthetized will and unconscious mental activity, medico-legal experts had begun to argue that some defendants could not be held fully responsible for acts that were committed while under hypnotic influence. Several famous criminal causes célèbres gave these issues national exposure, as popular audiences joined physicians and criminologists in speculating about the problem of self-control and the integrity of the *moi*.[96]

Charcot and his followers had argued that it was a condition of their hysteria that allowed his subjects to be hypnotized—that is, because of their hysteria, understood as a neurophysiological condition, they were both especially suggestible and already stripped of inhibitions. This theoretical posture, however, met with increasing opposition, particularly from the Nancy school, led by Hippolyte Bernheim, who insisted in contrast that the ability to be hypnotized was unrelated to the presence of disease. In fact, Bernheim saw hypnosis as a useful therapy for a wide range of physical and emotional disorders and encouraged its popularization.[97] Yet, in spite of the profound differences between these schools and the public challenges of each to the scientific credibility of the other, both groups recognized the potential dangers of hypnotic influence that was not supervised by trained medical personnel. Stories abounded of charlatans who had taken sexual advantage of young women, of married women who had been induced to commit adultery and even to sign over their property to unscrupulous amateurs, and of crowds driven wild by performing magnetizers.

In effect, the possibilities of hypnosis brought to the surface immediate anxieties about the reliability of the lower orders and the "contagion" of antisocial behaviors, and more abstract but connected worries about potential manipulations, by hypnotists and other dangerous types, of irrational and unconscious desires. Women were especially implicated, both symbolically and materially, in these concerns. Social theorists regularly identified the dangers of fin-de-siècle crowds in specifically feminized terms, while suggestibility itself had become a defining characteristic of femininity, articulated simultaneously in medical diagnoses and in republican anxieties about the undue influence of priests over their female followers. (Ironically, perhaps, the anticlerical thrust of much psychiatric theorizing sought to free women from priestly superstition even as it urged them toward greater openness to medical authority.)[98]

Most important, the integrity of the bourgeois family seemed to be threatened by a particularly female vulnerability to sexual violation while under hypnosis. Physicians speculated that female patients who engaged in apparently inexplicable or irregular sexual behavior must have done so as a result of hypnotic suggestion. The case of Mme Grille, who left her family for a younger man of lower social standing, provided the prototype. One medical commentator, for example, categorized her among the victims of suggestion "who lose all courage, whose resolution disappears, whose will is vanquished and who give themselves without enthusiasm, without passion, without love."[99] Most subjects in demonstrations of hypnosis were in fact women, whose essential suggestibility seemed so well established that medical advice characteristically urged women not to travel alone and never to meet the eyes of male strangers.[100] Assumptions about female nature, social danger, and political instability converged in a wide-ranging discussion of the implications of hypnosis that cut across social and ideological divisions. The links that medical discourse had drawn between female disorders (biological and sexual) and social disorder (criminal and political) had gained broad cultural authority.

An underlying concern with the potential dangers of unleashed and disordered female sexuality similarly runs through a broad spectrum of medical interpretations of female criminality. Especially in accounts of shoplifting, but also present in discussions of other crimes committed by women, there is a characteristic subtext that exceeds medical preoccupations with the reproductive female body and emerges in a (veiled) focus on the sexual body. Although it was the operation of her reproductive system that allegedly catapulted the woman into a state of mental disequilibrium, this clinical picture was inseparable from, and perhaps embedded in, pervasive and formulaic sexualized fantasies of female deviancy. In the construction of female deviants (the witch and the hysteric, for example), sexuality proliferates; the disordered woman is infinitely and problematically sexualized. We can find this subtext in its nineteenth-century mode of seeing and telling in a prominent alienist's discussion of department store theft:

The new stores contain and expose, competing for attention, the richest materials, the most sumptuous *objets de toilette* and the most seductive luxuries [*excesses*]. Women of every rank, attracted to this elegant milieu by the instinct that is natural to their sex, fascinated by so much imprudent provocation, dazzled by the profusion of laces and trinkets, find themselves surprised by a sudden incitement which is not premeditated and is nearly brutal: they place an inexpert but furtive hand on the exposed goods, and there it is; they cancel, in a thoughtless touch, the most respectable past, becoming thieves, making themselves into delinquents.[101]

This text operates on several levels. The department store becomes at once the scene of a sexual encounter and the occasion for a psychosexual discourse. The author links instincts with excesses, exposure, and imprudence; unpremeditated excitement with delinquency and punishment; touching with crime. What is it here that is stolen? Who is, in fact, the author of the furtive, fatal touch? What is the danger that links instinct and exposure? And whose fears and fantasies are most clearly in evidence here?

Zola's *Au Bonheur des Dames* captures, in a different medium, a similar expression of fantasy and projection. When we are introduced to his protagonist, Denise, a young and impoverished country woman, she has just arrived in Paris in the early morning hours; she is stopped short in her tentative search for relatives by the imposing sight of the department store, the Bonheur des Dames. "Zounds!" her younger brother exhales as Denise is drawn to the building by an "irresistible force." In the presence of the glittering displays in the showcase windows, "an endless perspective of spotless glass and brilliant gilding," presided over by two allegorical figures, "two laughing women with heads thrown back" unrolling the sign at the entrance, "she lingered, forgetting all else." From the very moment of her arrival in the city, Denise exists in a state that Zola describes as a kind of bewildered fascination generated by her first sensual confrontation with the department store. As she prepares to enter for the first time, Zola provides the appropriate *frisson*; she is both attracted and fearful: "Mingled with her desire to pass through those doors, there was also a vague fear, which was in itself almost a delight." (Again, whose desire? whose fear?) To complete the sexual charge, the store's owner, M. Mouret, understands his new marketing strategies explicitly as seduction:

It was women, [he said,] who were the mainspring of trade. It was they who were to be enticed, tempted and bewildered. They were attracted by bargains and tranquillized by the plain figures of the prices attached. They were vanquished at first by appeals to them as housekeepers, and then carried away by their love of novelty and fashion . . . "I am at your service, ladies," said Mouret with a smile. He was welcomed by the feminine group that opened to make room for him.[102]

The language of male desire inhabits the texts of both the novelist and the psychiatrist. Clearly, the department store had become the "*apanage des femmes*,"[103] women's privileged space, characterized by its dazzling sensuality and its capacity to arouse unexpected desires in middle-class women whose appetites would fuel the new mass consumption economy. But women were described in this new context not only as active consumers but as targets of a sensory attack, bombarded by stimuli from which they retreated "overheated" (*surchauffées*), "bewildered," and sometimes compromised.[104]

Discussions of disturbances in female reproductive functioning led, perhaps inevitably, to the mystery of female sexuality. Descriptions of the eroticized environment of the department store were but one strand of a larger medical investigation into the links between female biology and *folies érotiques*; ideas that remained merely latent and vaguely titillating in reports of kleptomania emerged explicitly in accounts of erotomania and nymphomania. The erotomaniac was a person suffering from a "delusion of the imagination" characterized by a morbid, obsessive love for another, a love that was typically chaste and unacknowledged. The illness produced psychological rather than physiological symptoms, although doctors claimed that the disease could be triggered especially by irregularities in the biological life cycles of women and by masturbation in men.[105] It was essentially a disease of modern life, provoked by the reading of erotic novels, the suggestive repertoire of contemporary theater, and the excesses of romantic poetry as they influenced "exalted," "overly sensitive" individuals who had become accustomed to a "feminized" life-style.[106]

Nymphomania, in contrast, was understood as a physical disorder, a "uterine furor" characterized by a "morbid excitement of the genital organs." The nymphomaniac could be recognized by a set of physical clues (noteworthy for their simultaneous specificity and imprecision) that signaled, in effect, a "genital temperament": fleshy, well-developed muscles; average plumpness; black, abundant body hair; an expressive face (physiognomy); a large mouth with thick red lips; white teeth; "a well-defined shape," with especially noticeable sexual parts.[107] The afflicted woman was at the mercy of her instincts, unable to control her desires or check her behavior. In the words of one medico-legal expert, "despite the most ingrained moral principles and habits of decency, despite the most sincere religious sentiments, the patient gives herself to the first person who presents himself, often seeks embraces with a person of the same sex . . . abandons her parents, and resorts to prostitution as a remedy to the furor that dominates her senses and her reason."[108] Such medical *histoires* proliferated: one woman could not sit because the heat irritated her genital parts and had to walk with her legs apart in order to avoid creating a morbid friction that would lead to an erotic crisis;[109] another demanded admission to a brothel with each menstrual period;[110] some men became ill and were even driven to suicide by women "with the nature of Don Juan," veritable Messalinas, who were finally insatiable.[111]

These medical case histories, with their combination of fantasmatic detail and scientific rhetoric, catalogue a pervasive anxiety about sexual excess located specifically in disordered women—what Alain Corbin has described as evidence of a wide-ranging effort "to exorcize the image of the excessive, devouring female."[112] Citing boastful accounts of visits to the bordello as well as "the anxious counting of conjugal couplings," growing performance anxiety, and attention to the getting and spending of a spermatic economy, Corbin argues that a masculine fear of sexual inferiority haunts the late nineteenth-century scientific demonization of the nymphomaniac, the hysteric, and the lesbian.[113] These types, especially frightening because pregnancy was not the manifest goal of their sexual "overflowing," figured prominently in medical descriptions of potentially pathological female sexuality, particularly of women in "the critical age" of menopause, when any signs of sexual activity, and especially sexual activity with a younger man, brought an automatic diagnosis of "delusion" and "mental debility." Women who, according to medical accounts, had had "moderate sexual instincts" or who had been "indifferent toward sexual encounters" often became tormented during menopause by "irresistible genital sensations" that caused them to ignore their domestic and familial responsibilities and to succumb to a violent "uterine furor."[114] If knowledge of the limits of female sexual desire remained elusive, medical theory could at least help to identify behavior that would be understood as undisputedly out of bounds.

But this effort to restore or reimagine sexual limits is perhaps only a part of the story. The language of the texts is somewhat more equivocal, suggesting a preoccupation with the release of female sexuality—with the opportunities for, and conditions of, a seduction—as well as with a desire to contain it. Nymphomania does not simply erupt, as do menstrual periods; within the rhetorical structure of the case history, the woman is seduced, struggles, and inevitably succumbs. According to one alienist:

[the ill woman] . . . resists at first the thoughts, the desires that besiege her; little by little she allows herself to be dominated by her inclinations . . . she pleases herself with the most lascivious ideas, the most voluptuous conversations, the most obscene reading, until finally . . . the most timid young girl [is transformed] into a lewd woman and the most delicate modesty into a furious audacity that approaches prostitution in its effrontery.[115]

· The seduction scenario, with its denouement in the act of succumbing, is predicated on the woman's inability to resist. The centrality of this theme as the device that moves the story forward is confirmed in Legrand de Saulle's advice to medical experts testifying in cases of kleptomania. He maintained that in evaluating responsibility for criminal behavior it was necessary to consider the defendant in terms of both a powerful incitement to act and an insufficient resistance to temptation. In the end, he urged doctors to focus on the pathological loss of will to resist, rather than on the strength of the compulsion.[116] In this scenario, the seduction was not complete unless it vanquished resistance. These descriptions of pathologies—sexual and criminal—provided the opportunity for a recurring discussion of the threshold, the point at which will is overcome, pointing to the moment in which female sexuality (and danger) is released, unbounded. We seem to have arrived here, in these scenarios of pleasure and danger, at the intersections of fantasy, myth, and medical science.

The medical narrative must be understood, then, as produced in a context in which the medical story gained its authority from its linkages with other, widely diffused ideological assumptions and cultural concerns. This type of dense cultural intersection is especially evident in the way that medical testimony worked in infanticide cases. As we have seen, physicians had generated an extensive literature that linked female reproductive biology, including childbirth and its aftermath, to mental illness. Yet this well-documented connection barely appeared in cases of alleged infanticide. In these cases, the medical expert typically provided the crucial autopsy report that specified the precise cause of death and speculated about the possible truth of the claims made by the defendant. He described the markings of strangulation, suffocation, and beating; he attested to the condition of the dead infant's lungs to determine if a live birth had in fact occurred; he speculated about the likely cause of bruises on the cadaver, seeking to assess whether the infant's skull fractures could have resulted from a fall during a delivery in which the mother was standing or crouching. But rarely did the forensic expert comment on the defendant's mental health. The defense of puerperal insanity was not raised by medical experts in infanticide cases and I found no medical report introduced into a criminal proceeding that specifically labeled the emotional distress of a defendant as mental disease.

Several women accused of infanticide—most often poor, unmarried domestics—did themselves describe a kind of temporary insanity following their delivery, provoked by physical exhaustion and emotional confusion. They spoke of a sense of extreme desolation, the horror of bringing dishonor on their families, and the certain knowledge that they would lose their jobs if the birth became known. They acknowledged smothering or strangling their unwanted newborns and hiding the cadavers, or more typically disposing of them via the sewer system, but claimed that, moved by despair and isolation, they had "lost their heads" and "succumbed to a sudden impulse." Many women who delivered alone, without assistance, reported that they had little memory of their delivery or subsequent behavior and described losing consciousness, only to awake to find a dead baby between their legs. Still others, who had delivered in a public hospital, seemed unclear about the welfare services to which they could have appealed; such a woman would recount wandering the city with her newborn for hours, until, overcome with desperation and barely conscious of what she was doing, she threw the child into the river.

In exploring the implications of these stories, it seems evident that no single set of factors can account adequately for the acts of infanticide—that the truths range through different emotional registers and material circumstances. In searching for the multiple realities embedded in accounts of infanticide, the historian must ask: Was it possible that some women were not even aware that they had delivered? Could labor be confused with intestinal cramps? Did babies die because their frightened mothers, still anxious to keep the birth secret, attempted to stifle their cries and instead smothered them? Could hopelessness and helplessness produce acute mental derangement?[117] In directing attention to the emotionally overwhelmed mother, I do not want to argue here for yet another disabling of the feminine. Rather, I want to emphasize the fact that certain kinds of emotional distress evoked sympathy (and were "normalized" by their assimilation to a medical condition) while others did not. The cases of women accused of infanticide present striking examples of women living without any protection; those women whose stories we know represent a particular group of women who were unable to preserve the necessary secrecy achieved by many others whose infanticides remained undetected.[118] They are the women turned over to the police by their employers, by midwives, by physicians, and by neighbors and concierges. Some sense of their isolation and disorientation may be gathered from the fact that many seemed to keep the incriminating cadavers near them for days after the death, suggesting both emotional distress and a kind of paralysis, an inability to save themselves. Why, then, was this "underexcitement" less disordered in the minds of examining physicians than the "overexcitement" of other criminal women?

In the end, questions about the defendant's emotional state were of quite secondary importance to the medico-legal experts who commented on infanticide cases. The inclination of physicians to confirm that women were responsible even when they had reduced capacity tipped decidedly in infanticide cases in the direction of an even greater emphasis on the defendant's fundamental sanity and responsibility. The "exalted sensitivities" and "nervous excitability" that described defendants in cases of homicide and theft simply disappeared from the medical rhetoric. More significant for the physician testifying in infanticide cases was the fact that many women had concealed their pregnancies, failed to prepare a layette, and delivered in secrecy—a pattern of behavior that seemed particularly calculating and thus apparently ruled out a discussion of nervous disorder.[119] Echoes of this perspective appeared in indictments speculating that women who killed their newborns were unwilling to accept the responsibilities of motherhood, were moved by the desire to "taste forbidden pleasures without bearing the consequences," a characterization that was expressed, by the 1890s, in a charge of "*égoisme*."[120] In infanticide cases, then, both the medico-legal expert and the prosecution emphasized the "knowingness" or consciousness of the defendants. Physicians had debated, somewhat more abstractly, about whether the possible insanity of postpartum women could only apply in legal terms to the first few moments following delivery or whether the period of vulnerability could extend for several months.[121] But this consideration was largely moot as individual infanticide cases moved through the court system where the mental equilibrium of the defendant did not carry particular weight.

The trial of Marie Victor for the murder of her child is useful in situating medical discourse within broader cultural assumptions about appropriate and believable female behavior.[122] Victor was convicted of involuntary homicide in the death of her seventeen-month-old daughter and was sentenced to six months in prison. The prosecution's case recited the following scenario: Marie had married Philadelphe Victor, a typographer, in 1880, had borne two children, and lived *une vie régulière* until 1886, when she developed a consuming passion for her neighbor Joseph Cordier, a cobbler. In despair of their ever being able to live together, they plotted a double suicide but, losing courage at the last moment, they abandoned the attempt. Instead, Joseph convinced Marie to leave her husband; with her youngest daughter in tow, she followed him to an apartment. This decision was succeeded by a series of increasingly bizarre developments. Almost immediately, Joseph's father and uncle convinced Joseph that he had acted imprudently, and, because he could not hope to find work at that time in Paris, they urged him to return to his native village. Without any explanation, Joseph abandoned Marie and her child, leaving them locked in the apartment. When Marie learned that Joseph had left her, she composed letters to both Joseph and her husband and attempted suicide by asphyxiation. Marie was discovered unconscious some time later; her infant daughter was dead.

The case against Marie Victor relied heavily on a story about passion and abandonment.[123] It was a selfish passion, the indictment suggested, that drove this woman to abandon her husband and older daughter, and it was passionate despair at losing her lover that provoked the suicide attempt. The prosecution emphasized especially what it considered to be the heated tone of the letter to the lover in comparison to the cooler message left for the husband. No physician was asked to evaluate Marie Victor's mental health. This omission seems especially noteworthy in light of the fact that Philadelphe Victor's deposition had described in some detail Marie's somberness and "dark thoughts" that had emerged after the birth of her first child and persisted for five years, leading her to talk periodically of throwing herself into the canal or hurling herself out the window. In fact, when he discovered that she had left, he searched for her first in the city's morgues. But Marie Victor's suicide attempt did not seem to require a medical explanation; rather, it emerged as "normal" behavior for a woman abandoned by her lover and, further, as a not inappropriate response for a woman who had so definitively breached her familial duties. In the context of these assumptions, Victor's lawyer did not request a medical report that might have attested to the reduced capacity of a woman who had lost her equilibrium; no expert testimony suggested heightened excitability as an extenuating circumstance. Infanticide cases, in general, did not call for an alienist's professional opinion. And in Victor's case as in others like it, women whose material circumstances were not desperate—especially women with husbands or with lovers allegedly willing to support their children—were more likely to be convicted of a crime, even when the infanticide was the incidental result of a suicide attempt.[124]

The terms in which Marie Victor's case were presented and its resounding silences suggest the ways in which medical opinion was at once inextricable from the culture of the moment and instrumental in shaping its outlines. The medico-legal report created a popular audience for its particular stories from a position already deeply immersed in culturally validated stories. While the specific language and assumptions of medico-legal reports in infanticide cases differed from the reports of other crimes, where physicians were more likely to claim that women's disturbed emotivity overcame their more rational selves, in both situations the medical report itself complemented broadly shared cultural expectations. The hysterical female was a widely recognized type; women's erratic, overexcited constitution, often driven by biology, was similarly widely acknowledged as the cause of criminal acts. But neither physicians nor the court could as readily assimilate the mother who murdered her newborn to the other types who, in the culture of the fin-de-siècle, were apparently both more disturbed in their psychophysiology and more benign in their criminality. Significantly, outcomes in infanticide trials did not differ greatly from outcomes in other criminal categories; in both situations, juries, responding as always to a set of extralegal rules and assumptions, granted high acquittal rates to female defendants, regardless of whether the court emphasized reason or unreason.[125] What is noteworthy about infanticide cases, however, is an absence of the kind of medical discussion about women's reproductive instability that was such a large part of the narrative repertoire of both gynecologists and alienists.

In the cases of poor, unmarried women who murdered their unwanted babies, the rationality of desperate acts in desperate material circumstances seemed so self-evident as to make irrelevant the extensive literature of medical case histories that could have been used to argue quite the opposite. When the crime was infanticide, a gap opens between discourse and social practice that brings into sharper focus the rhetorical qualities and cultural specificity of medico-legal expertise as applied to the behavior of deviant women. Perhaps the stories of infanticide were too sordid and mundane; perhaps they spoke too directly to the social rather than to the personal; perhaps because they evoked economics rather than the mysteries of the human soul, the poor and desperate murdering mother did not inhabit the same imaginative space as the hysteric and did not draw the same kind of medico-legal commentary. Most important, a culture preoccupied with worries about depopulation perhaps could not afford to offer murdering mothers the rhetorical leniency embedded in the medical discourse of diminished responsibility. The selective use of medico-legal expertise in infanticide cases suggests the conceptual and cultural constraints within which physicians operated as much as their ability to set the terms of debate.

Foucault has argued that nineteenth-century criminal psychiatry emerged by defining itself as a science of the monstrous, a knowledge that alone could penetrate the meaning of crimes against nature, against "those laws which are perceived to be inscribed directly on the human heart." But as we have seen, and as Foucault argues, by the end of the century the dangerous individual was more likely to be identified by a more diffuse pathology; rather than a monster, s/he was a degenerate. In Foucault's terms, forensic psychiatry moved from a focus on "the rare and monstrous figure of the monomaniac to the common everyday figure of the degenerate, of the pervert, of the constitutionally unbalanced, of the immature."[126] In focusing on the nature of the criminal rather than on the criminal act, alienists could present themselves as guarantors of a kind of public hygiene of the social body. But when we look at medical discourse about criminal women the pattern is considerably more complicated.

Alienists explained criminal women in both their monstrous and their more ordinary manifestations. It was, in fact, Henriette Cornier's grotesque homicide and inexplicable lack of remorse that introduced the defense of "menstrual psychosis." But as Foucault suggests, the speculation about human motivation provided by medical opinion found a deeper resonance in social theory than it did in individual therapeutics and clinical practice. What seems crucial in understanding the effects of medical expertise in cases of female criminality is the way that medical opinion spoke simultaneously about the individual defendant *and* about all women. More important in medical discourse than the nature of the individual criminal woman was the nature of femaleness.

Rarely did physicians argue that women ought to be absolved of all responsibility for their criminal behaviors. Such a claim was not congruent with their preoccupations with the periodicity of the female life cycle—a periodicity that suggested intermittent incapacity—nor was it likely to be acceptable in a system that had begun to worry about the "misguided philanthropy" of medical diagnoses that left society disarmed and criminals unpunished.[127] Rather, alienists searched the histories of accused women for biological evidence foreshadowing the extenuating circumstances that justified a conclusion of attenuated responsibility and a plea for judicial leniency. In attesting to this biologically grounded space of limited capacity, medical discourse closed the distance between body and behavior, constructing a female subject confined in an unstable system of physical responses and heightened suggestibility. Alienists were not alone in this project; they did not by themselves codify the meanings attributed to biological difference. But in their role as expert witnesses in the criminal justice system, they provided the specific language by which the "disabilities" of women could be interpreted.

Medico-legal reports on the mental condition and legal responsibility of female defendants produced a syndrome of femininity that underlined women's disequilibrium, grounded in their biological sex, in an age that based its hope and its future on moderation and balance, *le juste milieu*. Like the hysteric who was charming when not dangerous, the female criminal described by medical testimony was a woman at once reasonable and wholly unreliable—suffused by an unreliability that had become the hallmark of femaleness. The criminal stories popularized by physicians situated female defendants in an ambiguous zone that rendered their sanity precarious, in effect disabling the feminine. What would be the public role, the civic capacity of this woman who could not be held fully responsible but who was in part responsible—a woman not deprived of reason but not fully reasonable? In the end, medical discourse made of female criminals—and by extension of all women—beings worthy of sympathy, in need of the tutelary support of the court system and the medical profession, who remained, finally, disqualified for public life.

LOVE STORIES

Female Crimes of Passion

Have we not seen Paris—the Paris of frivolous liaisons, of furtive
scandals, of peaceful infidelities, the promised land of cosmopolitan dreams where wives who are half-married coexist with mistresses who are half-legitimate in a delicious promiscuity?

A. de Monzie, *Le Jury contemporain et les crimes passionels*, 1901

We love and suffer according to cultural imperatives.

Niklas Luhmann, *Love and Passion: The Codification of Intimacy*,
1986

The refrain of a ballad popular in the streets of Paris in the 1880s celebrated the recent murderess Gabrielle Bompard along with Joan of Arc
and Sarah Bernhardt.[1] This placing of Bompard in such illustrious com-
pany speaks to the ways in which crime had captured the popular imagination; it attests also to the special aura of heroic notoriety that surrounded the *femme criminelle*. As the nineteenth century progressed,
women, like men, were increasingly accused of *crimes crapuleux*—crimes
of greed, including theft, forgery, swindling, and the like. But the female
crimes that drew sustained public interest were crimes of passion—acts of
violence fueled by jealousy, vengeance, or madness and provoked by betrayal or disappointment in love. These crimes—appealing in their suggestion of sexual and emotional excess—invited explanations that defined women in terms of a set of predictable affective responses. Lawyers
and magistrates as well as social scientists, popularizers, and journalists
produced "love stories" that represented *criminelles passionnelles* as, quintessentially, women-in-love. These were women whose violence made
sense to their contemporaries, whose actions conformed to the codes
organizing the expected behaviors in the ordinary interactions of daily
life.

In looking at explanations of crimes of passion, it is crucial to ask
both what "love" meant and how its meanings were anchored culturally.

In a recent study of the historical functions of love as a symbolic code, Niklas Luhmann speaks of love not as a feeling but as a code of communication

according to the rules of which one can express, form and simulate feelings, deny them, impute them to others, and be prepared to face up to all the consequences which enacting such a communication may bring with it. . . . It is the enhancement of the meanings anchored in the code which enables love to be learned, tokens of it to be interpreted and small signs of it to convey deep feelings.[2]

The language of love, then, encourages the emergence of feelings judged appropriate by the culture, and specifies the connection between feelings and behavior that identifies behavior as either reasonable or erratic. Most important, "the semantics of love can," according to Luhmann, "provide an understanding of the relationship between the symbolic media and the social structure."[3] Luhmann's study surveys the development of different modes of speaking about and understanding "love" in order to identify changes in the conceptual resources of a culture that might facilitate or impede social change. It is precisely my interest here to explore, via the intensified language of romantic love, the connections between what I am calling the love discourse of crimes of passion and shifting sets of social relations—to see how the love discourse became a means to address unstable gender relations and perceived threats to the traditional family in the fin-de-siècle.

Embedded in contemporary discussions of love were the social codes that sought to regulate relations between men and women—codes that catalogued appropriate expectations and disappointments and rehearsed the "normal" behaviors of private life. But the crime of passion, because of its very publicity, carried domestic struggles into public venues where their connection to broader concerns could become visible. Public fascination with the crime of passion guaranteed that the more sensational stories of private frustrations and domestic tensions would provide the conceptual tools with which contemporaries considered the institution of the family and the implicit terms and conditions of marriage—the respective rights and responsibilities buried in the daily practices of ordinary life, and the family's relation to such regulatory institutions as the courts. In spite of deep divisions within the numerous political parties of the time, the bourgeoisie as a whole sought to consolidate its authority by protecting a hierarchical, patriarchal model of the middle-class family, by normalizing the working-class household, and by producing a shared,

gendered version of the right order of things. At the same time, the
women who attacked their seducers, spouses, lovers, and rivals were revising popular myths as they turned to private justice to enforce their
own domestic codes. The love stories deployed to interpret the crime of
passion attested to these disparate efforts. In retelling them here, I will
be exploring the intertwined history of love and social change.

true Neither the Code Pénal of 1791 nor the revised code of 1810 identified crimes of passion as specific legal entities;[4] nevertheless, popular opinion, seconded by judges and juries, continued to set apart crimes that
seemed to belong exclusively to a private realm of domestic relations regulated by customary social practice and outside the purview of public
authorities. In effect, the crime of passion was understood as "the epilogue to a long moral suffering" that engendered "a sudden exasperation," culminating in an "irresistible compulsion" that propelled the perpetrator into the criminal act.[5] While the spontaneous eruption of passion
was the identifying mark of the *crime passionnel*, a certain amount of premeditation was accepted if it could be shown that the defendant was the
victim of "an uncontrollable obsession" and had fought to resist an impulsion that would not go away. The true *criminel passionnel* was expected
to instantly and eternally regret the act—attempted suicide could attest to
such regret—and to make no effort to conceal the crime, asserting
thereby the essential legitimacy of the behavior. Thus, although they
were entirely extralegal, *affaires passionnelles* rigorously obeyed their own
protocols, which referred to method as well as motive. One commentator explained, for example, that a woman who killed her husband in his
sleep would be in much the same position as a duelist who used his left
hand; it simply was not done.[6]

In popular consciousness, the *crime passionnel* belonged as much to
the world of the "normal" as to the realm of the criminal, so much so
that Alexandre Dumas fils, dubbed "the evangelist of unhappy households," could end his play about an adulterous wife with the extraordinary
command to the betrayed spouse: "*Tue-la!*" (Kill her!)[7] Journals regularly
featured crimes of passion animated by full-page color illustrations in
their weekly supplements, and conducted investigative surveys that
queried the population at large about the appropriate response to adultery
and betrayal: Should one kill the lover? just the lover? the lover and one's
spouse?[8] Paradoxically, then, although the state brought criminal charges
for *crimes passionnels*, their resolution obeyed conventions and under-

standings that were external to criminal law. When the Président of the Cour d'Assises questioned Victorine Lelong, for example, about the lengthy preparation (and implied premeditation) of her assault on a former lover, she could sincerely reply, "I was not thinking of a crime, I was only thinking of disfiguring him,"[9] making explicit the cognitive disjunction that typically legitimized crimes of passion. Similarly, a fait divers of 1881 entitled "A Husband in a Hurry" reported the shooting of a laborer by a man who had earlier discovered the worker in a compromising situation with his wife. After hurrying to the office of the local police captain to make his declaration, the young husband sought to rush off so as not to miss his train. The anecdote ends with the observation that only with difficulty was the husband persuaded that he would be held accountable in criminal court for the shooting, while the victim, transported to the nearest hospital, shortly thereafter breathed his last breath.[10] The story entertains through its ironic juxtaposition of the death of the laborer with the worry about missed trains; it nevertheless pointedly refers to the possibility of missing the criminal implications of such acts. According to one jurist, the crime of passion had acquired such popular legitimacy that the murderer presented himself

not as the victim of some obscure fatality, but as a being endowed with free will, having accomplished his murder consciously and for reasons that he is compelled to explain. The crime of passion does not make excuses for itself, it justifies itself; one does not pardon it, one consecrates it; it is not a matter of indulgence but of theory.

This was a perspective that enabled the defense lawyer Charles Lachaud to urge: "Let us close the Codes, let us open our hearts."[11]

The *crime passionnel* confirmed a moral order that implicitly stood above the legal order. The crime itself and responses to it presumed that the victim had participated in creating the conditions that inevitably spilled over into violence.[12] Objecting to this alleged complicity on the part of the victim, one critic complained, for example, that defense lawyers typically transformed the seducer who had been shot into a "moral murderer," turning the victim, with a mere rhetorical flourish, into the defendant.[13] Popular opinion defended the crime of passion as the exercise of a right (this especially for men) or as an instrument of justice, a righting of wrongs (this especially for women).[14] Perpetrators were not, then, seen as beings apart from the "normal," noncriminal population; they presented no apparent social danger, nor were they likely to become recidivists.

Married men quite simply claimed the right to defend their honor, a right specifically identified in Article 324 of the penal code, which excused the murder of a wife caught with her lover, *flagrante delicto*.[15] In so doing, they represented themselves as defenders of the integrity of the family, of the proper upbringing of children, of the purity of *moeurs*. After killing his adulterous wife, M. Robert could report: "My wife knew that I am uncompromising on the question of honor, and that if I found her in someone else's arms, I would not be able to restrain my first instincts. . . . I have regrets but no remorse."[16] Commentators noted repeatedly that any person could, in such circumstances, be propelled by a surge of passion to similar violent acts. Jury verdicts typically evidenced a moral solidarity with husbands whose honor had been compromised, a solidarity that was not shaken even when a man who had murdered his unfaithful wife was confronted in the courtroom by his occasional paramour.[17] To a certain extent, crimes of passion by married men were assimilated to the normal because they represented the end point on a legitimate continuum of practices for controlling one's wife, a point of excess, perhaps, but different only in degree from behaviors that were expected and condoned.[18]

The same sense of entitlement did not apply automatically to married women. When Marie Sivadon appeared in court after having shot her husband's mistress, the presiding magistrate asked directly if she believed that a wife had the right to kill in such circumstances. She replied, somewhat equivocally, "It is probable that if my husband had found me in the same situation, he would have done as much." The judge persisted: "From where do you assume a comparable right?" Daunted, perhaps, by the implications of the question, Sivadon made her claim, in the end, on more contingent grounds: "I have suffered enough."[19] Married or not, the female *criminelle passionnelle* was seen, and often saw herself, as having acted to redress her dependent and victimized status—to recoup on her suffering. Juries acquitting such women acted on the same assumptions, offering women a right denied by the code. Where the code established that a husband's adultery could only be punished (by a fine) when the act had taken place within the marital home, an adulterous wife could be fined and imprisoned for her behavior (no matter where it took place) and her murder could be excused. In their leniency to female crimes of passion, juries authorized, according to one ironist, a *"Tue-le!"* (Kill him!), responding to Dumas's prescription by creating a system that maintained "an equilibrium in the delicate customs of the bedchamber."[20] Or, as another commentator noted, "the jury has placed justice in accord with the feminine heart."[21]

Within real-life dramas of domestic struggle, the themes of jealousy and vengeance had gained canonical status. Men and women of the period lived in a conceptual and social universe in which extreme jealousy was identified as a central component of normal love,[22] and violent death following betrayal or abandonment was neither horrifying nor absurd—was, in fact, part of the order of things. The magistrate Louis Proal lamented the fact that, "as revolutionary socialism had claimed the *right to insurrection* for the citizen, the *right to work, the right to credit* and *the right to capital* for the worker, the *right to pleasure* for the poor, novels, poetry and modern drama had invented the *right to suicide*, the *right to love*, the *right to adultery*, the *right to vengeance* for forsaken lovers and outraged husbands."[23] In a popular cartoon, a woman commented to her friend, "My husband has discovered my lover, but he has not yet tried to kill him or me." Echoing the same matter-of-fact assumptions, a father testifying in a legal deposition admonished his wayward daughter: "It is a disgrace; you have led a married man astray, a man who is the father of a family; you would deserve it if the wife should kill you."[24] This code was so pervasive that the *Gazette des Tribunaux* could introduce its account of an attempted homicide in a shorthand style that assumed a social imagination common to all its readership. Listen to the formula:

It is an intimate drama, painful and somber, that is unfolding before the Cour d'Assises: the irregular liaison of a young woman with a hardworking man; several years together, then the lover abandons his mistress; the misery and the suffering of the latter, whose maternal devotion is noted by all; the death of her infant, the despair, the jealousy that possesses her; finally the ambush and the criminal satisfactions of vengeance.[25]

The sequence of loss and despair was, in this scenario, finally and predictably ended with the release (and closure) provided by vengeance. In very much the same way that dueling had become an acceptable and even expected means whereby bourgeois and elite men responded to assaults on their honor in the fin-de-siècle,[26] the violent resolution of domestic conflicts became ordinary—a domestication based on broadly shared and fairly precise understandings of the conditions that separated crimes of passion warranting judicial tolerance from mere violence.

A particular discourse on love made the crime of passion legitimate and credible. From the literature of caricature to the literature of philos-

Le Petit Journal

Le Petit Journal

SUPPLÉMENT ILLUSTRÉ

ABONNEMENTS

Le Supplément illustré

Huit pages : CINQ centimes

Douzième année   DIMANCHE 11 AOUT 1901   Numéro 560

TRAGIQUE ÉPILOGUE D'UNE IDYLLE

"The tragic epilogue to an idyll."

ophy and medicine, writers elaborated exalted images of "love" that disdained more mundane feelings in favor of *la grande passion*. Such panegyrics to love appeared in a surprising variety of contexts. In his address to an audience of lawyers, for example, Joseph Sur grounded his discussion of crimes of passion in the principle that "love is an essentially dominating force that affects all the moral energies of the individual: reason, will, and sensibility."[27] Even so unpoetic a figure as a former Parisian chief of police wrote in 1899 that "alone among the human appetites, love remains irreducible, like death, immune to social conventions. . . . It is a natural, irresistible feeling which is in profound conflict with the laws and habits of society."[28] Whereas earlier conventions of loving suggested that one languished from love or was ruined by love, Parisians of the fin-de-siècle described themselves as driven mad by love. In their humorous treatment of Parisian fads, *Paris enragé*, Henry Buguet and Edmond Benjamin quipped that if all those maddened by love were to turn themselves over to science (that is, to Pasteur's prophylactic hand), the Palace of Industry, annexed to the central markets, annexed to the Magasins Réunis, and annexed to the Hippodrome would still be too small to hold these sufferers![29] Paraphrasing lines from a play by Dumas fils, one author summarized the widely proliferating romantic catechism: "the freedom to love no matter whom, no matter how, provided that one loved to the point of suicide and to the point of crime."[30] This was, then, a secular dogma that removed limits and consequences from behaviors that flowed from avowed feelings that were by definition dominating and excessive.

In the terms of this discourse, only a love that would risk death—either one's own or that of another—was worthy of the name; hence, ordinary people took extraordinary steps to produce convincing evidence of the depth and validity of their feelings. One witness commented, in a case that typifies the genre, that she and others had been harrassed by Emile Perrin, who routinely insisted that he loved each "to madness" while underscoring his commitment with continuous talk of suicide and assassination.[31] When words were not enough, both men and women attempted to express themselves through the symbolic forms associated with exalted love, a goal that produced sometimes successful but mostly failed attempts at suicide and murder that became near-parodies of the sentiments they sought to represent. Despairing of her ability to reconcile with her husband, Marie Koenig reported her decision to do away with herself. She lighted the carbon in her stove and placed herself beside it in

coal

a closed room; only her husband's return, she alleged, prevented her death. Thwarted once, she began again, this time by placing phosphorus matches in a glass of water for fifteen minutes and then drinking the water; but she failed to become ill and this seems to have ended her efforts.[32] Similarly, following a broken love affair and an attack on his former lover, Julien Meerts tried unsuccessfully to drown himself in the Seine; when this failed, he attempted to hang himself from a nearby tree.[33]

The judicial dossiers are replete with long descriptions of failed hangings, unsuccessful drownings, and bullets that missed their targets entirely. It is, of course, impossible to unravel the complicated social and psychological dynamics that pushed people to respond to disappointments in love in this particular way. How are we to understand the many assertions by defendants who had wounded their former lovers and spouses that they had actually wanted to take their own lives? What are we to make of the perhaps even more impenetrable claims that they had only intended to frighten their victims and not to harm them? It is striking, nevertheless, in spite of these obvious ambiguities, that the terms in which love and its disappointments were spoken and understood had gained a broad consensus by this period. An exalted language that encouraged extreme, stylized behaviors had become generally available, justifying specific words and actions and invoking well-articulated codes that could be enlisted to interpret a broad range of experiences.

As participants in the production of this melodramatic love discourse, scholars, social critics, and professionals sought to define the boundaries between normal love—heterosexual, attuned to reproducing the family, and promoting national grandeur—and morbid love: "perverse," homosexual, or psychically or physiologically obsessive.[34] Unable finally to establish clear and stable differences between healthy and pathological love, they concluded, somewhat ambiguously, that the emotions that triggered crimes of passion were, at bottom, normal. But within this framework, attention usually drifted to a focus on the limits of the normal, to the point where passions could become uncontrollable and dangerous. High and low literature, as well as scientific, philosophical, legal, and medical texts, exhaustively rehearsed the perils of thwarted love. The modern world seemed to have raised up romantic needs that could not be satisfied, *une disproportion entre les appetits amoureux et les resources amoureuses*.[35] Awareness of the dark side of love intruded on more idyllic images:

If poets have reason to represent blissful love as a young and beautiful woman, full of life and joy, criminologists can represent unhappy love, not less faithfully, through the features of Death holding a scissors or a Fury brandishing a dagger. In effect, one drowns oneself for love, one hangs oneself for love, one suffocates oneself for love, one's mind is consumed for love. One becomes mad for love, one dies of a disappointment in love. . . . Who will count the drops of poison, the blows of the dagger, the pistol shots generated by love, the pots of vitriol that it has caused to be thrown, the nooses that it has formed?[36]

Contemporaries had little doubt that thwarted love could indeed lead to violent or criminal behavior. It was to women that scenarios of seduction, abandonment, and betrayal were imaginatively linked. According to one magistrate, "abandonment represents the sum of a woman's moral suffering: that is, the loss of the loved one, disdain for her beauty, preference conceded to a rival, public humiliation rendered more painful by the fear of being mocked publicly in her grief."[37] The female emotional economy turned, it seems, on a love equilibrium. He continued: "Love satisfies her pride, her need for tenderness, and her need for domination," while the forsaken woman is thrown into disequilibrium (bouleversée), overtaken by rage and fury. Such judgments had broad currency. An article on female criminality in Le Matin concluded that women did not commit crimes out of greed but were drawn into crime by their need to protect their position in the world, a position that was invariably established by a relation to a man. A threat to the terms of the relationship became inevitably a threat to their social being. Hence it was "love, jealousy, the desire for exclusive possession of the loved one, the desire to kill her rival" that drove the female criminal to save, as it were, her life.[38] Within the terms of this argument, the relationship *was* her life. The criminologist Camille Granier codified these assumptions when he claimed that, in contrast to the experience of men, women who were driven to suicide, to violence against themselves, had been overwhelmed by "a thwarted passion" (une passion contrariée), not by "physical suffering, illness, misery, impoverishment," which they were better able to endure than were men.[39] The malady that overcame women, that drove them to despair, was not physical sickness but lovesickness.

The causes célèbres of both Jeanne Daniloff and Mme Grille (of the Chambige affair) provided a descriptive taxonomy of women subjugated by passion (detailed in Chapter 2). Perhaps some of the evocative power of their stories derived from the exotic ambiance of colonial Algeria. But even more, these cases provided the context for and enacted the elaboration of cultural myths about woman as love-slave. Although one doctor testified that Daniloff was sick, "a nymphomaniac,"[40] most accounts cast

Cinquième Année. — N° 240.　　　Huit pages : CINQ centimes　　　Dimanche 10 Septembre 1892

Le Petit Parisien

SUPPLÉMENT LITTÉRAIRE ILLUSTRÉ

TOUS LES JOURS
Le Petit Parisien
25 CENTIMES

DIRECTION : 18, rue d'Enghien, PARIS

TOUS LES SAMEDIS
SUPPLÉMENT LITTÉRAIRE
5 CENTIMES

UN DRAME DANS UNE ÉGLISE

"A drama in a church."

her as a normal woman whose behavior represented an intensification of more ordinary feelings. Daniloff's attorney argued that, in attempting to poison her husband, she had acted under the influence of her lover, presumably against her own inclinations, and had secretly even begun to decrease the doses of the poison that she administered, "fighting for a year against the force that had taken possession of her."[41] According to popular lore, Jeanne Daniloff was at once "the mistress and the slave." She had become "the instrument [*executrice persistante*] of the criminal will of her lover, [who was] master of her body, master of her soul. She had given herself to him. She belonged entirely to him. There was nothing that she did not agree to do for love. He commanded. She acted. And death for all."[42] Similarly, the apparent decision of Mme Grille, respectable bourgeois wife and mother, to abandon her husband and children for a younger, socially inferior lover, was only comprehensible if one recognized that she had lost her will, had become "intoxicated" by a grand passion.[43] Both women, according to the stories told about them, slipped into criminal behavior as they lost control of the darker potentialities of their (female) nature.

The same insistence on women's natural propensity for "lovesickness," and the same sexual subtext of dominance and submission, loss of self and will, is evident in a discussion by the Italian criminologist Ferrero of women's "need" to confess even their crimes to their lovers:

It is the need of the woman in love to show her devotion, her attachment to the man, by giving him something of herself, surrendering to him not only her body, but her whole self, her thoughts, her soul, her fate, her life. . . . [Hence her need to impart a secret through which her lover becomes] the master of her destiny [to whom] she abandons herself, hands and feet tied, fulfilling the most ardent desire of a woman taken [*éprise*] in love.[44]

Although this image of the surrendered female body, bound hand and foot, is particularly graphic, the representation of woman as love-slave was mundane in the popular and professional literature of the period. In his novel *La Bête humaine*, for example, Zola repeats these assumptions nearly to the letter. Following a silent, implied confession to murder by the woman he is beginning to love, the protagonist Jacques Lantier assesses the meaning of her as yet unspoken confidence: "He was deeply touched by this way of finding peace by confessing to him. . . . She was so confiding, so vulnerable, with her soft, periwinkle-blue eyes! She seemed to him so womanly, belonging entirely to man and always ready to submit to him."[45] Love and submission, (male) power and (female) vulnerability, male self-possession and women's loss of self, seem to have been the poles of this widely circulating fantasy.

In a study of cell graffiti, the criminologist Raymond de Ryckère confirmed the belief that religious sentiments and feelings of love dominated the emotional life of female prisoners, whose scribblings contrasted sharply with the evident pride and hatefulness that characterized those of their male counterparts.[46] But more telling for de Ryckère was the fact that even female prisoners could recognize "unnatural women"— those who had committed crimes *against* love. A case in point was that of the infamous Gabrielle Fenayrou, a woman who had helped her husband to kill her lover. When Martin Fenayrou discovered the adultery of his wife, he ordered her to become his accomplice in his plan to take revenge on his former friend and rival. The centerpiece of Gabrielle's trial was not, in the end, the murder itself, but her apparent unfeeling complicity. Commentators drew attention to her coldness and her lack of passion in the courtroom, traits that were then read backwards as an explanation of her role in the crime.[47] According to de Ryckère, when Gabrielle appeared in the courtyard of Saint-Lazare prison for the first time, she was nearly slashed by the other female inmates, whose implacable anger finally banished her from the prison's public spaces.[48] The fatal violation was, then, not legal but affective. In betraying her husband, she had broken a formal commitment; in betraying her lover, she had forfeited her humanity.

In contrast to the ready assumption of women's fragile love equilibrium, a man who was "*détraqué en amour*," disordered by love, was understood either as a hysteric—to have his equilibrium so shattered seemed patently a form of illness—or as a *déséquilibré* who might present an ongoing social danger. Men who committed crimes of passion typically excused their violence against rivals, wives, or mistresses as a legitimate and justifiable defense of male honor, a defense heightened in its emotional pitch by its invocation of the language of despair and madness. But for this defense to be successful, it was important to represent the violence as the product of a moment of temporary madness. Women, in contrast, were seen as more profoundly and essentially *exaltée*, with uncontrollable passions persistently threatening to break out. The female analogue of a person *détraqué* typically suggested, then, not a woman driven by an excess of feeling but an upper-class woman who had run off with a servant.[49] In fact, the criminologist Granier spoke of women who committed crimes out of "interest" as pathological, "the masculine type," with more sharply articulated characters than *criminelles passionnelles*.[50] While the male crime of passion was sometimes represented as an atavistic residue of a time when violence in the defense of honor had ordered social life (an act largely suppressed in more highly evolved contemporary societies),[51] the same crime committed by a woman seemed less anachronistic, emerging as it did quite naturally through her moral-affective-physiological economy.

Sabine Juratic has noted that a compilation of causes célèbres in the eighteenth century cited five cases in which wives murdered their husbands, but none in which husbands were the aggressors. She suggests both that the death of wives at their husbands' hands was too banal a subject to merit special attention and that contemporaries seemed to share a belief in women's suppressed inclination to assassinate their husbands.[52] I would argue, at least for the late nineteenth century, that the particular act of violence driven by disappointed or betrayed love was understood, except when clearly a case of vindicating male honor, as a quintessentially feminine act, regardless of the sex of the perpetrator. Men who did not decisively invoke the masculine code of honor in their defense could become effectively feminized in the opinion of the court and in their self-presentation as *criminels passionnels*. In the case of Georges-Charles Koenig, for example, accused of trying to murder his wife, the defendant confronted his victim in terms typically voiced by betrayed women, appropriating, in his references to domesticity, the justification marshaled by women who sought to position their husbands as the ones responsible for the breach of domestic contract, and hence ultimately responsible for the violence:

I was always good to you, I deprived myself of everything, I drank water so that you would have wine, I ate bread in order to provide you with food; deny that! . . . What can you reproach me with? Was I a drunkard? . . . Did I run around with women? . . . Did I not take care of household chores? Did I not wash your laundry with mine, saving you from fatiguing work?[53]

Koenig had offered a feminized representation of himself that earned the disdain of the prosecutor. In his summary of the case, he sharply criticized Koenig for ignoring the advice of friends who had warned him about his wife's loose morals, but especially for the fact that, "dominated by the affection he had for his wife," he took her back, even after confirming the truth of her ongoing relationship with a former lover—a lapse in gender-appropriate behavior that the prosecutor could not pass

over. Absent unequivocal references to masculine honor, Koenig's violence could be assimilated to the specifically female image of a person
"dominated" by love.

In a slightly different version of the coding of the crime of passion as
feminine, the psychiatrist Hélie Courtis opened his medico-legal treatise
with a riveting visual image, *"un spectacle hideux"*:

> A large young man is stretched out in the workshop; his life is escaping in a
> gushing scarlet stream from a gaping wound in his neck; a crowd of women has
> gathered, most of whom are howling as if intoxicated by the sight of blood, re-
> leasing in their cries all the rancor of the female toward the male dominator;
> however, their "tyrant" was lying outstretched, inanimate, killed in his youth by
> an older and tragically jealous mistress.[54]

Women represent here *the* act in its purest form. It is an act of the weaker
against the stronger, of the subordinate against the dominant, the disadvantaged and illegitimate against the privileged and legitimate: he is tied
to his workshop, to the right order of things, a tyrant only in quotation
marks; she to howling animals, to the frenzy of blood and jealousy, to
the latent chaos that threatens ordered social life. Significantly, Courtis
says little more about women in the remainder of his study of crimes of
passion; his examples are drawn almost exclusively from cases with male
defendants; yet he has succeeded in powerfully connecting passionate violence to female disorder. It was not the actor who gendered the crime,
but the quality of the act.

The construct of Woman defined by love, fully present only in love,
was pervasive and nearly unshakeable. It appeared as a structure of the
contemporary imagination, and further as an interpretive device that
shaped the presentation and outcomes of criminal cases. The murder trial
of Marie Fournet is exemplary. In June 1886, Fournet murdered her former lover and business partner.[55] During her preliminary interrogations,
Fournet explained: "I was outraged to see that all my savings were lost
and that I had been duped by Biver, and it was because of this that I
killed him." Her interrogator responded: "Weren't you, on the contrary,
particularly overexcited because Biver had refused to continue the intimate relations that you had established?" Again Fournet countered this
suggestion: "No, I had had relations with Biver when we were together
in the employ of M. Courtois; but these relations ceased when his wife
arrived in Paris." The interrogator, undeterred, continued: "When Biver
rebuffed your advances and announced the intention of living with his
wife, it was from this moment that your jealousy awoke and you began to

threaten him and his wife about money." Fournet repeated her story: "This is a two-faced man—telling his wife one thing and me another. I wanted to settle accounts and break with him."[56] In the hearing in the Cour d'Assises, the presiding judge persisted in the official line of inquiry: "You have killed this man for jealousy?" The defendant's response: "No, sir, because he had compromised my situation and dissipated my savings."[57] Finally, the impossibility of her story, the need to transform it, is evident in the account of the *Gazette des Tribunaux*, where the crime was recounted in the following terms:

It is a question again, this time, of a drama of jealousy; however, to see the importance that issues of financial interest have assumed in the debates, one might doubt that it is passion that has driven the author of this crime. But through all these complaints and business negotiations that have emerged to complicate the situation, one sees the single idea that has guided the accused, which was nothing but to retrieve a lover who had slipped through her hands. This sentiment comes through in all her words, in spite of her denials; and, in sum, it is the sole thought that is able to explain her conduct.[58]

Yes, her disappointment in love was indeed "the sole thought" that was able to explain her conduct; economic issues unduly "complicated" the picture, obscuring the "single idea" that continued to force itself forward. But, we might ask, whose single-mindedness is in evidence here? In the terms of the love discourse, passion, not money—jealousy, not economic vulnerability—provided the interpretive frame that would account for the crime. Alternative meanings were literally expunged, preserving intact the woman-in-love.

The case of Hélène Guillet, accused of wounding her former lover's mistress with vitriol, produced a similar contest between the defendant and her interrogators over the meaning of her attack, and demonstrates even more directly both the persistence of the love discourse and its effects as a filter through which the collected data passed.[59] At Guillet's court hearing, the questions of the presiding judge laid out the context for understanding the crime. He began with "You became his mistress," and continued with the link that drove the plot: "Cattiaux [the lover] says that the domestic troubles came from your exalted jealousy." The image conveyed was a familiar one: that of an overwrought, abandoned woman, deceived in love, taking vengeance. Guillet's statements, however, challenged this totalizing representation. Responding to the *fact* of becoming Cattiaux's mistress, she rejected the romantic language of the genre, offering instead a self-presentation characterized by its cool emotional register and its pragmatism: "Before becoming his mistress, I made some inquiries about him. Afterwards, I said to him, 'It is not a lover that I want. It is a husband who is a good worker. If you want a mistress, go elsewhere!'" The judge then asked: "In your inquiries, you learned that he had two children?" Again she replied through the same connection to the constraints of ordinary life: "Yes, I said to myself, if we both work, we can be happy."[60] Nevertheless, in her description of the abandonment that provoked the vitriol attack, Guillet used conventional formulas to express the despair she felt, ending with the decision on revenge only after contemplating suicide. What is particularly interesting in this case, however, is her careful and detailed financial accounting of the money that she had lent her lover and lost, which is interspersed with, and in fact overwhelms, her account of romantic despair and ruminations on suicide.[61]

What we see here, then, is the intersection of separate but joined understandings, at once contradictory and complementary, held by unequal opponents in a struggle for definition. In their separate efforts to convey the essence of the crime, officials and defendants each selected the details that made the event meaningful to him- or herself and credible to others. It is clear that Guillet and the investigating magistrate shared a system of meanings, common narrative fictions expressed through the love discourse. The story of thwarted love can literally "explain" criminal acts such as Guillet's. Accused women were as capable as their interrogators of filling in the conventional causal assumptions that linked the events of the plot in a believable way. It was not only male commentators who produced the melodramatic image of the "woman consumed by love"; female defendants also frequently justified their violence in terms of the paroxysms of despair, "overexcitement," or "exaltation" provoked by disappointments in love.

Several variations on the formula emerged. In one version, the abandoned woman vowed to punish her tormentor and then to take her own life. Marie Sivadon claimed, for example, that she had determined to murder her husband and his lover and then to kill herself,[62] a strategy echoed by Agathe Georges ("I have suffered for such a long time that the abandonment by the one I love has given me a deadly resolution. I have sworn to kill him and to kill myself afterwards").[63] Others, immersed in (and perhaps elevated by) images of their victimization, spoke only of dying, making explicit their belief that a suicide would accuse their lovers more painfully and publicly than could any other gesture.

The vengeance and/or suicide formula, in all its diverse articulations, had become *the* available language to explain women's domestic violence.

It should be readily apparent, however, that this condensed language of despair could not encompass or exhaust the complex material, psychological, and social dynamics that it was called upon to interpret. When a defendant claimed that she followed her intended victim for days, but the vial that she carried contained warm water and not vitriol, what are we to think of this assertion? When shots, fired at point-blank range, missed entirely, did the defendant in fact only want to scare her victim? Even when the shots were fired directly at his head? or from behind? These ambiguities are clouded further by references to *le petit revolver* as a "woman's weapon," presumably intended to be part of the staging of domestic melodramas, but without the force to kill. By invoking the formula, even when it was not compatible with other testimony, defendants further obscured the tangle of conditions that combined to produce the criminal act. For example, Rose Chervey spoke of herself pathetically as the faithful dog of her lover Paul Parquet: "I had wanted to kill myself at his feet as the faithful dog that I was." She insisted that she loved Parquet too much to do him harm, maintaining throughout that it was "inexplicable," "by mere chance" that when she attempted to kill herself, she instead shot him twice.[64] Such odd juxtapositions appear regularly. The judicial dossiers are profoundly anarchic in their messages, often providing clear evidence only of the incongruence between the words that were chosen and the emotional register and causal links they were meant to convey. We cannot, then, know with certainty how to interpret the complex motivations that emerge in individual dossiers. What we can more readily uncover, however, are the various cultural effects set into play by the love discourse.

To begin with, the image of love that authorized the crime of passion invited a clarification of difference—differences between men and women, between "normal" and "abnormal" passions, between "normal" and "unnatural" women. Seeking exact criteria by which to judge culpability, interrogators attempted to establish the precise levels of "overexcitement" (*surexcitation*) and despair experienced by alleged *criminelles passionnelles*; they counted bullets to verify the sincerity of defendants' professed desire to commit suicide; they assessed the seriousness with which promises of marriage were offered to determine the reasonableness of the accused's expectations; they pored over reports of past conduct, searching for either *une vie régulière* or a pattern of disreputable behavior; they evaluated the degree of responsibility shared by the victim. Such standards were useful in confirming deeply held beliefs about female nature. In effect, the discussion of female crimes of passion swung between a depiction of the normal woman, driven by a precarious love equilibrium, and the vicious woman, released by the same emotional economy. Women-in-love seemed at once natural and dangerous.

It is in the work of the jurist Louis Proal that the implications of this double image are most starkly outlined. In his study of women betrayed in love, Proal created two prototypical female types: those who suffer in silence and ultimately languish into death—women, in Proal's words, with a "fixed character" who are "gentle, sensitive, discreet"; and alternatively, those who kill, the woman here as "a fury who shrieks, stamps her feet, pulls out her hair, threatens, hits, smashes."[65] Proal is taken with the image of the languishing, despairing female who chooses ultimately to take her own life. He observes that these women express unending devotion to, and forgiveness of, their unfaithful lovers, and for him, "nothing is more touching than these final adieus, full of tenderness, of pardon, that they murmur even to their final breath":

"From the day that I saw that you would not be my husband I had only a single thought, to die. If I am not able to be your wife, at least I will no longer suffer."

"I love you always, I pardon you. Adieu, death torments me."

"Adieu, be happy! Let my memory accompany you only so that you will remember that I adored you."[66]

Even when the suicide notes contained reproaches ("Why have you made me suffer?" "Why have you deceived me?"), Proal insisted that these maudlin farewells end, *quand même*, with expressions of love. The note that Proal quotes at length to demonstrate his point is especially interesting in its emotional ambiguities, its mixture of assertiveness and submission:

My dear Louis, because your feeling for me is ended, I prefer to take my life. . . . Louis, come to my burial. I want you to be the last person to embrace me before I am put in my coffin. . . . Take good care of our daughter and kiss her for me. . . . If she asks why I died, tell her that it is from having loved too much. . . . I would like always to have flowers on my grave; come there every Sunday with our daughter.[67]

This text is at once despairing and manipulative, a woman struggling perhaps to realize some power in death that eluded her in life. Proal sees, nevertheless, only Woman, eternally constant and forgiving.

Proal's study represents a recurrent type among the many investigations into the meaning of love and loss, investigations that collectively suggested suicide as woman's natural and appropriate response to intense suffering—a response that at least derailed the fury. In fact, many of the texts presented suicide as the necessary outcome of true suffering, while taking revenge became a sign of "egoism." The philosopher and criminologist Gabriel Tarde observed that Jeanne Daniloff ought to have responded to her romantic desperation by taking her own life instead of trying to poison her husband. In her eventual suicide, he saw "the explication of her soul, the revelation of her energy, her sincerity, her suffering, the fatality of the overpowering sentiments that pushed her to crime . . . for these emotions were her essential being."[68] The lawyer Henri Robert echoed this perception, presenting Daniloff's suicide as an expiation through which she disarmed even her most severe judges.[69]

Both the cultural credibility and interpretive power of the despair-vengeance-suicide narrative are particularly evident in the case of Marie Louise Victor.[70] As I have already noted, in assessing Marie Victor's responsibility for the death of her infant daughter in a failed suicide attempt the court and her lawyer chose to ignore her history of depression and preoccupation with suicide, and did not order an examination by a psychiatrist. Instead, the judicial documents emphasized the disparity between the passionate tone of the suicide note left for the lover and the *froideur* of the note addressed to her husband. The summary of the pretrial investigation concluded that this difference showed, without a doubt, that Victor's behavior was the result of disappointment in love. Victor explained herself in quite different terms, claiming that she could not console herself for the injury she had done her husband and that she despaired of receiving his pardon. There was evidence to support her explanation. Victor's brother-in-law, who was the first to find her after her lover's departure, testified that she was obsessed with the thought that she could not return home after what she had done. Most tellingly, Victor had herself used similar terms during her interrogation. She claimed that her abandonment by her lover had caused her great grief; but "it was certainly not sorrow for the abandonment that made me decide on suicide. From the moment when I saw that he was not coming back, the obsession [*entraînement*] that I had for him ended. The only motive that pushed me to suicide was remorse and the feeling that my husband would not be able to forgive me."

The lover seems almost a minor player in this drama—the catalyst, or merely the excuse, rather than the cause. Yet because the abandonment-suicide story was so compelling and her behavior seemingly so transparent, no one even thought to question Victor's mental condition, not even her own lawyer, at a time when female behavior that appeared excessive was routinely subjected to medical scrutiny. The messiness of the story, including Victor's longstanding and persistent depression, was deleted or overlooked. (In fact, while recovering in the hospital, she continued to talk of suicide, and was restrained in a straitjacket for some time.) Instead, the trial preserved a tighter and more formulaic story line. It must have seemed appropriate and "normal" for Marie Victor to be *détraquée en amour*, responding to her loss in a most conventional way.

The despairing Marie Victor had, of course, as her shadow, the more threatening figure of the fury. Convictions about the naturalness of a suicidal response to despair inevitably opened a space for a discussion of the unnatural woman whose responses exceeded acceptable limits. One criminologist noted, for example, that although fewer bloody crimes were committed by women, "it would . . . be difficult to assemble a comparable list of murders committed by men having such frivolous motives. Is it not one of the striking characteristics of female criminality," he asks, "not to know how to make the vengeance proportionate to the injury?"[71] Such perceptions were ubiquitous. Granier insisted that female sadism had not been studied carefully enough;[72] Proal claimed that women experienced more pleasure in taking revenge than did men, exercising their retribution "with the most delicate or the most perverse refinements";[73] while de Ryckère described a woman's revenge as "a kind of voluptuousness that she nourishes, allows to smolder, and caresses."[74] Criminologists were convinced that "in her cruelties, [the vengeful woman] far surpasses the most ferocious man."[75]

Because vengeance, in this analysis, revealed something essentially sinister in the female character, explanations were offered in the language of familiar misogynistic stereotypes—ones that frequently joined the themes of (excessive) sexuality and violence. The "bellicose viragos" of the Commune provided an accessible model for making these links. Maxime du Camp's description of the *petroleuses*, women accused of setting fire to Paris in 1870, is representative. He begins with an idiom—"les femmes avaient lancé bien autre chose que leur bonnet par dessus les moulins" (women have thrown off all restraint)—but continues with a literal rendering of the idiom in a description that seeks to expose the essential nature of the women of the Commune by a physical (and rhetorical) uncovering:

Women have thrown more than their bonnets over the mills. They did not stop at such a trifling detail, and all the rest of their costume passed over as well. They laid bare their souls and one was stupefied by the quantity of natural perversity that one discovered there. Those who gave themselves to the Commune, and they were numerous, had only one ambition: to elevate themselves above man in exaggerating his vices.[76]

In disrobing (or lifting their skirts, as it were) and uncovering their "souls," the *petroleuses* revealed their natural perversity. Although du Camp displaces their sex with their souls, he nevertheless has imaginatively linked female sexuality with both perversity and violence, danger with women in public, revolution with women on top.

Taking his cue almost to the letter from these culturally available constructs of femininity, the physician Paul Aubry elaborated the familiar image of the vicious seductress who, "in simulating a caress, prepares an assassination":

Knowing the power of woman over man, the fatal trust that he has in her, they take their usual place near him, in their shared bed, or else in pretending to give him a kiss. We cannot remember encountering, in all of the accounts of crime that we have read, a man who does not recoil before this treachery.[77]

The celebrated case of Gabrielle Bompard, a prototype of the genre, seemed to confirm these associations. In a crime plotted with her lover, Bompard offered herself as sexual bait to draw their intended victim to an apartment where he could be robbed and murdered. In the midst of an embrace, Bompard slipped a rope around her victim's neck, permitting her accomplice to complete the deed. The intense popular interest elicited by this case arose from its quality as an adventure story that moved across several continents, and from its challenge to interpretations of criminal responsibility enacted in a confrontation between some of France's most prominent alienists of the time.[78] But one may speculate as well that the devious and dangerous sexuality that Bompard represented resonated broadly in the audience, both male and female, that made her a celebrity.

Various experts on women's crime attempted to establish criteria for separating the legitimate *criminelle passionnelle* from her more perverse counterpart. One magistrate wrote of the need to ferret out all "counterfeiting of love," by which he meant the "coarse love" that only satisfied the physical senses, a "love" that was an offense against morals; this was a distinction that would be made with particular care in crimes committed by women.[79] Jeanne Daniloff, for example, in whom sexual desire appeared to prevail over maternal responsibility, could only be understood as either sick or criminal. Such finely tuned calibration appears in the writings of Louis Proal, who spoke sympathetically of the dependent, abandoned *jeune fille* who took vengeance on her seducer, but specifically denied comparable rights to mothers, to widows who had seduced younger men, or to *femmes galantes* who had had children.[80] Similarly, the physician Aubry concluded that, while jealousy was one of the forms of love (pointing therefore to an acquittal for a woman who murdered the husband or lover who had left her for a mistress), he could countenance no similar leniency for a married woman who killed her husband in order to be with her lover. As prototypes of this kind of de facto divorce, Aubry cited two revealing examples: a virtuous woman who, in the throes of menopause, "under the influence of a uterine excitation," killed her husband in order to freely continue relations with her son; and a woman who turned her eleven-year-old daughter over to one of her lovers and, with the aid of her son, murdered her husband.[81] It is not merely that such murders could not be assimilated to the crime of passion, but that the married woman who had taken a lover became, here, not just a murderess but a monster.

This literature reads like fifteenth-century tirades against witches. In its symbols and language, it exemplifies a kind of transhistorical representation of the dangerous woman. It also has, however, a more specific historical referent in the social relations of the nineteenth century, and it is the local strategic possibilities that I want to highlight. In the fin-de-siècle, the familiar opposition between the "normal" and the "unnatural" woman invoked in explanations of female criminality worked to suggest timeless patterns, dislocating the stories revealed in the judicial dossiers from the socioeconomic and cultural realities out of which they emerged. The code that underwrote the crime of passion promoted explanations grounded in individual psychology. We have seen, for example, that the official version of the case of Marie Fournet effaced the inequities in social and economic power between the accused and her victim—an asymmetry that was the basis of so many crimes of passion.

Ironically, and perhaps tellingly, although the love discourse formally "explained" crimes spawned by domestic conflict, the aggrieved parties themselves rarely mentioned actual disappointment in love. Complaints

so the whole discourse was external to the people on trial? only a figment of bourg. observers' imagination?

referred rather to the performance of specific (gendered) roles that constituted the bottom line of acceptable behaviors—to the implied contract that underlay domestic relations. Female defendants spoke especially of their economic vulnerability, of the fact that their husbands or lovers did not work hard enough, did not contribute to their joint existence, abused them physically, and especially when the man was of a higher social stratum, took advantage of their dependency by refusing to honor the implicit codes of cross-class alliances. In these explanations, women who committed crimes of passion were effectively challenging a cultural myth of male chivalry through which various forms of male privilege emerged as the reward for their protection of women. Absent this protection, women felt entitled to assert their own claims, which they sometimes enforced by violence. Françoise Bechon, for example, falsely represented herself to her employers and to her lover as a widow, claiming in her depositions that her husband gave her nothing and ate up what little she had, hence the lie that was truer than the truth: "Because I could not count on him, I said that I did not have a husband."[82] Jeanne Bonnefous, a widow with four children who blinded her former lover with vitriol, admitted that her crime was produced by his abandonment; it is clear, however, that she also believed that *his* treachery exceeded (and perhaps justified) hers. She explained in her depositions that he had told her he was single, although in fact he was married, and had proposed taking her to America with him. Under the pretext of preparing for this trip, he sold off much of her furniture, keeping all the profits for himself; although she gave birth to his child and her economic situation became increasingly precarious, he failed to help her in any way.[83]

The working-class women who committed crimes of passion may indeed have been moved by paroxysms of passionate feeling, but it seems equally clear that the love discourse offered them a way to reassert the terms of domestic codes that were, in their minds, consistently being breached—to call into question the apparent immunity of men who escaped their responsibilities. The protocols required by the crime of passion suppressed these details that catalogued the expectations of ordinary life in favor of (in the words of Terry Eagleton) "affective mythologies that would permeate the texture of lived experience."[84] Such mythologies, rendered always in the language of natural and timeless universals, explicitly expunged economic and more broadly social concerns, presenting each crime as the act of a particular, unique individual in response to needs that were private and psychological. In the terms of the love discourse, women were anchored in an interiorized domestic space that was implicitly defined as distinct from the larger social world.

The way in which the formula dissolved the social context of women's criminality is particularly evident in the case of Louise Demaret. According to the indictment, the twenty-one-year-old cook shot and killed her lover, Victor Bernant, in the early morning hours of May 30, 1881.[85] Their relationship had been stormy during the preceding few months, occasionally requiring the intervention of neighbors. On May 29 Bernant had promised to take Demaret walking, asking her to leave work at 1 o'clock in the afternoon; she waited for him for four hours; when he finally arrived he said that he did not want to go out with her after all and was going, instead, to have dinner with his stepmother. Demaret reported that she was profoundly wounded by this slight, and returned to her employers' home where she removed a revolver from a cabinet and then went, in a state of great agitation, to spend the evening with a friend. She returned home to find her lover sleeping. When she approached him, seeking a reconciliation, he rebuffed her, and she had to spend the night in a chair. Throughout the night, she tried to return to their bed and, each time, he resisted her effort. At 5:00 A.M., she made a last attempt; when it appeared to her that the rupture was irreversible, she seized the revolver and shot him. He died immediately. Louise Demaret was condemned to six years in prison.

Much of the testimony in this case revolved around Demaret's supposed jealousy of Bernant's stepmother, with whom he was alleged to be having an affair, a focus that was repeated in the press reports: "Again, a drama of jealousy. Before it was vitriol that served as the instrument of vengeance; today it is the revolver. As we see, the means change, but the goal is the same—to avenge oneself for the abandonment of a lover."[86] Demaret does speak of her jealousy, but her testimony places the issue of jealousy in the context of her pregnancy and its economic implications. In her account, the couple's troubles intensified as she began to resist Bernant's efforts to hold all her earnings, telling him that she needed to save for her confinement.[87] When she refused to turn over her wages, he beat her. In her description of their last interaction, she claimed that she had asked to stay with him until after her delivery, promising that she would then give the child to a wet nurse and look for a new position. According to her testimony, Bernant insisted that, from that moment, he had decided to live with his stepmother and would not let her remain with him. When the prosecutor questioned Demaret about whether she intended to murder her lover, she replied: "My existence had become impossible. I had given him all my money. . . . He was going to abandon me although I was pregnant and without resources. . . . It is his ingratitude on the one hand, and jealousy on the other, that made me decide to kill him." And later, describing their final encounter, Demaret reported in the courtroom: "I was thinking of my situation, and of what I would become if he abandoned me as he said, and I kept returning without respite to this burden."[88] She does, in the end, speak of an intense jealousy; but in all of her accounts, it is impossible not to hear also her rage at her social and economic vulnerability.

In fact, the various moves that had brought Demaret to her last employer suggest a woman who was hardworking, even self-consciously ambitious. She had followed her sister to Paris where she changed employment many times, sometimes making use of a placement agency, each time increasing her wages, moving always closer to *les grands quartiers*. She also appears to have been quite independent, leaving jobs in which her employers sought to supervise her social life too closely, as she had resisted similar intervention by her parents. When Demaret was asked to explain the basis of her quarrels with Bernant, she attributed the intensity of their confrontations first to his violent nature, then to the fact that he took all her money, and finally to his affair with his stepmother. Thus, while Demaret admitted to jealousy, and responded affirmatively and perhaps obligatorily to direct questioning about whether she regretted her crime, it is clear that the court's presentation of the case in terms of jealousy and revenge (and the echo of this judgment in the press) obscured the social context and social meaning of her act. Demaret's crime had become, in these versions, emphatically personal; the complexities of her life were swallowed up by the love discourse.

What, then, did contemporaries make of these "love stories"? When a journalist called for the acquittal of Marie Bière, he wrote of her as a woman whom the law could consider guilty but who could only be understood, "in the light of human conscience, as a martyr for her heart."[89] Or, as a jurist wrote, the crime of passion was the legitimate response of "a woman in the thrall of a sacred delusion . . . in whom the cry of the flesh spoke as a duty."[90] But there is also clear evidence that in spite of endless repetitions of the precise formula that defined the crime of passion, these formulas were understood to depart radically from social experience. In fact, contemporary observers were both naive and cynical in their responses to this romanticized mode of explanation. They clearly *did* see that the stories of seduction and abandonment were frequently about social and economic precariousness—about disparities in power between men and women—even when they refused to tell the story in these terms. According to one Parisian lawyer, the essentially peaceable bourgeois men who sat on the jury did not necessarily believe in the innocence of the seduced girl, were too cynical to accept the formulaic scenarios presented to the court, accepted extramarital liaisons without qualm or moral outrage, yet regularly joined, through some unspoken shared commitment, to acquit the *criminelle passionnelle*.[91] "Have we not seen Paris," he mused, "the Paris of frivolous liaisons, of furtive scandals, of peaceful infidelities, the promised land of cosmopolitan dreams where wives who are half-married coexist with mistresses who are half-legitimate in a delicious promiscuity?"[92] The Paris he knew did not seem the natural setting for the script put into circulation by crimes of passion. But in the end he could not, or would not, think outside of the conventions that he was describing, and his analysis moved ultimately in a circle, concluding that the acquittals offered by juries were, at bottom, a secular poem to Love. We can, however, try to read between the lines of this poem in order to discover why "love" so often prevailed, at least publicly and rhetorically, over cynicism.

I want to argue here that the love discourse, in its intensification of the language of romantic feelings (love, jealousy, vengeance) worked to construct appropriate gender relations and to secure the bourgeois family as the basis of the social order. The focus in these criminal stories on the emotions of the individual woman obscured the fact that the talk about love was more fundamentally about the institution of the family at a time when the family had become an object of intense concern in Third Republic France. For social authorities across the political spectrum, *la famille* stood for *la patrie*—in the apt words of one writer, the "fatherland is none other than *le plus grand foyer*";[93] acts against the family were equated with threats to the nation. The subtext that made this conflation both credible and powerful was provided by the new divorce law of 1884, which reversed prohibitions in effect since 1803, and by growing alarm about the declining birth rate, attributed especially to the same "egoism" that promoted divorce and symbolizing the same perceived national decadence. Theresa McBride points out that the potential implications of the divorce law remained frightening decades after the law was passed. Even republicans who considered marriage reform to be the emblem and expression of republican freedom were cautious, ultimately passing a law that reinstituted divorce, but circumscribed the new freedom with restrictions designed to protect the patriarchal family.[94] Newspapers regularly featured debates about the effects of divorce and family limitation, couched in apocalyptic language that warned of social decay and national decline. Not surprisingly, then, questions about male authority and women's independence, about sexuality inside and outside of marriage, as well as more generalized worries about the working-class milieu, could be expressed through this widespread concern for the traditional family.

The crime of passion brought together these quite different familial issues. As bourgeois authorities and ordinary working people looked to the family as the source of both public and private well-being, the Cour d'Assises became an important arena for articulating, consolidating, and even revising the codes that underpinned domestic life. Like melodramas, courtroom proceedings recited a dramatic story, fueled by emotional hyperbole, that sought to make the moral universe visible.[95] The courtroom narrative provided an opportunity for ethical clarification in which behavior was simplified, stripped of ambiguity and complexity in order to underline the ethical imperatives. The presiding magistrate typically spoke *ex officio* to reiterate his understanding of the informal assumptions that organized social relationships, defining: the obligations between unmarried persons from the same social stratum; the differences in these obligations in cross-class alliances; the criteria for what constituted a promise; the differences between a legitimate and an illegitimate abandonment, and so on. There were clearly rules. Some kinds of jealousy were more worthy than others, some instances of jealousy more believable than others;[96] some promises were more real than others. Only certain kinds of women could legitimately feel despair as a result of abandonment.[97] Criminal stories became, in effect, exemplars—morality tales that weighed the rights and worth of each party and commented on appropriate gender roles and expectations. By example and by prescription, the courtroom narratives sought to constitute desired social relations, ordering and explaining social interactions according to specific narrative and behavioral codes.

The most sympathetic *criminelle passionnelle* was the bourgeois woman whose passion was driven by family concerns—that is, whose excesses were maternal and not sexual. Marie Bière symbolized not just the wronged woman but the wronged mother. The special poignancy of her case lay in the death of her child and Gentien's callous response to this loss. Similarly, the case of Comtesse de T became famous not only because its protagonists were from the upper classes, whose stories were especially titillating in the popular press, but because of the comtesse's much-repeated claim that she had hurled vitriol at her husband's working-class mistress in order to prevent this woman from becoming the mother to her children at her death.[98] Even the feisty Melanie Lerondeau was transformed at her second trial into a *bonne mère de famille* by her lawyer, although new toxicological evidence had apparently made such rhetorical embellishment unnecessary (see Chapter 2). Seeking to create an image of beleaguered motherhood, Lachaud insisted that Melanie was sharp-tongued, perhaps even fiery, but a good housewife, an unfortunate whose only crime was "to have wanted her husband to save for his daughter's dowry and to have been, for her, the true husband of a woman who loved him."[99]

For Lachaud, this strategy was a familiar one. In an earlier case, he had moved toward his concluding arguments by evoking for the court the miserable spectacle of an imprisoned mother forced to confront her child:

When this child comes to see her mother in prison, what agony! "Come, mama, let's not stay here, it is cold, it is dark, come, come to our home, come then." "Tomorrow, my daughter!" and tomorrow never comes. Poor child! They had promised that she would have her mother last night! Oh! gentlemen of the jury, we have waited too long, speak, speak quickly and your voice will be blessed.[100]

Lachaud's editor noted that this statement produced a general explosion in the courtroom: "There were cries, sobs, moaning, tears." Several years later, Lachaud repeated his earlier success:

Poor mother! she has two angels, two small daughters whom everyone loves and pities, and she has not seen them for seven months! Ah! she would like to see them. But to have these poor innocents enter a glacial cell; to have them hear the grinding of keys; to give them the maternal embrace in this suffocating air; to not be able to bring them home afterwards; finally, to see one's children in the midst of this environment of shame and dishonor, this would have been too horrible. . . . Oh! gentlemen, these are terrible sufferings that rend the heart . . . But I hesitate, I do not want to move this audience; I, myself, would not be master of my emotions.[101]

In response to this carefully crafted speech, the defendant sustained "a nervous crisis" during which she cried out repeatedly, "My children! my poor children!" Fulfilling its own role in the drama, the courtroom audience responded with an outburst of applause. At bottom, real mothers could not be criminal.

This focus on motherhood legitimized women's distress—justifying the seduced and abandoned (pregnant) unmarried woman in her violence and giving married women standing to resist a husband's betrayal. It recuperated women from the public world of crime and restored them to a privatized and asocial domestic space. In cases such as those of Melanie Lerondeau, Louise Demaret, and Marie Fournet, the love story that explained their behavior rendered them more passive, more dependent, less ambitious, and more fully inscribed within a love relationship—that is, within expectations defined by femininity and domesticity—than we might expect from a reading of their criminal dossiers. By contrast, women who could be seen as "unnatural" mothers or those whose acts seemed to reveal some hidden "sexual depravity" (disqualifying them as mothers) were denied the leniency afforded by an alleged crime of passion.[102] *She has it both ways.*

The formulaic love stories that explained crimes of passion did not, however, merely reconfirm traditional values; they could also facilitate the assimilation of change. The jury, as well as courtroom spectators and public officials, both created and responded to shifting popular opinions about such issues as the responsibilities of paternity, standards for judging adultery, and the rights of individuals engaged in irregular liaisons. For working-class and middle-class men and women, marriage involved both personal feelings and economic considerations. The women who committed acts of violence against lovers, spouses, and rivals were producing a kind of polemic that attested to their profound sense of frustration with existing practices and customs, to their experience of extreme vulnerability, and to the loss of their hopes for the future. Arlette Farge has made a similar argument in her study of eighteenth-century violence, in which she suggests that we need to read women's complaints on two levels: as descriptions of the material conditions and events of their lives and as evidence of their illusions—their hopes, dreams, and expectations.[103] Crimes of passion had become social texts that pointed to unsettled expectations about interpersonal relations and to unclear ideas about how to address issues that crossed back and forth between public and private spheres. This was a "text" that revealed the convergence of intimate stories of domestic life with several loosely related public developments: increasing discussion of woman's place and woman's rights; a perceived disruption of the equilibrium in relations between men and women; height-

ened demands by women for the legal right to support for their illegitimate children; and growing evidence that direct action and private justice,
with the complicity of juries, were substituting for clear public policies or
legal remedies for the problems expressed through women's criminal acts.

While the court clearly sought to promote the "natural family," it was
forced in the process to reexamine the viability of existing codes. Marie
Bière's is a case in point. The prosecutor in the Bière case had appealed to
the code of *galanterie* to absolve Gentien of responsibility in terms that
he believed were well understood. According to the prosecutor, Bière
belonged to the world of the theater and knew perfectly well what she
was doing, while Gentien had promised her nothing. Perhaps, he argued,
she had hoped for marriage, but when Gentien left her, he was well
within his rights. And, finally, the moral of the tale: "When one moves
outside of the laws of morality . . . one has only the protection of the
code of gallantry of fashionable society, and this code is not harsh."[104] In
this instance, however, the prosecutor's invocation of Gentien's conventionally protected position backfired, angering spectators in its "callous-
ness" and "cruelty." A journalist reporting the popular support that
greeted Marie Bière's acquittal noted that public opinion had come to
insist that the responsibilities of paternity existed outside of formal legal
definitions.[105] Fueled especially by anxieties about depopulation, recognition seemed to be growing that fathers could no longer automatically
expect the abandonment of illegitimate children to go unnoticed or unpunished.

The desperate circumstances of unmarried working-class mothers and
the irresponsibility of men who refused to acknowledge or support their
illegitimate children were constant themes in accounts of women's violent
crime. Most women's efforts to secure some protection stopped short of
crime, of course, and often engaged whole families in the project. Both
Rosalie Velay and her mother followed Rosalie's ex-lover in the street to
harrass him for refusing to honor his promise of marriage, a promise that
his parents opposed.[106] More than women, perhaps, men seemed concerned with the status implications of marriage, especially skilled workers, petty merchants, and functionaries who might have been upwardly
mobile. Friends of M. Torlotin commented, for example, that they never
believed that he would marry his mistress or recognize their child because her family was not sufficiently honorable.[107] Similarly, when
Blanche Béchard asked her lover of two years, Paul Longne, to regularize
their union after the birth of their child, he left her. Disconsolate,

Béchard appealed to Longne's aunt, who rebuffed her with the admonition that she should have come eighteen months ago when she began the affair, because "my nephew is not from a family in which one marries one's mistress."[108] Longne repeated this dictum as well; but it seems that he had not always understood so clearly the rules of the game. When he was seventeen, he had wanted to marry a young girl whom he had impregnated, earning the mockery of his family in the process. He would not make the same mistake twice.

By the turn of the century, however, politicians and reformers had begun to be more concerned with the demographic consequences of fragile working-class unions than with protecting male prerogatives. Increasingly, high infant mortality rates among the poor were attributed to the insufficient protections afforded unwed mothers by either the state or private philanthropy; the legal prohibition against the search for paternity, preserved until 1912 in Article 340 of the civil code, was deemed especially deficient.[109] While reformers continued to worry that a change in the code would disrupt "normal families"—that is, would embarrass bourgeois married men identified as the fathers of illegitimate children—and that augmenting the rights of unwed mothers would promote illegitimacy, many had come to believe that some changes were necessary to enable single mothers to seek the necessary child support that would prevent abortion, infanticide, child abandonment, or early death.[110] The impassioned words of the politician Paul Strauss in 1896, in response to an infanticide committed by a single mother, attested to the presence in public discourse of a powerful new perspective: "Where is the seducer, the cause of the pregnancy? Why isn't he with the accused? If the seduced girl has so odiously violated the laws of nature and of humanity . . . the fault is especially with the one who has abused her weakness and tenderness. . . . The seducer remains unknown . . . Responsibility belongs to both."[111]

It was in the context of these broader debates about depopulation and paternity that presiding magistrates in the Cour d'Assises frequently lectured working-class men on their responsibilities to the women whom they had impregnated and responded harshly to clear evidence that promises of marriage had been violated. While women often explained their violence against former lovers in terms of their lost honor, the high rates of acquittal for female defendants had less to do with honor than with the court's efforts to encourage working-class couples to marry and produce legitimate children. As a corollary to this position, the court was particularly unsympathetic to perceived "crimes against the family." For example, in the case of a failed suicide attempt that left her infant son dead, Marie Louise Vasseur was condemned to five years in prison.[112] In this case, the defendant had been accused of stealing small sums from her employer. She became desperate in the face of this charge and despaired of ever being able to support her two children. The case differs from so many like it in that her lover claimed that he had proposed marriage and had agreed to recognize the two children. It is indeed possible that Vasseur drew such a harsh sentence not just because she had caused her small son's death, but because she had refused to form a regular family.

The Cour d'Assises became, then, a privileged site for the articulation of a set of fine-tuned distinctions that would, in principle, stabilize domestic life. As these codes were worked out through the judicial process, women did gain some implicit recognition of specifically female vulnerabilities that were built into both law and custom. But even as the court acknowledged women's grievances, it returned female defendants to a state of dependency that had been temporarily suspended by their acts of violence. By interpreting crimes of passion in psychological terms, the trials became melodramas, constructing stories in which the plot turned on a problematic created by the situation of a pivotal female character who was most often a heroine-victim.[113] Hence, although typical nineteenth-century melodramatic scenarios insisted on the moral (sexual) probity of the woman—insisted either on her virginity if unmarried or her fidelity if married—an implicit code backed up by the threat of punishment, it was even more important for the narrative to emphasize her dependency and powerlessness. Léon Métayer has argued, for example, that within the formula of melodramatic narrative, the appropriate power relations are fixed by the right of a male character to pardon as well as to punish—"the fate of the woman is only assured by the good will of the man."[114] According to Métayer, the symbolic importance of the pardon derives from the assumption that a woman is naturally tender and forgiving, while the pardon of the male, less readily available, more discriminating, stands in for the will of Society. The analogy to the courtroom seems evident. The accused—seduced, abandoned or betrayed, the victim of an overpowering male will—arrived in the courtroom where, once again, her fate would be decided by the will (and perhaps generosity) of more powerful men.

In actual practice, prominent defense lawyers such as Charles Lachaud spoke directly to this point, reminding jurors of their prescribed role in the courtroom drama. In a style that came to define the genre, Lachaud first established the image of the victim: "Have courage, *my child*, life is difficult because this man has taken everything from you, your honor, your future, your spiritual peace. You have suffered greatly." His conclusion then, with inexorable logic, directed attention to the paternal power of the court: "I deliver this unfortunate [woman] to your hands, gentlemen of the jury, and I await your verdict with confidence."[115] In evidence here is what Judith Walkowitz has called the erotic triangle of nineteenth-century melodrama: the villain, the daughter, and the outraged father who acts to restore (patriarchal) order, resetting the terms of relationships that had become slippery, unstable, threatening.[116]

Yet the desired order remained elusive. At the turn of the century, critics reacted with growing dismay to the unanticipated consequences produced by the special status afforded crimes of passion. To some extent, this more skeptical stance was part of a larger worry that juries had become too powerful. In acquitting so many *criminelles passionnelles*, jurors had claimed to be bringing the law into harmony with public opinion, providing extralegal recourse in cases where the legal code seemed outdated and inflexible. But critics increasingly interpreted the independent judgments of juries as an inappropriate exercise of authority by the petit bourgeois men who dominated jury lists. In the words of the judicial press, the Parisian who sat on a jury was a "*Parisien frondeur*," a rebel who by temperament would oppose the representatives of the state.[117] Responding to what they saw as an unsystematic or idiosyncratic rendering of justice, some critics lobbied for the reform of criminal procedures, arguing that if juries had more leeway in graduating penalties, the paradoxical acquittal of defendants who readily confessed to their crimes would disappear. As it stood, the jury frequently had to decide between an extremely harsh sentence or an acquittal; in such a situation, a sympathetic defendant, particularly a woman, could expect to be acquitted.[118] Others, including the prominent prosecutor Adolphe Guillot, recommended higher standards for jury duty, such as some sort of requirement in higher education or token of professional accomplishment that would assure the presence of men with a "clearer" and "more refined" sense of social duty.[119] The goal was to mute the voice of popular opinion in favor of a more formal system that would speak authoritatively as the voice of the state.

Embedded in this discussion (and seconded by critics who wanted to eliminate the jury altogether) was the suspicion that the jury, a premier symbol of political democracy, shared in one of democracy's greatest inherent dangers—the risk borne by institutions in a mass society of becoming weak, irrational—in fact, feminized. Contemporary wisdom held that verdicts in Paris reflected, above all, an *"esthétique théâtrale,"*[120] romantic and melodramatic, that encouraged jurors to "applaud the acquittal of a murderer as if at the end of the third act, forgetting that, in the theater, the victim gets up to take a curtain call with the rest."[121] Commentators repeated with some regularity stories such as that of Mme P, who decided to delay the murder of her rival until they had both returned to Paris from the provinces, anticipating, of course, the acquittal more readily available in the city.[122] Underneath this discourse was the fear that the jury was too susceptible to manipulation by skillful defense lawyers, irrationally responsive to sentimental appeals. Juries, critics observed, produced merely "an echo of popular opinion"; they were capable of reflecting but not leading, were "dazzled" by the spectacles of the street and unhealthy works of literature, and finally were unable to discriminate among the issues put before them.[123] Coded feminine, the contemporary jury engendered "a legitimate disquiet among reasonable men" who began to build a case against the license enabled by the jury's extralegal decisions and informal practices, which they believed had become all too common.[124]

Equally problematic was the growing immunity of women. By the end of the century, many of the professionals who had participated in the construction of the criminal woman—*surexcitée*, driven by disappointed love—had themselves come to recognize the ways in which the resolution of these domestic melodramas in the courts departed from their goals of social hygiene or social defense. Increasingly they began to resist the particular kind of justice delivered by the Cour d'Assises—extralegal but officially sanctioned—not because they were prepared to recant their ideas about the irresistible force of love or its centrality in the female emotional economy, but because they were forced to confront more and more the contradictory implications of the definitions they had put into circulation.

Lawyers began to argue more forcefully that the jealousy supposedly justifying the crime of passion was more often than not the manifestation of an "unrestrained egoism" that rendered one's own desires more important than those of the alleged loved one.[125] In this moment of intense anxiety around the viability of the traditional family, and in a political context inflected by public commitments to "social solidarity," the charge of egoism was particularly damaging. The indiscriminate judicial leniency afforded women who committed crimes of passion seemed to critics to obscure the crucial distinction between good (selfless) women and their egoistic, immoral, and shameless opposites.[126] To redress the balance in both rhetorical and social terms the lawyer Louis Holtz wrote in 1904, for example, that the seduced girl "is ordinarily *une jeune fille coquette* whose parents gave her tastes disproportionate to her condition; she is more refined than the men of her social class; her aspirations are higher."[127] Presumably had she been more willing to accept her fate and station, she would not have found herself accused of murder. The popular novelist Paul Bourget echoed these sentiments. For him,

whenever it is a question of a mean or base vengeance, . . . almost always the heroine is a woman whose pride has been wounded: an actress who has failed to win applause, a schoolteacher who has not gotten published, a girl of the demimonde who has not succeeded in getting married. And the lover attacked with vitriol was merely the revenge exacted for these failed lives.[128]

These images associated with ambition gone amok—ambition self-evidently inappropriate, in the authors' minds, on grounds of both gender and class—seem quite removed from the mundane stories of economic exigency and emotional distress suggested by the judicial dossiers. Yet their very distance from the details of actual crimes attests to a perceived need for an alternative story to counter the one that had legitimized female crimes of passion. The construct of the woman as love-victim had worked, as we have seen, to retrieve and consolidate practices, symbols, and even myths that seemed to have lost their secure cultural moorings. It anchored women's lives in the domestic, interpreting grievances and rebellions exclusively in terms of love and its disappointments. And it reiterated the terms of bourgeois respectability, producing difference: between good women and bad women, between men and women, between middle-class and working-class women. Nevertheless, by the close of the century critics had begun to be as much preoccupied with the alleged "contagion" of crime—with the possibility of growing female lawlessness—as with the nature or character of the individual female criminal. As rates of acquittal (for women especially) continued to increase, so did alarm over women out of control, taking the law into their own hands, defining justice themselves.[129] Somehow women seemed to be getting away with murder.

The trajectory from approval to anxiety in response to the *criminelle passionnel* is charted with uncanny precision in "Le Poison," a story that appeared in the *Revue des Deux Mondes* in 1891.[130] The author, Jean Reibrach, presents the story of Marie Morisset, a woman accused of poisoning her husband while conducting an adulterous affair. Throughout the judicial investigation, she remained impassive—no feeling, no tears, no denials—eventually asserting that the only viable action was to take her own life. As a result of an impassioned defense by her lawyer, Daguerre, Marie Morisset was acquitted, evoking an ovation in the courtroom. Daguerre rescued Morisset from her despair, married her, and restored her to respectability, having established with her an "ideal love" based on "the weakness and gratitude" of the woman and the "strength and protectiveness" of the man. She gradually banished her awful memories—seeing only at a great distance "the pride that had allowed her to usurp the powers of justice."

But, the text warns, she became more and more aware of a vague malaise, "a latent force, a continuous presence, not to be appeased, that soon became inexorable." The return of the repressed—sinister echoes of an unpunished crime—came in the parting words of a servant who had been dismissed: "I will not stay to be poisoned!" Soon, press reports of another case of poisoning seemed to exhume Morisset's past, assaulting her with memories "as if a sudden beam of light were directed at the shadowed corner in which she had taken refuge." The conviction of this unknown woman, her condemnation to twenty years of forced labor, shattered the calm of Marie Morisset's life. She became nervous, bizarre, swinging between torpor and forced gaiety. Her husband began to doubt her happiness and her love for him, suspecting that perhaps, once again, she had taken a lover. The "bad seed" was bearing fruit. In anguish, he became obsessive about his health, compulsively cataloguing his symptoms and checking the pallor of his skin. He retrieved Morisset's criminal dossier, rereading each piece, searching for signs of his own blindness and finding, he believed, with a belated clarity, the truth that had eluded him: "Of the woman, nothing remained but the adulteress. Of the novel, nothing but odious machinations; of the poetic heroine, only the criminal—a common criminal, the most cowardly of all, the most contemptible, *une empoisonneuse*." Inevitably, their life together became silent, oppressive, as each became imprisoned by anxieties that could not be alleviated. While Morisset suffered from her crushing guilt, Daguerre wondered to himself, "Is she a monomaniac of poisoning?"

In the denouement that becomes increasingly inevitable, Daguerre

Poison

refused to drink the coffee that his wife had prepared, examining its color and odor with a look of disgust, and finally suggesting with some malice that he was tempted to have it analyzed. Pushed by her own profound despair, Morisset insisted on an explanation. "It was in the coffee, wasn't it," Daguerre asked with ferocious irony, "that you poured the poison for your first husband?" Following the overdetermined thesis of the story, taking the only truly acceptable action, Morisset provided the closure that she had inappropriately sidestepped; this time she took her own life. Daguerre felt first a sense of deliverance, and then pity. He believed that she had at last rendered justice.

We are returned, here, to Louis Proal's choice between the "discreet woman" whose despair leads to suicide and the fury whose dangerous temperament leads to crime. In her final act of self-policing, Marie Morisset confirmed the moral (and legal) order that her marriage to Daguerre had undermined. In this story, poison, like the *femme criminelle* herself, raised a problem of interpretation; and a poisoning, like the unpunished criminal woman, symbolized a systemic pathology, inexorable and lethal, that could be disguised in any number of visible forms. *L'empoisonneuse*, a figure with broad cultural resonance, needed to be exorcised according to the logic of the plot, even if the necessary punishment was rendered by poetic justice standing in for official justice.

Within the context suggested by this story, legal scholars and criminologists began to make finer and finer distinctions between the kinds of cases that warranted judicial leniency and those that did not. In a growing chorus of voices that suspected that women made use of theories of female criminality for their own purposes (that is, feigned uncontrollable passion, irresistible impulses), magistrates demanded to know whether defendants had, from their reading of press reports, assumed that they would automatically be pardoned in the Cour d'Assises. Worried critics noted that some women flaunted their criminal acts, making themselves heroes of their own lives, refusing the role of victim, refusing even the required remorse. It seems that women who had acted on their anger found in the love discourse a narrative that legitimated their pain and urged them to revenge, but, even more, invited them to tell their own stories. Medical experts and lawyers complained that many female criminals looked forward expectantly to their day in court and, in a perverse refusal to express the obligatory devastation and regret, only lamented that they had not succeeded in killing their victims. Commentators such as Louis Puibaraud worried that in taking vengeance, they believe that they are taking vengeance for all betrayed women. They imagine that they are accomplishing an act of integrity. You will nearly never meet a woman repenting for having assassinated or attempted to assassinate the one who has been unfaithful or treacherous. The words "my conscience reproaches me for nothing" are frequently on their lips.[131]

Humorists noted with sharp-edged irony that seduced and abandoned women no longer thought of asphyxiation or of throwing themselves into the Seine—"games" that had become *démodé*—but chose instead to vitriolize their former lovers.[132] The woman who suffered in silence seemed to be disappearing. A satirical novelist alerted his readers to a changing cultural scene. Before, he noted,

when you wanted to break with a woman . . . [you would] simply take the train without making a song and dance of it and allow 24 hours for her to get over wanting to shoot you. During these 48 hours she shrieks, she storms, she buys laudanum, she poisons herself, she makes a mess of it. As in all things, she doubles the dose, but when you return, you have been replaced. But today, *les revolveriennes* are no longer so nice; the 24 hours of the revolver has elongated considerably; they no longer buy laudanum but the latest model pistol and wait patiently; if you take the train, they are capable of following you.[133]

Some legislators had hoped that the new divorce law would make most female violence unnecessary. But this did not seem to be the case; angry, violent women had not disappeared. Case after case in the Cour d'Assises suggested the possibility that women might reject the role of victim required by melodrama—might, in fact, substitute a more heroic scenario while escaping legal restraint.

Rather than restoring the familiar gender hierarchy or securing the traditional family, the effects of the love discourse were ultimately more ambiguous. An infamous crime of passion in 1914, the Caillaux affair, focused all of the arguments with which critics had begun to resist this extralegal indulgence that had effectively decriminalized certain violent acts. This time the resistence emerged in the context of a case that featured the most powerful political figures of the period, and unfolded under a spotlight of unrelenting national publicity, rivaling—indeed, surpassing—coverage of the international tensions leading to the outbreak of war. Henriette Caillaux shot and killed Gaston Calmette, editor of the conservative daily *Le Figaro*, who had been running a scathing political attack on her husband, Joseph Caillaux, a former prime minister and leader of the Radical party.[134] Apprehended instantly, literally holding the smoking gun, Henriette's only hope was to argue that she had acted in the throes of an emotional crisis that propelled her into actions she was unable to control.

The protocols of the crime of passion that had been elaborated and refined over several decades shaped the presentations of both the prosecution and the defense. Henriette and her attorney fashioned an account focused on the pain and humiliation caused by Le Figaro's vendetta, and especially on the emotional shock produced by Calmette's breach of journalistic etiquette in publishing an embarrassing love letter that Caillaux had sent Henriette while married to his first wife—an action experienced by Henriette as an assault on her honor. Most important was Henriette's borrowing from contemporary psychology to depict herself as a woman who, as Edward Berenson has described, saw herself pushed over an emotional edge, invaded, and ultimately vanquished by a conflict between two competing wills. Henriette had told the investigating magistrate:

It was like having two separate beings inside myself, like two separate wills. On the one hand I wanted to go to an afternoon tea a friend had invited me to, and I put on a dressy dress; if I had been [meant to go] to Le Figaro to accomplish the deed that I accomplished, I wouldn't have dressed up. On the other hand I felt a greater force take hold of me and it was the one that drove me.[135]

Within the terms of this argument, what appeared to be calculating premeditation became only one component of an intrapsychic struggle that the "real" Henriette had lost.

The state, in contrast, insisted that Henriette Caillaux's self-presentation was entirely manipulative. The public prosecutor described her as hard, emotionless, not at all the type of fragile woman who was subject to nervous crises; in fact, he argued, she was manlike, self-confident, methodical, and had acted with deliberation to silence a political rival who might thwart her husband's ambitions. This willful, self-possessed, unfeminine murderer could not qualify for judicial leniency.

Henriette Caillaux's acquittal (the jury voted eleven to one) produced pandemonium among the crowds, split between supporters and opponents, waiting in the streets; but unlike the popular celebration over which Marie Bière had presided in 1880, Henriette's vindication seems to be less complete. Although her acquittal did signal an affirmation of traditional feminine qualities, there was nothing traditional in the publicized stories of the Caillaux's extramarital affair, nor in Henriette's stepping in to fight for her husband's honor, nor even in the fact that prominent feminists argued that Henriette's violence was *not* the act of an independent woman as the prosecution had argued, but rather a marker of the limited options of traditional, dependent women, unprotected by custom or law. If, as Berenson comments, the trial of Mme Caillaux marked the end of an era, it did so in cultural as well as political terms; the mores and assumptions that had legitimized the crime of passion had begun to wear thin.

The "love stories" told about female crime had emerged in the opening decades of the Third Republic to interpret and manage unstable social relations. They had seemed convincing because they grounded women in their emotivity and placed the fate of "overexcited" wronged women, in the style of true melodrama, in the hands of male juries with the power to forgive and pardon. By focusing on the female love equilibrium, they kept the social and material inequities between men and women from a political analysis. And, in their provision of a kind of rough justice, they forestalled a more systematic consideration of women's rights within the republican order. This discourse, however, ultimately succumbed to the internal contradictions that it had evoked. If women, acting through their femaleness, could kill with impunity, how were social relations and social roles to be made finally secure? If women were justified generically by the love discourse, how would distinctions between good and bad women be preserved? If women could set their own terms of justice, what happened to male authority?

In effect, the love stories produced to account for *crimes passionnels* seemed always to lead away from problems of intimacy and private life—and even from individual psychology—and to turn themselves, inevitably, into political discourse. If we look at an *Enquête sur l'amour*, compiled by Ph. Pagnat in 1906, we can observe the explosion of the love story.[136] By the turn of the century, the *enquête*, or survey of opinion, had become a characteristic format for discussions of important social issues.[137] Pagnat brought together a large group of important intellectuals—literary figures, doctors, politicians—to reflect on such questions as: Is love an illness? Has love evolved? Which maxims about love ought we to interfere with? The underlying premise of this enterprise was that there was something that could be identified as "the problem of love" and that it was the business of the elites to solve it—a problem tellingly but unselfconsciously identified in the text as "the most important after that of subsistence in the class struggle."[138]

Within this *enquête*, various commentators addressed questions of changing expectations among women and men, worries about depopulation and the "disorganization of the family," theories of attraction, and so on. But a look at Pagnat's summary recommendations about how to solve the "problem" of love reveals an agenda that refers most immediately to that which remained unspoken. Pagnat sought to "rehabilitate" love, remove it from the rhetoric of infirmity and intoxication. He does not proceed, however, by affirming love as a spiritual or social construct, but by proposing a specific set of concrete policies: to establish coeduation as the norm everywhere; to enact legislation that would allow women to bring paternity suits; to pay men and women equal wages; to put an end to hypocrisy by promoting respect for *courtisanes*. He claimed that his goal was to reformulate ideas about love by enacting economic measures and by transforming popular opinion. Embedded in this project, then, is the recognition that discussions of love were fundamentally about unequal relationships of power between men and women, about the social and economic disabilities of women in the civil code, about double standards of sexual morality. Once again, meditations on love turn out to refer directly to tensions in the public realm that had become visible through the contradictory status of the *criminelle passionnelle* and the conflicting stories told about her.

In the end, the love stories of the Cour d'Assises were not melodramas. They could not provide the ethical clarity required of a melodramatic text, nor could they restabilize gender relations in fin-de-siècle society. Instead, the plots exceeded the formulas that sought to constrain their meaning, so that even when the court dismissed or ignored the larger issues raised by cases of domestic violence, these issues intruded. The obscure female defendants whom we have looked at in this chapter became, in the end, witting participants, and perhaps unwitting catalysts, in processes of social change through which women's position and rights were being renegotiated. They regularly refused to accept, without qualification, the official story of their "love" crime, even when it secured their acquittal. Instead, they offered accounts of their lives that foregrounded disparities in social and economic power between women and men. In their determination to revise and enforce the terms of an implicit domestic contract, they posed questions about the effects of contemporary tolerance for the privileges and irresponsibility of men. Juries responded inevitably to the social dimensions of these stories as much as to their personal aspect. Patterns of acquittal had, after all, recognized inequities that were understood, if not acknowledged, as a primary source of women's criminal behavior. While highlighting female dependency, then, these trials also raised questions about the causes of such dependency that referred as much to social as to individual conditions.

So it seems the melodramatic text could lead to unintended outcomes—to a recognition of the connections between women's "passionate" violence and questions of economics and power. The *criminelle passionnelle* was not, after all, confined to a depoliticized social space where she would exist as a social category awaiting analysis and intervention by a host of expert authorities. She remained an ambiguous figure, the repository of ideological conflicts and social uncertainties. As the contradictions of the discourse about her were exposed in growing anxieties about rising acquittal rates for female defendants, the *crime passionnel* revealed itself to be the cultural product that it had been all along—one that merged fact, myth, fantasy, and ideology. The closure provided by the love story could only be unstable and temporary, undermined by its own inconsistencies and by its apparently inevitable slide from intimacy into politics. While the cultural meanings of the crime of passion would continue to be shaped in the judicial process and by its popular and scholarly commentators, the issues that it raised ultimately spilled over into other public arenas.

5

THE SEXUAL POLITICS OF FEMALE CRIMINALITY

Society is afraid of both the feminist and the murderer, for each of
them, in her own way, tests society's established boundaries . . .
Nor is it surprising that the panic provoked by feminism and the
alarm at female criminality coincide almost perfectly, as though
according to some plan.

Ann Jones, *Women Who Kill*, 1980

As gateway to the Great Exposition of 1889, the Eiffel Tower transformed
the Parisian landscape—asserting republican confidence, celebrating republican unity, and claiming the legacy of the Great Revolution for the
new republican regime. Designed to "show our sons what their fathers
have accomplished in the space of a century," the tower spoke to ideals of
citizenship and national strength that were to be realized through the republic's promotion of liberty, secularism, and science. In the direct, universal language of its monumentality, and in its incarnation as a kind of
"baroque dream" that invited imaginative license, the tower called on
millions to bear witness to the ascent of man.[1]

In the context of the national malaise that followed France's defeat in
1870, this dream depended on a restored national identity—one that
pointed to former French glory and looked aggressively to the future.
The promises of republicanism were to be guaranteed, as Robert Nye
has argued, by the new republican man, embodying the qualities of "citizen, worker, and father"; these men would constitute a republic secured
not only by political principles but by a specifically masculine civic identity.[2] Their female counterparts were to be republican mothers—women
freed from the manipulations of priestly authority, dedicated to the domestic hearth, and trained to raise republican *citoyens*. The corrupt, clerical, infertile Empire would be replaced by a morally regenerate, secular,
and fecund Republic.

This was less an era of settled social roles, however, than a moment of
conflict and transition in relations between men and women; in its symbols and programs, the Exposition of 1889 ironically captured both the

gendered dream of national harmony and its frustration. Even as the Eiffel Tower asserted masculine accomplishment, Paris was, in this symbolically dense year marking the anniversary of the Revolution of 1789, simultaneously the site of two women's congresses: the officially sponsored first International Congress on Women's Rights and Feminine Institutions, designed to celebrate women's philanthropic and charitable activities, and the French and International Congress on the Rights of Women, organized as an alternative and specifically feminist response to the government-subsidized conference.[3] Although the program of the second conference was considerably more political than its official counterpart and its demands were couched in more radical terms, contemporaries did not see the two as necessarily in opposition; in fact, many men and women participated in both congresses. More important than the differences in outlook and strategy between the two groups was the extensive press coverage that both received and the growing audience attentive to feminist concerns that they represented. If, as social critics had argued throughout the century, the "condition of women" could be read as a barometer measuring the viability of the social order, what did this new preoccupation with women's issues connote?

Questions about the meaning of the republic for women increased as the new regime became more firmly established. Feminists who had begun to organize in the closing years of the Second Empire had been forced to retreat in the backlash that followed the defeat of the Commune. But with the republican order ensconced by 1879, they began to hope that the new government would realize the promises of republican rhetoric through concrete gains for women. According to feminist Maria Deraismes, "the liberation of half of humanity is, like the republic, in its third incarnation. . . . The republic seems, this time, determined to confirm its existence, and the rights of women are now a question that it must address."[4] In similar terms, urging the republic to honor its heritage, another feminist noted that "the revolutionary idea has only been half realized; women await with confidence the great anniversary of 1789."[5]

Yet republican politicians did not as a group line up behind feminist goals, nor did feminist issues form a part of a republican political platform. The legislative and institutional gains that were achieved (such as the creation of a system of secondary education for girls in 1880 and the divorce law of 1884), were the work of particular, typically quite cautious individuals; politicians had no desire to turn attention to the legal inequities against which feminists were organizing, preferring rather to "modernize" women's condition, promoting *une citoyenne au foyer*, a female citizen whose realm was the domestic sphere.[6] Thus, though historians have characteristically identified the primary division in fin-de-siècle society as between the "two Frances"—the secular, liberal, republican France led by the progressive bourgeoisie; and the religious, conservative, monarchical France of the Church, army, and aristocratic *notables*—this descriptive dichotomy obscures the degree to which traditional, even patriarchal values were shared across the political spectrum.[7] It therefore misses the way that "the condition of women" question revealed contradictions within republican rhetoric, as conflicts about how to address women's status undercut clear understandings of the meaning of republican egalitarianism and rattled republican sensitivities in both deeply personal and more public matters. In fact, republicans (and socialists) were as adamant as conservatives in their defense of the family and were reluctant to compromise their political capital by supporting any position that could be construed as undermining traditional familial patterns.

The growth of an organized movement for women's rights, however, exposed the paradox of a republicanism that asserted democratic principles and at the same time based its claim to legitimacy on a model of social organization derived from hierarchical, "normal" families that guaranteed men's rights and women's dependence. As men and women sought to find their balance within the possibilities opened by republican rhetoric and feminist challenges, some reformers began to argue that improvements in the condition of women—especially in the status of women within marriage—were a necessary prerequisite to national regeneration. But in the context of intense national anxieties about depopulation, there was also increasing concern about a new type of disordered woman: the autonomous bourgeois woman who, in one version, became an adulteress or a lesbian, rejecting the sexual confines of marriage; or, in another, the egoist who refused to have children, a woman barely distinguishable in her imagined social effects from the working-class *fille mère*, linked to abortion, infanticide, and murder. These were women—represented by the feminist and her presumed alter ego, the lesbian—who were dangerous in their independence and nonreproductivity. As recent additions to the social landscape and social imagination of the 1880s and 1890s, these two resonant female figures joined the cast of female deviants who seemed in some measure responsible for (and symbolic of) both domestic conflict and national decline.

Each became, in her own way, emblematic of a profound *désordre des moeurs* that threatened the patterns of private life while calling into question the organizing principles of the public realm. Although contemporaries shared a fairly consistent image of the ideal republican man, the presence of feminist women making civil and political claims unsettled easy assumptions about domestic order and national politics. It was these new female types who pressed republican authorities most insistently with questions about the attributes of citizenship and patterns of hierarchy in domestic and public spheres. And it was feminist women who represented the nearly unthinkable possibility of unstable gender difference, raising the double spectre of converging gender roles and slipping male authority. By calling into question inequalities established at law and sanctioned by tradition, by challenging the exclusions imposed on women and the protected privileges enjoyed by men, the feminist and the lesbian became, finally, the metaphorical shadows of the criminal women brought to account in the Cour d'Assises. Like the female criminal, the feminist contested deeply held beliefs about gender hierarchies and raised questions about women's rights; and both the feminist and the female criminal brought their grievances—which, by the end of the century, seemed to be couched in similar terms—to national attention, dramatizing the ways that contemporary policy and practice failed to secure their well-being as women. In her recent study of female criminals, Ann Jones has made an argument similar to the one I am making here. The quote that served as this chapter's epigraph is worth repeating here:

Society is afraid of both the feminist and the murderer, for each of them, in her own way, tests society's established boundaries . . . Nor is it surprising that the panic provoked by feminism and the alarm at female criminality coincide almost perfectly, as though according to some plan.[8]

This chapter will explore the conceptual web that naturalized the connections between criminal women and independent feminist women so as to reveal the intersections of gender, culture, and politics in the context of fin-de-siècle republicanism.

There was no unified feminist movement in the fin-de-siècle; but, although most French feminists were reluctant to follow the more radical groups in demanding suffrage, nearly all organized to rescind the legal disabilities of women formalized in the Civil Code—especially the infamous Article 213 on the authority of the husband in marriage (*l'autorité marital*), which stipulated that men owed their wives protection while women pledged obedience. Promulgated under Napoleon in 1804, the code effectively placed married women under the tutelary supervision of their husbands: a husband had control of all his wife's assets and property, which she could not dispose of without his consent; in marriages controlled by community property (and this included the vast majority), the husband could sell off (aside from real estate) his wife's personal belongings without her agreement; a woman could not live apart from her husband or open a business without his formal approval; any money that she earned belonged to him; the husband had custody of minor children of the marriage, a right passed to his family if his widow remarried; women could not initiate paternity suits, nor did they have equal rights to prosecute their spouses for adultery. Only widows and some single adult women enjoyed slightly more control over their own lives. Drawing out the political implications of these formal differences in status, one reformer wondered, rhetorically, whether such blatant inequality could be compatible with republican principles. In the end, he concluded, "we must assure the abdication of this conjugal king who is the husband and the succession of this citizen who is a woman; in a word, we have to make of marriage a republic."[9]

Public opinion about the respective rights and duties of spouses was galvanized in 1872 by a widely publicized Parisian crime of passion that provided the occasion for intense debate about the status of women and men in marriage and, more broadly, in the civil code. M. Du Bourg had murdered his adulterous wife—an essentially banal case that was rendered notorious by the fact that, instead of the expected acquittal, Du Bourg was sentenced to five years in prison. Among the outpourings of criticism that greeted this unlikely decision was an explosive pamphlet by Alexandre Dumas fils, L'Homme-Femme, that was reedited thirty-five times in the six months after it appeared, selling 50,000 copies after only three months and provoking impassioned responses from at least thirty-three writers across the full political spectrum.[10] In a dramatic and inflammatory rhetorical flourish, Dumas had placed the bourgeois adulteress alongside the more familiar figure of the working woman / prostitute as a signifier of social decay. According to Dumas, a husband has the right to say to his judges: "I have killed this creature . . . in order to extinguish in her the germ of a child that she is going to impose on my trust . . . on my labor, on my legitimate children, on my name and on all my posterity." At the conclusion of this tract, Dumas takes his son to the summit of a mountain, and, speaking as God the Father, delivers his sermon:

Marry [a woman] from whichever class, provided that the one that you marry is religious, chaste, hard-working, healthy, and gay, without irony. Never marry a mocking woman. Bantering by a woman is a sign of hell . . . ; if she betrays you, KILL HER![11]

Dumas had thrown down the challenge, reasserting traditional values and expectations. But would traditional hierarchies be able to sustain the challenges raised by feminists and reformers? What were women's rights to be in the new political order? How were the conflictual claims of men and women, husbands and wives, to be negotiated? And who would be the arbiters? In one of the most aggressive replies to Dumas, the feminist Maria Deraismes parodied her adversary. Taking her hypothetical daughter to a mountaintop, in "a solemn and sure tone" she lectured:

My child . . . you who are young, beautiful, educated, endowed with talent and virtue, do not forget that if this man, who appropriates all of this for himself, who takes as well your dowry, your fortune, in order to make himself a notary, a banker or deputy . . . if he keeps mistresses . . . if it happens that he even succeeds in corrupting the purity of your blood, do not forget that this man spoils the divine plan . . . he is Darwin's ape, he is Cain in person; kill him; do not hesitate.[12]

The debate could not, of course, stay within the terms of the polemics laid out by Dumas and Deraismes. In succeeding decades feminists and their opponents would attempt to come to grips with the implications of the specific issues and alternative definitions of rights implicated in these notorious incitements to murder. Women and men who supported broadly feminist objectives held a wide range of opinions on specific issues.[13] Only a small faction were willing to support full political rights for women. These feminists, identified as radicals by their contemporaries, argued that nothing short of identical rights for both sexes would be compatible with republican liberty. The majority, however, did not share a specific program, but determined to dismantle piecemeal the most inequitable aspects of the legal and social codes that had been constructed over time according to patriarchal principles. Different groups organized around different goals, which included: the removal, one by one, of the disabilities of women legislated by the civil code; the pursuit of advanced secular education for women; the development of broader economic opportunities for women; the abolition of state-regulated prostitution; an end to the practice of arranged marriages; and the provision of public assistance to pregnant women, whatever their marital status. None of these causes automatically excluded any one of the others; feminist discourse intervened in public debates not as a uniform program but through the multiplicity of its commitments. In an interesting example of the possible, even contradictory, combinations of sensibilities and programmatic concerns, Marie Terrisse divided her feminist agenda into three parts: the first, presented as a series of sentimental vignettes of the lives of seduced and abandoned women, reads like a roman feuilleton and ends with a call for the right to initiate paternity suits; the second, a plea for an end to the system of state-sanctioned prostitution, is rendered in terms that echoed conventional, socially conservative reform literature—that is, by describing prostitution as a problem of "corrupted and corrupting women"; and the third, a demand for political rights for women, is expressed in the language of radical feminism.[14]

In spite of their small numbers, typically respectable social position, and predominantly moderate discourse, feminists had, it seems, become both visible and alarming as debate over "the woman question" heated up in the 1880s and 1890s. In his doctoral thesis, the lawyer Paul Granotier echoed contemporary sentiments when he referred to feminism as "an irresistible wave," a force "assailing governments like a mounting tide" and embodying less a fixed doctrine than a spirit that had penetrated nearly every social stratum and had found voices along the whole spectrum of political opinion.[15] In Granotier's terms, "in the public world, woman establishes her headquarters everywhere." While feminism never became a mass movement in France, the gains made by women in a short period of time, in terms of both organizational strength and substantive changes, were significant. International congresses on women's rights were held in Paris in 1889, 1892, 1896, and 1900, and feminist journals began to be published throughout the country.[16] The numbers of women pursuing higher education increased dramatically, as did the count of women seeking entrance into the professions.[17]

Even as republicans pursued a fairly conservative social agenda, a pattern of small, continuing, maybe even unrelenting, changes emerged in the space opened by more general republican commitments to equality. In 1880 new legislation mandated free public secondary education for girls, followed (1881) by the creation of teacher training schools for women, eligibility for women on Departmental Councils of Public Education (1886), and the entry of women into positions as inspectors of primary education (1889). In 1884 divorce was reinstituted, and the new law abandoned the legal distinction between a man's adultery and that of his wife. In 1893 women separated from their husbands but not divorced gained full civil capacity; four years later all women, married or not, could act as witnesses in a civil court, that is, were considered to have a separate legal identity. Women won the right to open their own old-age pension accounts (1886) and savings accounts (1895). From 1895 women could be named as administrators of charity boards; in 1898 they gained similar rights on commercial boards and in mutual aid societies and, two years later, on elected boards for labor arbitration. In 1900 women won the right to accede to the bar, and in 1907, equal rights over minor children. While several important issues remained contested—the right to initiate paternity suits, the right to marry the named party in a divorce-for-adultery case, divorce by mutual consent, and political rights—it is clear that established customs were being dismantled. The glue that had maintained a fairly stable equilibrium between the sexes for nearly a century had been loosened.

While it is usual for historians to describe the position of women in French society during this period in terms of their legal disabilities and second-class citizenship, it seems equally accurate and perhaps more revealing to see these decades as a time when men correctly perceived that they were losing many of the traditional prerogatives that had defined their superior status, validated their authority, and secured their masculinity. Du Camp's hyberbolic warnings in 1861 about the subversive campaign of prostitutes to "cretinize the aristocracy"—that is, his image of the female deviant as social solvent—could be (and was) readily rewritten in reference to a perceived invasion of feminists who appeared to be pulling down the edifice of male privilege. It should be no surprise that bourgeois men spoke explicitly of sex wars that envisioned the overturning of all that made social life familiar and possible, while conservatives wrote angrily and derogatorily of Marianne, the symbolic representation of what seemed to be a feminized republic, presiding over the loss of masculine power. In his study of republican imagery in the nineteenth century, Maurice Agulhon notes that the figure of Marianne remained, as she had been for critics since the time of the Revolution, a whore, "'naturally' called a woman selling her favours every time that the State could be reproached for any weakness, compromise or alleged corruption."[18] Antifeminist discourse in this period did not, then, merely reflect the voice of a powerful male establishment seeking to exercise control over a subordinate group. We can only understand this literature if we interpret it as informed by both power and perceived powerlessness, inflected by anxiety as much as by authority.

The most intractable arguments against women's rights warned against violating traditional social practices that allegedly originated in "natural" or biological laws. Some appealed to the lessons of history—that is, the longstanding exclusion of women from public life—that were alleged to be necessary and eternally valid. Blaming the fall of Rome on the emancipation of women and the infiltration of foreign customs, for example, a Parisian lawyer offered a "natural law": "The Greek hid his wife in the *gynécée*, the Roman placed her under the guard of two *lares* (domestic spirits), the Moslem enclosed her in his harem, our society shelters her under the protective roof of the home."[19] Another lawyer referred to the submission of women to men, to men's "protection" of women, as a principle consented to by all people in every age, "one of the primordial axioms that are beyond question."[20] Evoking a similar inevitability, an alienist who presented himself as an expert in *la science intersexuelle*, claimed that women in mental institutions sought solitude more than did men; women, he insisted, "naturally" prefer to be alone, "a bit as a recluse in the home."[21] Antifeminists parodied women's demands as the expression of the "vain and hysterical" aspirations of a very few "egoistic" individuals; they catalogued the dangers women's emancipation presented to children and the family, citing especially the litany encapsulated in natality statistics from around the world; they worried about the effects of female naiveté and "impressionability" in political life, invoking Broca's studies of women's inferior cranial capacity and discussions of the limited range of female education; they elaborated sensational images of women in military life. It was practically an article of faith for political analysts of every persuasion that enfranchised French women would "take their orders from the confessional,"[22] a conviction that placed female emancipation with other threats to the future of the secular republic.

A somewhat more conciliatory position couched the discussion of women's rights in the context of "progressive" change, applauding the improved status of women but cautioning against too rapid progress, for which the appropriate ground had not been laid. These voices thus emphasized "legitimate ambitions," subscribing to projects based on notions of "equivalence" rather than equality—emphasizing the special, distinct attributes of each sex and retaining what they saw as gender-appropriate differences in civic life. The prominent law professor Raymond Saleilles, for example, proposed a compromise. In place of a "false feminism" that might produce female lawyers, he offered a social and juridical role to women that expanded the arenas for their appropriate social service without undermining conventional gender hierarchies. He reasoned that, as punishments in the criminal justice system were more and more tailored to fit the criminal (the individualization of penalties), there would be a natural function for women in providing the psychological analysis that would classify offenders, an activity described in familiar gendered terms as a "work of the heart."[23] Women could, then, enter public service in appropriate, supporting roles. In a similar attempt to respond to women's "legitimate" desires, another author noted that women fulfilled a patriotic duty in motherhood that exceeded men's responsibilities to the state both in its value and in its bloody toll, which was as brutal as any military service. Women's public duties, in his terms, were and should remain separate but superior.[24]

A consensus was beginning to emerge that promoted specific, limited reforms in the status of women, motivated on the one hand by the principles of republicanism—by what Odile Krakovitch has called a *prise de conscience*—and on the other by a desire to foreclose more fundamental changes. The *académicien* Ernest Legouvé captured the essence of this implicit bargain in a preface that he wrote in 1893 to a conservative tract by L. Roger-Milès.[25] Legouvé begins by noting that it might seem a bit odd for a progressive person such as he to be writing a preface to a book by a conservative who had persisted in his unqualified support of a discriminatory civil code. In contrast, Legouvé presents himself as "nearly a revolutionary" in his ardent insistence that the civil code, "iniquitous and immoral" with regard to women, must be reformed. He even goes so far as to recognize the legitimacy of women's demands for greater rights in the workplace. Claiming, then, his right to the label of "revolutionary," he asserts that for the past forty years he has promoted the independence of women—"an independence that is defined, measured, proportionate, but real and legal." Legouvé explains his collaboration with Roger-Milès, however, by acknowledging that the two men, in spite of serious differences, share certain fundamental convictions. It is in their common opposition to certain "disastrous ambitions"—that of the free woman, the woman voter, the female deputy—that the "revolutionary" and the conservative come together.

Legouvé is particularly piqued by the direction that women's education has taken. He complains that although he has been a partisan of lycées for young women, he finds that the program has become "too serious [*chargé*], too scientific, too masculine." In its place, Legouvé proposes "to feminize female education, to make it proportionate [*proportionner*]," to provide "an education that HAS A SEX" (emphasis in original). Legouvé's comments on education introduce his most pressing concern: the demands of some women for a kind of liberty "that would overturn the social order," for a liberty in their physical person that inheres in the appeal for full citizenship. Legouvé rejects out of hand the patriotic justification offered by feminists to explain women's demands for political rights, and sees instead a desire for personal freedom that reflects "some jealousy, some lassitude, but mainly curiosity. . . . Woman wants to lead the life of a boy."

I have paraphrased Legouvé's preface at some length because it conveys so effectively the tone of much of the literature around possible changes in the civil code. His repetition of the verb *proportionner*, "to make proportionate," used without the need to make explicit its male referent, suggests the degree to which the emergence of feminist women promoting a political agenda challenged conventional ways of accommodating what Karen Offen has described as the familial feminism that so often framed debates on the woman question in the late nineteenth century.[26] Republicans who supported an improved status for women looked, as Legouvé's remarks suggest, to the educational system to find the kind of proportion that would secure the social order—a proportion based upon conventional definitions of gender difference. The Sée Law of 1880, which established state-sponsored secondary education for women, was designed to free women from the pernicious influence of the Church; nevertheless, republican sponsors clearly did not intend to promote a single, ungendered curriculum or to open a path to professional careers for women. Sée himself stipulated that "I do not want women lawyers, and I worry about the possibility of having women doctors. The education of young women will certainly be set apart from all that which, in educating young men, is geared toward preparing them for a career."[27] Yet, in spite of the pressures to limit women's gains to those that supported motherhood and family, debates extended beyond these limits as feminists emerged to challenge traditional assumptions about their social roles that were, at that moment, being reinscribed by contemporary politicians and reformers as a kind of republican civic mandate.

The fierce controversy surrounding the request of Jeanne Chauvin to be admitted to the bar in 1897 epitomized the intensity of the struggles among different constituencies to come to terms with the meaning of gender roles in a context that at least rhetorically promoted individual rights. Chauvin had pursued an elite education, typically available only to men, receiving a bachelor of letters degree in 1883, a bachelor of sciences in 1885, a degree in philosophy in 1890, and a doctorate in law in 1892, when she passed her exams with the highest distinction.[28] That her candidacy raised more than just professional anxieties may be seen in the direct question posed to her by one of her examiners at the Faculty of Law on the occasion of Chauvin's defense of her thesis: "We have only two genders in the French language, masculine and feminine. Do you wish to introduce a neuter gender?" Following up this theme, a second questioner made explicit the inevitable trade-off he foresaw between maternal (social) interests on the one hand and professional (individual) ones on the other: "The Yankees said, 'When we want to have children, we will bring women from the other side of the Atlantic.' And we, Mademoiselle, from where will we bring them?" Chauvin is reported to have replied, "But my dear sir, the women who are around you now will give you more children than you wish."[29]

After receiving her law degree, Chauvin taught in lycées for young women for five years, after having been passed over for a university appointment. Frustrated by her inability to secure positions for which she was clearly qualified, Chauvin decided to apply for entry into the legal profession, a step that would allow her to practice law. In a packed courtroom of the appellate court in Paris, Chauvin, accompanied by her mother, argued her case before the attorney general (*procureur général*). The court denied her request, but the case had become famous and was not likely to end there. *Gil Blas* reported (July 2, 1899) that the agency that excerpted articles on celebrities from the daily press counted 6,935 references to Chauvin in the year 1898, that is, 119 references per day!— more publicity perhaps than that enjoyed by even the most sensational criminal story. In 1900 a bill was introduced in the legislature to support Chauvin's request. Following a favorable vote in the Chamber of Deputies (304 to 100) and the Senate (172 to 34), the legal profession was opened to women; Chauvin became a practicing lawyer shortly thereafter.

The technical issues about professional capacity and standing raised by Chauvin's case—issues that circulated through all the specialized law journals, in theses submitted for doctorates in law, and in the popular and feminist press—were immediately buried under the more emotionally charged questions about gender-appropriate roles and behavior. In a lecture essentially supporting the merits of Chauvin's position delivered at the opening of a court session, one jurist, Pierre-Julien Ravail, cited disparagingly the recent conclusions of a Belgian court that had rejected the appeal of a woman to join its bar. The Belgian court held that

the special nature of a woman, her weakness relative to her constitution, the reserve inherent in her sex, the protection that she requires, her special mission for humanity, the exigencies and constraints of maternity, the education that she owes her children, the direction of the household that is consigned to her care, all place her in conditions that are not compatible with the professional duties of a lawyer and give her neither the leisure, nor the strength, nor the necessary aptitude to engage in the struggles and the hardships of the bar.[30]

Ravail's lecture, in contrast, exposed the illogic of this decision. Such reasoning was untenable, he countered, because it was blatantly inconsistent. What, he asked, would one say about female weakness to women who worked on farms and in factories? Should women be removed from these positions because of their frailty? Is greater strength required to study judicial dossiers, to peruse works of jurisprudence, and to enter pleas in a courtroom? Moreover, what of the many women who had no household to oversee, no children to raise?[31] Ravail concluded this impassioned defense of Chauvin's right to enter the profession, his insistence that professional status could not be a privilege reserved exclusively to men, with an equally fervent wish that women would, in the end, renounce a professional life. "How much more worthy is the Frenchwoman," he asks, "who can say enthusiastically: 'that man is my son; it is I who formed his spirit and fashioned his heart. I will reap my share of honors from those bestowed on him.'"[32]

While Ravail rejected the specific disabilities attributed to women, he nevertheless resisted condoning a world that did not guarantee gender difference and preserve women's domestic roles. Chauvin herself explicitly seconded such sentiments. In an interview in 1899, she identified her professional goals in terms that affirmed conventional expectations: "This will be my goal: to defend children, to defend unfortunate mothers, abandoned ones and even guilty ones. Who knows if a kind word, a wise counsel, an encouragement, a support, will not lead a woman who has gone astray back to the straight and narrow path? What a noble task, what a noble role!"[33] In another context, Chauvin argued for the special suitability of women for careers in medicine and law—a suitability predicated on their "feminine tenderness," their "spirit of justice," and their "devotion."[34] Both Ravail and Chauvin also articulated more abstract defenses of women's rights; but both suggest as well some of their culture's uncertainties about how far the limits of gender definition could be stretched. They are important, therefore, not because they did not go far enough in their visions of reform, but because their respective writings reveal the struggle within individuals (as well as within the culture) to find viable boundaries even as older ones were exceeded and transgressed.

At stake in these discussions was the meaning and consequence of gender ambiguity in both social and personal terms. The feminist writer Marya Chéliga tried to defuse the emotional charge that surrounded these issues in an essay entitled "Childish Fears."[35] She noted that many men seemed to think that if women were endowed with the same rights as men, they would become men. How, she asks, will women become men? And why is it that men who pursue so-called feminine occupations do not endlessly have to assert their firm intention of remaining men? To demonstrate her point, Chéliga pointed to the celebrated fashion designer Worth, who, in a milieu rustling with silk and lace, had never been asked to attest to his having and preserving the personal qualities appropriate to his sex. In effect, she is arguing that social roles are not determined by, or coextensive with, biological sex; but this concept was deeply troubling in a culture that was built on quite opposite assumptions. As Foucault has shown in his discussion of the fate of a nineteenth-century hermaphrodite, contemporaries shared a powerful investment in establishing the "true sex" of an individual and in silencing or erasing elements of ambiguity.[36] And biological sex, once fixed, was believed to determine both personality and possibility in the world.

The physician Dr. J. Chevalier was closer than Marya Chéliga to his culture's deepest convictions when he described homosexuality (sexual inversion) in terms of gender roles and behaviors rather than in terms of sexual desire. For him, inverts were, first and especially, men who crocheted, sewed, knitted, embroidered, occupied themselves with cooking and household chores, and women who sought the out-of-doors, abandoned the hearth—men characterized by coquettishness and women by "virile sentiments," causing them to disdain female suffering in favor of strength and courage.[37] Inversion was not, then, exclusively or even especially a description of men and women who sought sexual relationships with partners of their own sex. Sex difference was, in this historical moment, as much grounded in social behavior and gendered roles as it was in erotic desire or sexual preferences.

It was, then, the instability of boundaries around appropriate behaviors that seemed profoundly dangerous. Whatever the manifest content of antifeminist arguments, anxieties about the consequences of gender slippage saturated these discussions. Feminism seemed to connote masculinism. Particularly in the 1890s, the "new woman" became a subject of intense discussion in the Parisian press—from the established *Journal des Débats* and the *Revue des Deux Mondes* to the avant-garde press, more middlebrow magazines, and popular satirical revues.[38] This *femme nouvelle*, depicted as either Amazon or *hommesse*, seemed in revolt against the social order, rejecting female roles, defying every manifestation of femininity or domesticity. She was, according to one observer, "not beautiful. She looks rather like a boy. . . . They are no longer women of pleasure and leisure but women who study, of very sober comportment. And nothing suits them better than heavy and somber colors . . . that express firmness, . . . roughness, and decisiveness."[39] Feminism meant, *tout court*, androgyny.

Examples such as this one excerpted by Debora Silverman from the late-nineteenth-century art world can be found, with slightly different inflections, in nearly any body of literature that surveyed the contemporary social scene. Almost any subject could become a vehicle for the discussion of what seemed to many an alarming blurring of sexual difference. In 1899, a piece in the weekly illustrated supplement to *Le Petit Journal* managed to bring nearly all the pieces of this litany together in a single short story entitled "Feminism."[40] The author describes a sitting room/office, severely (that is, unattractively) furnished, strewn with books and pamphlets. The walls are covered with framed diplomas and, instead of a mirror over the fireplace, there is a huge poster titled in bold capital letters "Declaration of the Rights of Woman." The mistress of the house is seated, working on a legislative proposal on the enlistment of women in the military in time of war. With three gentle knocks on the door (the wife responds "Enter" without looking up), the husband enters to begin a series of brief emblematic conversations. Throughout he is humorous and whimsical; she is harsh and humorless. In the climactic (and perhaps most characteristically French) moment, she forbids him to address her with the familiar "*tu*" and insists on the formal "*vous*": "It was fine before when we were slaves. But times have changed." She brusquely opens her robe and reveals a cycling outfit: "We now wear pants, my husband!" "So do we," he responds somewhat helplessly. In the closing vignette, she lectures him on taxes while he rings for the children who embrace him passionately.

"Feminist demands: 'I am going to a feminist congress. Prepare dinner for eight o'clock sharp, do you understand? And especially be sure that nothing goes wrong!'"

Dr. Chevalier provided a medical analogue to this story, reframing in medical terms the lowbrow version presented in the popular press. Not only was the modern woman winning her freedom, he argued, she was, more importantly, becoming masculinized. He noted that the dualities that had ordered social life had become precarious, that "in a multitude of matters, feelings, ways of thinking, activities, there is a resemblance" between men and women:

Little by little woman tends to approximate man, to appropriate his ways of being, his kind of independent and free existence. Instead of woman's life being constituted, as it was not long ago, by calm, by private life, by intimacy, the life of the woman of today is lived beyond her home, within preoccupations where the family does not count. . . . Determined, she affects in everything the independence, the turbulent audacity, the self-confidence of a boy. She shocks and disconcerts without being shocked or disconcerted herself.[41]

In a series of unsettling visual images, Chevalier described the unprecedented possibilities opened by the new urban milieu: female artists drawing from male and female nude models; mime shows that included play between female lovers; female dance partners parodying the "natural couple." He talked of "priestesses of a new cult" that was drawing ever more converts. These were women "without limits" who symbolized a society that had become unrecognizable and, in effect, sick.

Concerns about secure gender identity extended as well to issues centered on masculinity and manliness. Edward Berenson and Robert Nye have written extensively about fin-de-siècle preoccupations with codes of male conduct, emphasizing the ways in which the defeat of France by the Prussians in 1870 intensified worries that modern French civilization was fundamentally emasculating.[42] Critics characterized contemporary culture as on the one hand overintellectualized, enervated, and effete, and on the other overbureaucratized and mundane, hostile to the virtues of courage and daring. In the words of the moralist F. A. Vuillermet, "there are no longer any men."[43] Equally pointedly, a conservative opponent of the republic offered a most damning criticism by charging the leadership with sexual impotence: "The center-left has no sex."[44] A culture of honor and sport—institutionalized in dueling, fencing, and gymnastics societies—emerged as the antidote for perceived male weakness. The invocation of chivalry and training for physical aggression were called upon to produce a revival at once masculine and national, a reinvigorated patriotic virility. But as Berenson argues, the upsurge of dueling during this period testified to a sense of manhood lost as much as it guaranteed manhood regained.[45] While the duel encouraged a desired spirit of combat, its proponents unwittingly recapitulated depictions of elite men as prone to an effeminate sensitivity that rendered them particularly vulnerable to the slightest assault against their honor. In effect, the justifications for the code of honor led back onto the slippery terrain of converging gender identities.

Perhaps not surprisingly, one of the most resonant symbols of gender slippage was the most visible—"*une petite armée de femmes en culottes*," women on bicycles who made regular appearances in the urban landscape.[46] Getting directly to the heart of the matter, one author suggested that women's participation in the new sport represented "an important step in their emancipation," a step particularly captured in their giving up the skirt in favor of *le pantalon*: "the first time that women have challenged the monopoly on the quintessential attribute of masculinity." When Sarah Bernhardt, herself a cultural icon, was called upon to comment on this issue, she mused that "the bicycle is in the process of transforming the culture more profoundly than one might imagine. All the young women and all the girls who are out devouring public space [*devorant l'espace*] renounce in good part *la vie intérieure*, life within the family."[47] The link to emancipation seemed self-evident. Both the cyclist and the feminist in their "masculine" aspirations foretold the end of familiar patterns both in domestic and in public life—undoing the charged sexual/spatial oppositions of interior/exterior, and specifically embodying some of the forces disturbing the equilibrium of fin-de-siècle culture and producing its pervasive malaise.

The feminist Madeline Pelletier was uncharacteristic in her embracing of these destabilizing tendencies. Outraged by events at a feminist meeting, for example, she chastised her colleagues for their timidity. It seems that one woman had urged a group planning a demonstration for female suffrage to hire a carriage filled with flowers to accompany the march so that demonstrators could, in a most feminine fashion, throw bouquets to the crowd. Pelletier insisted that women needed to abandon such frivolous and ultimately retrograde behaviors and instead to become more masculine, creating a single standard of conduct without which the goal of equality remained elusive.[48] Few, however, were willing to contemplate such a prospect. Drawing out the implications of this threatened loss of gender clarity in terms of both love and politics, Henri Thulié was more typical. He warned that family life and heterosexual love were ultimately incompatible with women's political rights, that female bodies would become unrecognizable (even denatured) as women abandoned their "appropriate" function. The political woman became, in Thulié's analysis, both a subversive and a grotesque:

[Emancipation] will mark the beginning of the woman without breasts, for . . . it will not be long before these organs begin to disappear. . . . Soon, [women] will no longer want to be mothers; this will mean the organization of abortion, and, for the prudent, the triumph of lesbianism. Once sterility has been organized and *les politiciennes* refuse to offer their wombs for maternity, we will be obliged to have women whose special function is reproduction so as to prevent the race from being extinguished while *les citoyennes* engage in politics and homosexuality.[49]

The connection between the emancipated woman and lesbianism that Thulié elaborated had become a commonplace by the 1890s. Like earlier symbols of female deviancy, "the lesbian" worked as the condensed image that fused multiple and overlapping anxieties. One commentator noted, for example, that it had become usual to witness women arriving in fine carriages at brothels once reserved to men; he speculated that vice was spreading out from its contained quarters as prostitutes communicated their taste for lesbianism, not just to women of the theater, but to ordinary married women.[50] Making a similar point, Dr. Chevalier wrote extensively about the excesses of civilization that pushed women out of their protected naiveté into a world of sexual and political emancipation, ending finally, inevitably, in lesbianism. In fact, for Chevalier, while male homosexuality arose from a kind of aristocratic depravity that required ever more exotic pleasures for its satisfaction, "the story of sapphism for women is the story of the emancipated woman."[51] He prophesied that the end for the woman who had the confidence and the independence of a man, who no longer needed the guardianship of men—that is, the end of *la vrai jeune fille*—could only be lesbianism. Doing without a man's protection, she would do without his love.

In Chevalier's description of the emancipated-woman-as-lesbian, he sounds themes representative of his period; but the tone of his writing stands somewhat apart. While he laments the passing of "the true young woman"—simple, deferential, modest—he speaks respectfully of the modern woman, "a complex being, well-spoken, straightforward, perceptive," "whose practical sense does not readily accommodate daydreams and idle fancies."[52] His articles are intriguing because of the ambivalence conveyed in his vacillation between anxiety and admiration. Sometimes he seems to sound a note of wistfulness, or perhaps even of longing or

"La Garçonnière."

envy, when he describes the way that the modern woman has made the whole world her own. The tone is hard to read and impossible finally to pin down. Yet it is clear that his is a work that ranges over several social and emotional realities. For every description of loss—the loss of charming innocence, the loss of freshness and the carefree ignorance of speculative questions—Chevalier presents a picture of competence and accomplishment. The modern woman has succeeded, he claims, in the world of sports, in the art world, in the professions; she has reached her goals through keen judgment, lively curiosity, and talent, and has become, in Chevalier's words, "sufficient unto herself."[53] This is not un-ambiguous praise. He is clearly disturbed by the blurring of gender difference, and in the end asserts that "[the modern woman] has not succeeded in penetrating the secret of virility although physically and morally she has managed to unsex herself."[54]

In contrast to the shifting ground from which he represents the modern woman, Chevalier is unambivalent about what he sees as a dangerous revolution that had occurred in the relationship *between* men and women —a social transformation that did nothing less than erase the reciprocal relationship between the two sexes, placing them instead "on a footing of absolute equality."[55] It is the possibility of this equality, so unprecedented and disruptive, that seems to have left men like Chevalier without a secure sense of their role or place in society and especially without a secure identity grounded in sexual difference. Pointing directly to this typically unacknowledged dimension of the discussion around gender and political equality, Maria Deraismes observed that contemporary men could not imagine an identity that was not complementary—that in making women their legal equals, they seemed to think that they ceased being men. Deraismes claimed that men saw the world as a kind of zero-sum game in which any gain for women constituted a loss for men. In her terms, if women were to be granted equal rights, men would believe that women have/are everything and they have/are nothing.[56] Writings such as those of the sociologist Jacques Lourbet reassured his contemporaries that, while men and women might achieve juridical equality, "psychic parity was happily a chimera."[57] Similarly, Dr. Michel Bourgas provided scientific confirmation of the inevitability of complementarity, claiming that it was, in fact, a law of nature that "men and women who possess an attribute of the other sex prefer a partner deprived of that attribute. Thus a large woman seeks a small man, a fat seeks a slim, a virago seeks an effeminate."[58] In his terms, nature guaranteed complementary sexual difference, even if the precise terms of the difference fluctuated, confirming the couple as the complete social organism and providing a model for social arrangements that would both mirror and secure this complementarity. But women's demands for political rights raised confusing issues about the relationship between the assumptions that underpinned claims to equality and more conventional assumptions about gender complementarity.

In fact, feminist women and men as well as antifeminists often argued for equivalence rather than equality as the measure of justice—seeking to identify a standard that repudiated a sexual hierarchy while recognizing the apparent reality of gender difference and the specificity of women's needs and attributes, the special qualities that they would bring to public life. Feminists and reformers were caught in the contradiction between the individualist, egalitarian principles that justified claims for universal political rights and their own sense of (and often, defense of) women's difference. It was unclear on what grounds women could claim to be Frenchmen. Their political demands exposed the conundrum generated by the seeming opposition between the claims of equality and difference, and unsettled the model of natural complementarity.[59]

While Chevalier's writing is interesting because of the ways in which it explicitly presented the relationship between gender difference and other kinds of equality as a problem, it also pointed to the undercurrent of sexual anxiety that slipped into so many discussions of the emancipated woman. A Parisian lawyer observed in 1898, for example, that "the feminist is in revolt against love"—at least, against "love" as it had been conventionally understood.[60] The novelist Marcel Prévost echoed these worries, describing the *bourgeoise* of the fin-de-siècle as more sensible but less passionate than her earlier incarnations, having more reason and less tenderness, and possessing a clear sense of personal interests that made her less charming and more *égoiste*. In his tract insisting that women must not have the same freedoms as men, the conservative Roger-Milès dramatized the theme of sexual danger in two opposing scenarios that epitomized the social-sexual implications of women's political emancipation. The first vignette narrates the experience of a young woman who has lived by herself, *en garçon*. For her, the promise of marriage no longer held any secrets; she has loved and has been loved. What does she bring to her husband?

A withered soul; a sullied body. A man no longer needs to protect her; she is his equal—physically, morally and immorally. As for surprises, she no longer finds any. Her education is complete in all regards . . . since she brings to marriage the independence of a bachelor.

This image of damaged goods is juxtaposed against another: that of a naive young woman who waits for the companion that she has chosen to reveal to her "the great mystery." This woman "is amazed; the other compares. This one loves; the other judges."[61] It is striking that these images immediately follow a discussion of women's demands for political rights. For Roger-Milès and for many of his contemporaries, the slide from political emancipation to sexual freedom was automatic; the implied losses for men were both political and sexual. Many concluded, like the philosopher Charles Bos, that feminism made marriage impossible. Bos argued that young women who came under the influence of feminists would no longer see marriage as the only means of emancipation; would no longer be terrified of the label "old maid"; and would be less willing to make the sacrifices required by marriage. With the veils removed from their eyes and their romantic illusions gone, they might, he suggested, find their husbands to be mediocre, not worthy of love. In the end, Bos concluded that "the truth can be insidious." He suggested, instead, a "vital lie" that would suppress arguments about justice, about rights to which women were reasonably entitled, about women's aptitudes, in order to preserve the general well-being of society against the devastating effects of women's freedom.

Threaded through these discussions of changes in "love" were pervasive anxieties about sexual relations in marriage. With disarming directness, one commentator noted that "women's newly refined images of love present a grave danger for our times." He worried that with all the new ideas about love, women would not be able to accept or endure reality. "A day does not go by," he noted, when one does not meet young, beautiful women—some experienced, some virgins—who are asking, 'Is that all there is?'"[62] For decades, French doctors had encouraged husbands to please their wives sexually—advice offered in the interests of health and fertility. The coincidence of worries about increasing rates of divorce, depopulation, and the growth of feminism, however, increasingly thrust this discussion into a new context in which cultural authorities began to promote the eroticization of bourgeois marriage and to discuss women's sexual satisfaction as a right. Echoing the language of political struggle, Dr. Bourgas wrote, for example, about the need to achieve "equality in the work of the flesh," to find justice in sexual relations. Men must recognize, he argued, women's "right to love." Making the most direct links between the tenor of the bedroom and the quality of public life, Bourgas attributed the scourges of jealousy, adultery, murder, prostitution, and depopulation to female sexual frustration. In response to this new sensibility, faits divers and medical texts began to recount stories of morning-after suicides—characterized as a "postnuptial insanity" to which women were especially prone—in which new brides, overcome with aversion for their husbands, violently took their own lives.[63] Not surprisingly, then, doctors sought to teach husbands about the physiology of sex. Bourgas wanted to substitute women's right to sexual pleasure—the true woman's right—for feminists' demands for the "rights of men." In a veritable eulogy to the simultaneous orgasm, he concluded that when men learned how to please their wives, there would no longer be a "woman question."[64]

It is impossible fully to comprehend this literature without recognizing the extent to which depictions of women (their character, needs, desires) are inseparable from the needs and desires of the mostly male authors who were producing these documents. In his critique of the masculinist bias of the nineteenth-century sources available for writing the history of women, Alain Corbin has underscored what he calls a "sexual asymmetry in the fabrication of images."[65] He argues that historians necessarily rely on sources compiled by nineteenth-century men who were preoccupied with the possibility of male sexual inferiority—a preoccupation that haunts the scientific vision of women. According to Corbin, it is this set of sexual anxieties that accounts for the symbolic resonance of the figures of the nymphomaniac (the insatiable woman), the hysteric (whose sexuality is out of control), and the lesbian (who disdains men)—figures who proliferated in medical and prescriptive literature, masking (or perhaps revealing) male feelings of inadequacy.[66] Taking this argument further, Robert Nye has theorized that bourgeois male identity in the nineteenth century was rooted in reproductive capacity, centering around the ability of the bourgeois man to establish a vigorous lineage. Hence, fears of impotence and sexual exhaustion, exacerbated in the fin-de-siècle by greater public acknowledgement of women's right to sexual satisfaction, became a leitmotif in medical discussions in which "the dyad female orgasm / male impotence [was] always a latent feature."[67] Following the lines of thought opened by the work of Corbin and Nye, we need to recognize the preeminence of the (masculine or androgynous) feminist on the list of women who evoked sexual danger at the end of the century. In her, male commentators located worries about the woman who could not be satisfied, who, newly positioned to judge male adequacy, was immune to the "surprise" and "the great mystery," who upended all comfortable assumptions about gender, and who might decide for herself what she wanted and needed.

By the 1890s, then, speculations about women's independence had generated a discussion of "love" that crossed back and forth across the rhetorical boundaries between sex and politics. Although a large share

of the writing about the "problem" of love comes from the contemporary reporting of men, there is considerable evidence that women were
themselves talking about redefinitions of love (and sex). In a study of lit-
tle-known feminist novelists of the *belle époque*, Jennifer Waelti-Walters
notes that, while feminist novels tended to follow fairly conventional plot
lines and gave little credibility to women who sought a future outside of
marriage, they were at the same time "carefully subversive," suggesting
women's disappointments and dissatisfaction with the choices that love
and marriage forced upon them.[68] The novelist Réné Marcil complained
directly that "we have grown weary of not finding either in our fiancés,
or in our husbands, or in our sons that which we have dreamed of finding."[69] And Maria Deraismes cautioned that, in short-sighted justification of their casual adultery, "men deceived themselves into thinking that
a respectable woman was content with so little." In an effort to set the
record straight, she explained that adulterous women were women who
had been prematurely turned into "widows" by neglectful husbands.[70]
Madeline Pelletier once again took the most radical position. She argued
that female sexuality would be, and should be, liberated by economic independence. The woman who was able to support herself, claimed Pelletier, would be able to experience sex as a right rather than a duty. She
pointed to a new category of single women who had come to realize
that their respectability derived neither from their virginity nor their fidelity in marriage, but from their financial independence. For these
women, sexual freedom was inseparable from emancipation.[71]

What we are seeing here, at the end of the century, are new kinds of
"love stories"—not the story of passionate, obsessive, and vengeful love
codified in the *crime passionnel*, ultimately so conservative and normalizing, but stories that told of disappointment in love, of changing mores,
and of an unstable balance in the sexual equilibrium between men and
women. Moreover, in writing about "love," these various social critics
effectively shifted the discussion of political subjectivity that had been
raised by feminists onto more conventional ground, displacing the public
dialogue about republican citizenship with discussions of love and marriage. In making this substitution, the complicated ways in which gender
identities constructed political life were obscured by the more mundane
concerns encapsulated in anecdotes about heterosexual relations. Analyzing twentieth-century resistances to feminism, Janice Doane and Devon Hodges have described this kind of displacement as essentially nostalgic, seeking to restore a more comfortable "reality" than the "deteri-

orating" world of the present. Rewriting history in this way, nostalgic authors typically identify the disorder of the present as a sexual or gender disorder and create a mythic past that substitutes an alternative vision of the way things ought to be. In this writing, sexual meanings stand in for political ones.[72]

The frenzied discussions of the future of marriage in the first decade of the twentieth century exemplify this genre. Highbrow and mass-circulation newspapers repeatedly sponsored surveys of opinion to chart popular and elite sentiments on all aspects of the "crisis" of marriage—and, indeed, to set the terms of the debate.[73] An *enquête* conducted by Hugues Le Roux and sponsored by *Le Matin* in 1911 was typical. Le Roux solicited opinions among the newspaper's readership as to whether there was a "crisis in love," later publishing this material as a book that included both the letters received in response and his conclusions. Le Roux summarized and commented on the *cahiers de doléances* (grievance lists) of both men and women,[74] seeking ostensibly to discover: What do women want? What do men dream of in a wife? And what has inhibited the growth of love? To respond to these issues, he provided a series of telling anecdotes that allegedly recounted the particular dilemmas and disappointments of the current generation of young people—anecdotes that, in their intimate detail and calculated emotional effect, turned political and economic questions into a problem of *moeurs*, producing a conservative polemic that invited readers to witness the damage wrought by the disintegration of older values.

Le Roux noted that women's letters complained especially that they could experience no passion in situations in which they felt themselves, in so many ways, identical to their male suitors, that there could be only tepid attraction of like to like. For their part, men whose wives worked outside the home told of some small financial gains that were dwarfed by the loss of all domestic harmony. In reviewing these accounts, Le Roux concluded that "Frenchmen of every class want restored to them the homemaker of former times, a woman whose solid qualities had been formed by tradition, a woman who resembled their mothers."[75] He advised young men not to be fooled by the apparent independence of their women friends: "Today, as in the past, young women want, more than anything in the world, the strong arm of a man to lean on. If they appear independent, it is because they have not had this support in hard times. . . . What women really want is a master."[76] Through an evocative series of sentimental vignettes, Le Roux constructed an indictment of the present and a rationale for the restoration of traditional practices.

In contrast, however, to the substitution of personal stories for political ones accomplished in the nostalgic genre described by Doane and Hodges and exemplified by Le Roux, the link between sexual and political developments was often explicitly drawn by writers in late-nineteenth-century France. In an era obsessed with worries about depopulation, feminism, with its iconic Amazons and *hommesses*, could readily be identified with national decline. Gender slippage and national deterioration were experienced as paired phenomena; the sexual did not precisely displace the political, but rather was considered to be inseparable from it. For contemporaries, the link between gender equilibrium and France's future appeared self-evident. The connections between female independence and male weakness on the one hand and between male sexual potency and French national strength on the other seemed beyond dispute and all of a piece. Of all the symbolic women who represented the pain of the present, the possibility of "fatal women and impotent men,"[77] the feminist (haunted by her shadow twin, the lesbian) was best able to represent the most intimate and the most public anxieties.

Less evident and most interesting for our purposes is the fact that writers from very different positions began to speak of the feminist and the female criminal in exactly the same terms. The two seemed to merge culturally, exemplifying only slightly different versions of the same social malady, posing the same challenge to authority and convention. Some authors seemed to make the connection almost unconsciously, offering little or no explanation. The first sentence of a criminological study of women in prison stated, without further clarification, "In this time of feminism, this book has found its moment." Similarly, and even more cryptically, an appendix of supporting documents for a general study of "crime and debauchery" in Paris included a list of women who had received university degrees between 1870 and 1878.[78] All of the other tables and lists referred to the organization of the police force, the operations of the morgue, typical punishments, numbers of recidivists, and so on. The author clearly saw the higher education of women as connected to crime or debauchery (including divorce), but did not feel the need to elaborate or to explain the connection.

Often the mere existence of gender slippage seemed proof of immanent criminality. According to one forensic expert, "It is when, in one or the other sex, the characteristics are inverted that the aptitude for criminality reveals itself. In men, it appears with the characteristics of femininity; in women, with those of masculinity."[79] Although the French had not been particularly sympathetic to the Italian school of criminal anthropology, which posited a direct link between criminal women and "unfeminine" or masculine women, contemporary social criticism began nevertheless to think of feminists and criminals in the same conceptual and moral universe; lesbianism and feminism, like prostitution, had become the cultural equivalent of criminality. This kind of blurred association is evident in the concerns of one journalist who observed that, having reached the end of fantasies inspired by the image of the romantic consumptive, contemporary imagination (created, he claimed, by elite writers) had substituted the neurotic, the hysteric, and the disturbed (*détraquée*)—figures whose impact could be measured both in the increase of women's crime and "in the morbid desire to experience the unknown, to resuscitate the world of Lesbos."[80] The precise connections that would support the logic of this argument remained unaddressed; rather, the author describes a set of contemporary developments whose interdependence seems so real and self-evident as not to require elaboration. In effect, the perceived moral lassitude of the age—often described as a crisis in love and evident in various kinds of disorderly women—suggested to many a syndrome in which crime was linked, via loose and essentially affective associations, to lesbians and new women.[81]

Once again, it was Alexandre Dumas fils who brought these issues into sharpest focus and who popularized the intriguing connection between criminal women and women's emancipation. In his 1880 essay with the evocative title *Les Femmes qui tuent et les femmes qui votent* (Women who kill and women who vote), Dumas makes visible some of the ways in which his contemporaries understood, if only unconsciously, the social and political subtext of their discourse about female criminality in general and crimes of passion in particular. With this piece, Dumas, "the great consulting lawyer for bloody crimes," entered the growing debate over the acquittal of criminal women. He argued essentially that this kind of extralegal justice, "in which juries found victims odious and defendants interesting," had become so pervasive because the legal system lagged fatefully behind customs. In his terms, when an idea filled the air, when it reached a point of cultural saturation, it made itself material, visible, and active—in short, "when an idea must live, it makes itself human."[82] To prove his point, demonstrating the human embodiment of an idea whose time had come, Dumas discussed the criminal cases of three women (Mlle Marie Bière, Mlle Virginie Dumaire, Mme de Tilly), each from a different social stratum (actress, domestic, aristocrat), each accused of attempted murder. Each woman would have been uncomfortable in the others' presence; yet all found themselves before the same court, escorted by the same *gendarmes*, for essentially the same crime:

Mlle Marie Bière, Mlle Virginie Dumaire, Mme de Tilly . . . are they isolated beings, separated from the community by their temperaments, their customs, their specific and purely individual crimes? No. They are the effective living and at the same time unconscious incarnation of certain ideas generated by intellectuals, moralists, politicians, writers and philosophers—ideas that are just, logical, protective [*tutélaire*], whose time has come, according to these men of reflection, to become law.[83]

For Dumas, these three women, separated by their different milieus and by their different positions vis-à-vis their male victims, were no longer individuals, but had become through their criminal behavior *la Femme*, violently and publicly demanding justice from *l'Homme*. Women had, he argued, turned to private retribution because they were not sufficiently protected in their essential female roles by civil law. Dumas posited a law of nature that preceded both the legal codes and society's moral code. In each case, he claimed, it was the urgency of maternal concerns that drove each woman to crime—that behind the joined women's voices were the voices of three children.[84] Women's honor, located in their maternal function, was, in this argument, their "moral capital." The law—which did not protect the virginity of young girls, the honor of the married woman, or the rights of the (illegitimate) child—must be changed, Dumas argued, to provide the same guarantees that were in place to protect material capital against theft.

But Dumas's argument went well beyond his insistence that the time had come to revise the civil code in order to end the bizarre pattern of murder and acquittal that had, which such élan, installed itself in the popular theater of the Cour d'Assises. He observed that women who watched their "capital" dissipate would turn not only to crime but also to demands for more fundamental (and more fundamentally dangerous) changes in the social and political order:

Wearied of seeing men take from them, with impunity, their honor, their freedom, their love, they want to take from him his work and his place. . . . Women are actually not anxious to assume the business of men; their calling as women is entirely sufficient. It is only that they want to pursue this calling fully, in which they have a point. Thus, they say to men: "Either give us that which nature has told you to give us—love, respect, protection, the normal family—or give us that which you have kept for yourself—freedom."[85]

For Dumas, the *femme criminelle* was, quite literally, a feminist wielding a powerful bargaining chip. What was at stake in the resolution of these criminal domestic dramas was nothing less than the work and the place of men and the security of the patriarchal family. By receiving greater protections in her domestic domain, Dumas assured his readers, the contemporary woman, so disruptive in her behavior, would be led to relinquish her violent claims to justice as well as her demands for greater participation in a public arena (the freedom of men); satisfied, she would return to her natural domestic milieu, restoring the world, in Dr. Chevalier's apt phrase, "as it was not long ago."

We have been following here a paradoxically circular argument that underpinned the parallel development of the problem of female criminality and "the woman question." In this trajectory, the Mother—fecund, moral, and domestic—seemed the antidote to national decadence. But at the same time and in Dumas's terms, mothering, in the context of Third Republic legal codes, social policy, and contemporary practice, could also be the inspiration for women's lawlessness. Instead of two figures (the criminal and the feminist) we find three: the criminal, the disappointed mother / unprotected woman-as-criminal, and the feminist. In the center term of this triad, the problem identified its own solution. In defining his formula for a kind of de-criminalized "feminism," Dumas explicitly dismissed "those vociferous ones prone to exaggeration, with an exalted imagination and overblown pride," who were clamoring publicly for political rights. In their place, he substituted his maternal criminals, those "who have all the qualities that make them worthy of equal treatment."[86] Following this formula, commentators across the political spectrum recommended a broad range of legal changes to extend protections to women in the service of goals that were traditional and familial, at least in part to foreclose the possibility of more radical change. The progressive revision of the civil code was to be the means by which to purge society of both the female criminal and her more dangerous alter ego, the feminist. Both would be disarmed in the same move.

A tract by Anna Levinck, *Women Who Neither Kill Nor Vote*, although written to disrupt the connections between demands for women's rights and female crime, attested to the currency of Dumas's argument within the culture. Already in its third edition by 1882, Levinck's pamphlet sought to counteract "the arguments penetrated by vitriol and gunpowder," *les revendications homicides* that were validated by the acquittals voted by male juries "as an homage to women's right to vote."[87] Levinck observed that, in order to awaken male sympathy for the miserable condition of women—a condition inflicted in large part as a consequence of male pride—a woman had to be lewd, an assassin, or an arsonist. She rejected the rationale that allowed a guilty act, "sealed with blood and vitriol," to lead to a demand for suffrage; rejected a system that acquitted guilty criminals in the name of rights for honest women. Levinck's purpose was to solicit support for "real" women, that is, respectable women who accepted their place in the home, who recognized the public forum as an appropriately male preserve; but in making her argument she suggests, perhaps inadvertently, that it is the women standing before the Cour d'Assises—lewd women, assassins, and arsonists—who had in fact brought women's issues to public attention.

It is particularly interesting that feminist writers participated as well in this conflation of the feminist and the criminal woman. Many began to write about women's issues and to demand women's rights in ways informed by the cultural information produced in accounts of female criminality. Such links emerged implicitly, for example, in a pamphlet by the popular feminist novelist Daniel Lesueur that was commissioned for the International Congress of Commerce and Industry for the Universal Exposition of 1900.[88] Although ostensibly a technical examination of economic competition between women and men, Lesueur opened her study with a general discussion of the most important problems that constrained the lives of working women. She listed three critical reforms: the elimination of costly and complicated bureaucratic procedures in the application for marriage licenses; modification of the civil code so that the system of community property would not weigh so heavily on working women; and the institution of women's right to bring paternity suits. Lesueur's agenda could have been directly lifted out of the judicial de-- *Hardly!* positions of women accused of violent crime. In each case, she has underscored the very issues that female defendants identified as the grounds for their criminal acts against men who, in failing to marry them, in taking (and squandering) their income and property, and in abandoning the children produced in irregular liaisons, fatally compromised their economic viability and left them without legal recourse. Women's crimes were, then, but another version of a feminist text, and feminist texts took their message from women's crimes.

These same connections were made even more explicitly in Marie

Terrisse's exploration of the condition of women, *Notes et impressions à travers le féminisme*.[89] Terrisse speaks of her feminism as a "light that will illuminate the most obscure corners of the situation of women"; she recounts her feminist stories through similar plots and in precisely the same idiom as might be found in the depositions of female defendants (or in the criminal stories circulated in romans feuilletons). Posing as a self-consciously female *flâneur*, Terrisse structures her text around visits to Parisian landmarks, offering in each locale a story of female victimization and, often, of female violence. She tells, for example, of an abandoned mistress violently intruding on the church ceremony celebrating the marriage of her former lover, naming the new husband as the father of her child. She describes an infanticide executed on the banks of the Seine by a desperate, abandoned mother who, Terrisse claims, would surely have shot her betrayer in the temple or hurled vitriol in his face if she had been able to find him. In each case, the boundaries between the feminist text, the roman feuilleton, and the judicial deposition have disappeared as the author claimed for feminism the interpretations offered in archetypal criminal stories.

Both the female criminal and the feminist were understood as "problems," straining the boundaries of ideological certainty in the ways that they broke down distinctions between public and private realms and disrupted assumptions about the naturalness of gender identities; in their similar challenges to male privilege, both suggested an upheaval in social conventions and potential losses for men; both found the legal codes inadequate, and, in demanding substantive change, both threatened to overturn not only conventional gender relations but the terms of gender difference that secured these relations. As Edward Berenson has shown, each could be defined in terms of the other: women's familiarity with guns could in itself be seen as a sign of a dangerously blurred gender identity.[90] In the notorious trial of Mme Caillaux for the murder of the newspaper editor Gaston Calmette, the prosecution had based its case on the representation of Henriette Caillaux as a man-woman—cold, calculating, and, most tellingly, a woman able to select and maneuver a complicated firearm to execute a willful homicide. Such a characterization, including extensive testimony about Mme Caillaux's careful purchase of her weapon and her skill on the firing range, was designed to undercut the defense's version of the murder as a *crime passionnel* effected by a distraught (and thus more sympathetic) woman. In the state's case, the feminist-criminal was set in opposition to the real woman, whose passionate criminality would be, in effect, erased.

Feminists were not necessarily willing to confirm the prosecutor's depiction of Mme Caillaux as a powerful, independent woman. Jane Misme argued, for example, that Mme Caillaux was not at all a feminist but, on the contrary, represented a frustrated and dependent woman who had little knowledge of the public world.[91] On another occasion, however, she used the *crime passionnel* to present a more explicitly political analysis of female rage. When Mme Bassarabo killed her adulterous husband and cut him up in pieces, feminists joined the chorus of horror. Yet, writing in *La Française*, Misme did not lose the opportunity to make a larger point:

We have said, and we repeat, that we abhor the act of Mme Bassarabo. But men must do their part. The spirit of resignation seems to have definitively left women and if [men] want to feel secure in their homes, they must be converted, definitively as well, to the practice of conjugal probity. Family life will become impossible if the enlightenment of men does not correspond to the emancipation of women.[92]

If the goal here was loosely familial, the tone (and implications) surely were not. Similarly, Madeline Pelletier did not hesitate to appropriate the link between independent women and dangerous women for feminist purposes. She drove the point home with characteristic force in her recommendation that "women should adopt the habit of carrying revolvers for evening outings and walks in the country," which would make available to women the same sense of power that men derived from wielding weapons of self-defense.[93] The criminologist Granier turned this point to a slightly different end. There was nothing new about abandoned women taking vengeance, he argued. What was new was the belief, confirmed by juries, that this vengeance was a *right*—that it only awaited a law that would formalize "the rights of women over men."[94] Violent women acting to redress a wrong—criminal women as *justicières*—in this analysis became feminists, manipulating juries and politicians in their position as standard-bearers in a political struggle with men.

These diverse examples of the rhetorical merging of the feminist and the criminal woman suggest the different effects that could be accomplished by this association. With each small turn of the narrative, with just slightly different inflections, the basic story, like a kaleidoscope, registered multiply refracted impressions that joined in different ways the stories of feminists and female criminals. By the 1890s, this connection had begun to be articulated in terms of the problem of unpunished female crime. Concerns about problems of accountability and responsibility—medical, moral, and legal—were increasingly accompanied by a discussion of the devious *hommesse*. Worries that high acquittal rates for women spawned the "contagion" of crime were increasingly likely to be inflected by a new anger about the growing power of feminists to turn the world upside down. The regularly available acquittals offered to female defendants—*ces touchants faveurs*—appeared to have backfired; what had seemed benign had become malignant.

We can see something of the shifting attitudes toward the acquitted female defendant in *L'Acquittée*, a play performed at the turn of the century in the Grand Guignol, a theater specializing in bloody terror and "sordid realism." The story is about a provincial trial of a governess, Mme Ménard, for the strangulation murder of her six-year-old charge.[95] Defended by the famous Parisian lawyer Henri Robert, Mme Ménard was acquitted by a jury that deliberated less than fifteen minutes. It is the presiding magistrate who remains dissatisfied, worried about a system that had acquitted three defendants in one session. In a conversation with a local doctor, he observes that children had died in three of the households in which Ménard had served as governess, although the defense had each time succeeded in convincing the jury that there was no motive for the alleged crime. To satisfy the presiding judge's curiosity, they bring Ménard into his chambers, where the doctor hypnotizes her. Under hypnosis, she in fact reenacts the strangulation of which she had been accused. The play ends with Mme Ménard leaving the court with a menacing expression on her face as the doctor and the judge watch helplessly from the window.

In a theater dedicated exclusively to the macabre, one that did not flinch from the most graphic scenes of bodily mutilation and psychological horror, this play seems quite tame. We can only speculate that the fearsomeness of the story emerges from its closeness to very immediate fears shared by the presumed audience. It seems that the acquitted murderess had outlived her time; she had become not the grateful recipient of the court's largesse but a menacing female figure who had overpowered the men who judged her. Voicing this more cynical perspective, Maurice Talmeyr complained that the *fille-mère* of the roman feuilleton was always falsely rendered as an innocent, her misconduct cast in poetic terms, so that her "fall" became somehow a "legitimate fall."[96] Others insisted similarly that seduced and abandoned women were rarely the inexperienced victims created by the popular press, and characterized abortions and infanticides not as desperate moves to conceal dishonor but as the product of *"une terreur égoiste,"* a cowardice that drove women to experience forbidden pleasures without bearing the consequences.[97] One columnist observed, for example, that the "childlike" and "fragile" defendant who stood before the court was, in fact, "calculating" and "forceful," manipulating an acquittal from jurors who were, finally, "ultra-feminists."[98] He imagined the post-courtroom scene: "She will leave the Cour d'Assises, her face uplifted . . . to hold forth in the evening at some meeting of the League for the Rights of Women where she will superbly retell her feelings as a person who has rendered justice, who has redressed wrongs."[99] Merging the unpunished *femme criminelle* and the feminist, he described a new "despotism of women."

The defendants in the Cour d'Assises were not, however, self-identified feminists, nor did they present themselves in the terms attributed to them by worried commentators. As we have seen, they told their stories in personal terms that outlined especially the socioeconomic and emotional conditions of their lives, justifying their behavior as a legitimate response to men's failure to honor common understandings of a domestic contract in a context where women had few modes of recourse. But the actual and symbolic presence of the feminist as a cultural marker increasingly reframed these accounts of domestic conflict. Because feminists had provided a political analysis of the consequences of women's civil disabilities, and because their writings recapitulated and recast the kinds of stories told by female defendants, the slide between feminist discourse and the testimony of working-class defendants made cultural sense. Instead of positioning women more clearly as victims (that is, instead of following the melodramatic script), the sympathy accorded women defendants by juries came to be seen as a female victory in a larger sex war. This context of belligerency necessarily called forth a more concerted defense against what was increasingly perceived as a conspiratorial "freemasonry of women."[100]

In sum, the assimilation of the criminal woman to the feminist was not casual or accidental, but integral to the social, cultural, and political transitions of the fin-de-siècle. Both the feminist and the *femme criminelle* pointed to the weakening of the ordered oppositions that had organized social life—male/female, public/private, autonomous/dependent—and challenged the hierarchies and privileges that had guaranteed that order. We have already noted the regularity of the passage of laws that extended women's public roles. At the same time, male authority within the household was losing its unquestioned hegemony. Depopulationist worries opened the door to state involvement in the workings of the family that intruded on areas of private life traditionally believed to be fully and permanently beyond the purview of public authorities. The republican government had begun to reinvent, in terms of specifically fin-de-siècle concerns, the relationship between state and family, transforming in the process conventional understandings of both. Sylvia Schafer has argued, for example, that the child welfare legislation of 1889 must be seen as a pivotal moment in a redistribution of power. In assuming the role of protector of the "best interests" of the child—and hence the best interests of the nation—and placing that role above even the authority of biological parents, the state penetrated the sanctity and privacy of the home, violating parental and especially paternal rights that had seemed above society and beyond history. This legislation was, Schafer argues, part of a transformation in the state's *imaginaire*, preparing the way for increased regulation in the name of protection.[101] The unquestioned rule of the *bon père de famille* was passing.

Even masculine notions of honor were unraveling. One critic noted facetiously that in earlier times, "when the door was locked," a deceived husband was indeed ridiculous if he could not see a lover coming through the window. But in the present liberated society, a society in which the door was inevitably open, he wondered if there was any possibility of deception left![102] The irony of the situation did not change the fact that it recorded an arena of diminished power for men. Both Karen Offen and Robert Nye have shown that men of the fin-de-siècle understood depopulation as a man's issue—one that called into question their sexual potency and their familial authority.[103] And physicians were increasingly asserting the importance of female sexual pleasure in marriage, explicitly alerting men to a higher level of responsibility for assuring domestic tranquillity. There can be little doubt that the closing decades of the century were decades when bourgeois men might reasonably feel that the *mal de siècle* was, after all, a male malady.

The fin-de-siècle was, then, a period in which gender relations were particularly volatile—disruptive in ways that crossed back and forth across public and private realms. Republican aspirations to unity and stability notwithstanding, unresolved issues about the gender order persisted, starkly identified by the *femme nouvelle* and symbolized by her conflation with the *femme criminelle*. Crimes of passion did not cease with the passage of the divorce law as proponents had hoped; in fact, the numbers of such cases climbed steadily through at least the first decade of the twentieth century, as did cases of adultery and petitions for divorce. Abortion and infanticide eluded legal controls and birth rates continued to fall. The regulations surrounding prostitution were gradually loosening, but prostitution was neither eliminated nor effectively controlled; the numbers of clandestine prostitutes seemed, in fact, to be increasing, marking a failure to confine sexuality within the normal family. At the turn of the century, twenty-one feminist periodicals were being published in France;[104] and middle-class women continued to enter the professions in ever larger numbers. It had not been possible, after all, to recuperate deviant women. The shifts in gender relations produced by changes in law and social practice were incremental, not revolutionary. But as this examination of the criminal-as-feminist and feminist-as-criminal has shown, these shifts challenged fundamental values that had informed expectations and behaviors in both public and private life for a century.

The sexual politics that situated the *femme criminelle* within a cultural frame were inseparable from public politics. The preferred symbolic representation of the republic in 1880 was a domesticated Marianne, a demure figure who conveyed visually the moderate aspirations of the republic's founders. In keeping with this image, the sculptor Doriot produced a bust of the personified republic, chosen to adorn government buildings, which depicted a grave and motionless Marianne, wearing robes and a crown of vegetation above a headband with the engraved message "Honor and the Motherland"; eight medallions formed a necklace inscribed with the words Agriculture, Trade, Fine Arts, Education, Justice, Science, Shipping, Industry.[105] But realities did not match these normalizing aspirations; the image of republican order in its female personification was illusory and perhaps ironic. The year 1880 marked both the moment when the republic rested more securely after a decade of turmoil—a security celebrated in the *grande fête* of July 14—*and* the publication of Dumas's tract on women who kill and women who vote, inaugurating decades in which disorderly women, feminist women, and criminal women would be at the center of public concerns, challenging republican commitments and practices and the authority of men to rule both the family and the state.

Although women's rights were by no means complete by the closing years of the century, the republic had begun to redefine the meaning of citizenship and the parameters of state authority. The danger of the emancipated woman was effectively brought home in the figure of the *femme criminelle*, a figure who embodied for both feminists and social conservatives the nexus of concerns that informed "the woman question." There was no closure on the issue of women's place in French society at the turn of the century; rather, there was an ongoing series of small transformations and continuous debate in which the female criminal and the feminist marked profound transitions in domestic relations and civic life. In the midst of these shifts, men and women of the fin-de-siècle found themselves in new positions with regard to each other and to the state, as boundaries between public and private life were shown to be permeable and gender hierarchies, presumed natural and immutable, appeared, after all, to be subject to change.

Conclusion

The criminal trials of women in the fin-de-siècle not only offered compelling entertainment—*une justice théâtrale*, as contemporaries suspected—but also provided the occasion for repeated performances of the cultural conflicts and preoccupations of the moment, drawing a large and diverse audience into active engagement with current debates. These "performances" and the commentary they provoked open a window for us onto a culture in transition—a culture in the process of reinventing itself. By addressing the "problem" of women's crime and in making sense of criminal stories, men and women of the fin-de-siècle were also making sense of broader questions. The celebrity enjoyed by a fairly large repertoire of causes célèbres and the pervasive discussion of female violence meant that criminal stories moved quite regularly between "the serene halls of science" and the heady tumult of popular journalism and more general social commentary. In this fluid circulation between various forms of high and mass culture, late-nineteenth-century articulations of the symbolic possibilities of "femaleness" were brought to bear on specific contemporary concerns.

By focusing on the *femaleness* of female criminality—by putting gender at the center of my analysis—I have been able to demonstrate the connections among various cultural developments that were simultaneously unsettling and remaking the bourgeois culture of fin-de-siècle Paris. This close look at different manifestations of the organization of gender has produced not a new history of women, nor even a history of the way "women" figured in the symbolic economy of the late nineteenth century (although both of these topics do arise). This investigation explicates, rather, the ways in which gender(ed) considerations were centrally

implicated in several of the most important cultural and political redefinitions of the period.

In its first level of signification, a foregrounding of gender in the larger
debates about criminality reveals complex sets of relations between men
and women—intimate, domestic relations, but also relations between officials charged with enforcing the codes and ordinary women charged
with breaking them, between various professionals and their clients or
patients, between authors and the objects of their study, between cultural
and civic authorities and their popular audiences/constituencies, between
the politically empowered and the disenfranchised. This exploration of
different sets of relations discusses symbolic and strategic meanings attributed to women's behavior—its function as cultural marker or discursive sign—and the efforts by women to frame the terms in which to account for their own lives, thus presenting women as historical actors af-
fecting the social conventions of the period while inevitably bound by
them. In all of these interactions, in both physical space and in the social
imagination, threats to the conventional gender equilibrium lay at the
center of contemporary perceptions; efforts to establish a set of stable expectations document both what was at stake in the shifting relations between men and women and the available strategies for securing (and challenging) the practices that produced gender difference.

But understandings of gender operated as powerfully in providing
conceptual models for the operations of institutions and in defining the
commonsenseness of social practices as they did in organizing relations
between men and women. The specific meanings attributed to "femaleness" and to "maleness" provided a critical set of criteria for assessing contemporary culture and politics—a means by which to distinguish
between the legitimate-normal-healthy and the illegitimate-aberrant-
degenerate aspects of contemporary life. Deviant women seemed to offer
a particularly vivid mirror in which to recognize the ills of modern urban
life, and the specific answers to each version of "the woman question"
seemed to hold the fate of France in the balance. Emerging perceptions
of mass culture, the authority sought by the new social sciences, the consolidation and effects of medical expertise, changing notions of citizenship, and the unfolding implications of republicanism all relied on implicit gendered categories to establish their contemporary meanings.

Each individual strand of this story of fin-de-siècle cultural transition
suggests the ways in which using the lens of gender reframes our vision of
old material, allowing us to see in new ways. But perhaps more important

than the individual themes that emerge in this analysis is the way that the use of gender as an analytic category enables a bringing together of the subjects of cultural, social, and political history, producing a more integrated historical narrative. To probe the meaning of female criminality in the fin-de-siècle it has been necessary to interpret the various criminal stories in the context of the complexities and banalities of daily domestic life on the one hand and the preoccupations of public life on the other. In fact, turn-of-the-century commentators claimed explicitly that the stability of the traditional gender order was directly linked to national strength. It is ironic that it has been the work of historians that has tended to drive apart the very connections that were so immediate and palpable for the men and women of the period. In dividing up the discipline into "political history," "social history," and, more recently, "women's history," historians have inadvertently ignored the overlaps and commonalities that linked apparently different aspects of fin-de-siècle culture, and have obscured the ways that contemporaries depended on stable understandings of gender difference to make sense of both public and private life.

In this study I have tried instead to demonstrate the inadequacy of the categories of "public" and "private" as they have been conventionally used to segregate the subjects of historical inquiry. In the fin-de-siècle, the pervasive discussion of social questions in the popular press blurred the distinctions between the voices of traditional authorities commenting on public issues and the newer expressions of popular opinion often derived from private experiences. Women's decisions to resort to private justice as well as their own accounts of the expectations and desires that pushed them to violence must be understood in terms of their recognition of the inadequacy of formal (that is, public) protections or remedies. And, if we invert this perspective, we can see that debates about depopulation, divorce legislation, and changes in the civil code were inflected throughout by the cultural information generated in accounts of women's crime that turned largely on domestic issues. Discussions of the responsibilities and entitlements of citizenship were inseparable from parallel reflections on rights and responsibilities in marriage; the fate of the family carried the burden of the fate of the nation; love and politics, murder and suffrage, were inextricably intertwined issues in contemporary consciousness and in the emerging self-definitions of the Third Republic.

To say that a study of the imbrication of public and private behaviors and concerns produces a more integrated story is not to claim to have uncovered a linear or even coherent account of the period. Rather,

I have tried to trace the effects of competing cultural narratives, disintegrating models of top-down cultural prescription and bottom-up complicity or resistance in favor of a more kaleidoscopic image of cultural exchanges among differently empowered historical subjects. I have followed diverse voices as they crisscrossed through different media, genres, and institutions, glimpsing the processes that put various meanings into circulation. At the center of this study is the assumption that images, myths, and linguistic categories matter—that they must be seen as the source and effect of relations of power, revealing especially the ways in which different individuals positioned themselves and were positioned within and through specific cultural debates. I have sought to read these symbolic and discursive practices (in this case, representations of female criminality) in terms of competing images, myths, and linguistic categories as they functioned in the context of the specific historical developments of the fin-de-siècle.

These stories were, then, both instrumental and interpretive, revealing the contours and conflicts of the cultural landscape as lived in the moment and as refracted for us through different analytic lenses. In retelling them, attentive to their production, mobilization, and effects, we can see the dense web of cultural concerns that stretched across the social distance between elites and masses, oblivious to the (rhetorical) boundaries between public and private worlds, which allowed criminal women to be the carriers of so much symbolic weight. Perhaps those who identified the *femme criminelle* as the clearest embodiment of the tendencies and discontents of the modern age were not wrong after all.

REFERENCE MATTER

NOTES

Abbreviations

The following abbreviations are used in the notes:

APP   Archives de la Préfecture de Police, Paris
AVP   Archives de la Ville de Paris et du Département de la Seine, Série D2
       U8
BMD   Bibliothèque Marguerite Durand, Paris

Introduction

1. See especially Williams, *Dream Worlds*; Levin, *When the Eiffel Tower Was New*; Rearick, *Pleasures of the Belle Epoque*; Weber, *France*.

2. Rearick, *Pleasures of the Belle Epoque*, 199.

3. Chevalier, *Laboring Classes*.

4. Hay et al., eds., *Albion's Fatal Tree*.

5. Foucault, *Discipline and Punish*; *Madness and Civilization*; ed., *I, Pierre Rivière*.

6. Cixous and Clément, *Newly Born Woman*, 7.

7. Armstrong, *Desire and Domestic Fiction*.

8. For an interesting discussion of the historian's task in analyzing discursive struggles and the material and political context that produces cultural authority, see Walkowitz, "Patrolling the Borders," 25–31.

9. Walkowitz, *City of Dreadful Delight*, 10.

10. The phrase "stories-in-tension" is Steedman's in *Landscape for a Good Woman*, 12.

11. Nye, *Crime, Madness and Politics*; O'Brien, *Promise of Punishment*; Perrot, ed., *L'Impossible prison*.

12. Notable exceptions include the work of Harris, *Murders and Madness*; Fuchs, *Poor and Pregnant*; Schafer, "Children in Moral Danger."

13. Ouerd, "Dans la forge à cauchemars mythologiques."

Chapter 1

1. Grisson, *Paris horrible*, 4.
2. Perrot, "Delinquency and the Penitentiary System," 219.
3. Porter, *Pursuit of Crime*, 121.
4. Guillot, *Le Jury et les moeurs*, 11.
5. Rearick, *Pleasures of the Belle Epoque*, 102, 114.
6. *Compte général*, 1880, 1900.
7. In 1860, men committed 79 percent of crimes against persons and 84 percent of crimes against property, while comparable statistics for women's crime were 21 percent and 16 percent, respectively. Male crime constituted 82 percent and female crime 18 percent of the total crimes against persons and property. In 1890, female crime represented 20 percent of crimes against persons, 12 percent of crimes against property, and 15 percent of the total. Yvernès, *Le Crime et le criminel*, 9.
8. Ibid., 5.
9. Increasingly, condemned women were awarded milder sentences. In the period 1896–1900, 34 percent of men and 18 percent of women were condemned to the most serious punishments (peines afflictives et infamantes); in 1910 the figures had dropped to 31 percent and 11 percent, respectively. Dhavernas, "La Délinquance des femmes," n. 16. According to Patricia O'Brien, the percentage of women detained in central prisons declined precipitously in the final quarter of the century, dropping more rapidly than the overall decline of all detained prisoners. By the end of the century, women represented 12 to 13 percent of the total prison population, as compared to the 16 to 18 percent figure of twenty-five years earlier. Even in institutions holding those awaiting judgment and serving short sentences, there was an absolute and relative decline in the number of women detained. O'Brien, *Promise of Punishment*, 59–60.
10. Dhavernas, "La Délinquance des femmes," 56.
11. Smart, *Women, Crime and Criminology*, 2.
12. Poovey, *Uneven Developments*, 12. See also Scott, *Gender*.
13. Pick, *Faces of Degeneration*, 230.
14. Ibid., 54.
15. Maxwell, *Manuel du juré*, 54.
16. Sighele, *Littérature et criminalité*, 195.
17. Alexandre Lacassagne cited in De Ryckère, *La Servante criminelle*, 402.
18. Tarde, *La Criminalité comparée*, v–vi.
19. Ibid., 195–96.
20. Goron, *L'Amour à Paris*, 4.
21. APP, Dossier Macé: 1165.
22. Riley, *"Am I That Name?,"* 49–51.
23. Sighele, *Littérature et criminalité*, 203.
24. Mareille, *La Plaidoirie sentimentale*, 349.

25. *"De notre moi"*: of one's self. In Sighele, *Littérature et criminalité*, 200.

26. See Rudinesco, *La Bataille de cent ans*; Perrot, "Faits divers," 911–19.

27. See Proal, *Les Médecins positivistes*; Dallemagne, *Les Théories de la crimi-nalité*; Caignart de Mailly, *L'Evolution*; Tarde, *La Criminalité comparée*. Lombroso's positivist school of criminology (the Italian school) had focused attention espe-cially on the "born criminal," emphasizing the biological and physical basis of criminality that made the criminal an atavistic remnant of a primitive type, read-ily recognizable by anatomical stigmata that clearly marked her/him off from the rest of the population. French theorists worried that Lombrosian positivism left no room either for free will or for the rehabilitation of the prisoner, and ar-gued instead for the importance of both environmental and hereditarian factors that together determined which individuals would fall into antisocial behavior. This line of argument was nearly homologous to Pasteurian notions of disease that emphasized the development of the microbe in a hospitable terrain, and was equally compatible with hereditarian explanations of disease that included theories of both innate and acquired susceptibilities. For a more complete dis-cussion of these issues, see Harris, *Murders and Madness*, 100–101.

28. Foucault, "About the Concept of the 'Dangerous Individual'," 1.

29. Ibid., 3.

30. See, for example, Scott, "'L'ouvrière!'."

31. Dartigues, *De l'amour experimental*, 17. See also Schafer, "When the Child Is the Father of the Man."

32. Dartigues, *De l'amour experimental*, 17.

33. See, for example, Holtz, *Les Crimes passionnels*, 144.

34. Desmaze, *Le Crime et le débauche*, iii.

35. Puibaraud, *La Femme criminelle*, 399.

36. Riley, *"Am I That Name?,"* 57.

37. Scott, "'L'Ouvrière!'" 142.

38. Ibid., 147.

39. Zola, *Nana*, 221.

40. See especially Corbin, "Commercial Sexuality"; Hertz, "Medusa's Head."

41. Gullickson, "The Unruly Woman," 136.

42. Gabriel Tarde, *L'Opinion et la foule*, as quoted in Pick, *Faces of Degenera-tion*, 93. See also Barrows, *Distorting Mirrors*.

43. Granier, *La Femme criminelle*, vi.

44. C. Lombroso and G. Ferrero, *La Femme criminelle*, as quoted in Elissa Gelfand, *Imagination in Confinement*, 50. Following this general presumption, the criminologist Paul Aubry explained that his study of homicides committed by women would not include a discussion of either attacks with vitriol (*le vitrio-lage*) or infanticide because "the motives in each of these crimes were always identical."

45. Thulié, *La Femme*, i.

46. Wajeman, *Le Maître et l'hystérique*, 3, 9.

47. Scott, *Gender*, 2.

48. Miller, *The Novel and the Police*, 18.

49. Guillot, *Le Jury et nos moeurs*, 7.

50. Granotier, *L'Autorité de mari*, 50.

51. Ibid., 157.

52. Baradez, *L'Anthropologie criminelle*, 12–14.

53. Brunetière, *Questions de critique*, 172, 179.

54. See, for example, Laurent, "Les Suggestions criminelles"; Tarde, "L'Affaire Chambige."

55. Sighele, *Littérature et criminalité*, 171–72.

56. Ibid., 168.

57. In fact, Paris was not a particularly dangerous city at this time. Criminologists worried especially about recidivism, juvenile crime, and women's crime—worries that stemmed more from concerns about the apparent pathologies of modern urban society than from growing rates of crime and violence. See Chesnais, *Histoire de la violence*.

58. Aubry, *La Contagion du meurtre*, 3.

59. Moreau de Tours, *De la contagion*; Aubry, *La Contagion du meurtre*.

60. Macé, *La Femme criminelle*, 12–13.

61. Allen, *In the Public Eye*, 42.

62. Thiesse, *Le Roman du quotidien*, 17.

63. Romi, *Histoire des faits divers*. In 1848, there were approximately 10,000 *crieurs publics* in Paris. Perrot, "Faits divers," 912.

64. Romi, *Histoire des faits divers*, 164; Perrot, "Faits divers," 913.

65. Seguin, *Nouvelles à sensation*, 159.

66. *Le Petit Parisien*, April 18, 1897.

67. *Le Fait divers*, 110.

68. The roman feuilleton took 12.5 percent of the printed surface of popular journals. Thiesse, "Mutations et permanences de la culture populaire," 89, n. 8.

69. Although contemporaries often assumed that the romans feuilletons were read only by women while men attended to the more weighty sections of the paper, recent analyses suggest that men also followed the novel's installments, as did members of the bourgeoisie of both sexes, even as they expressed disdain for this popular form. Thiesse, *Le Roman du quotidien*, 17; Goimard, "Quelques structures formelles du roman feuilleton," 21.

70. Thiesse, *Le Roman du quotidien*, 142.

71. Ibid., 107; *Le Fait divers*, 53.

72. Sighele, *Littérature et criminalité*, 204–5.

73. Aubry, "De l'influence contagieuse."

74. Institut Général psychologique.

75. Corre, cited in Aubry, *La Contagion du meurtre*, xxi. Aubry wrote, for

example, that even though criminologists, magistrates, and doctors were bombarded daily by accounts of violent crimes, they did not succumb to the power of suggestion "because their level-headed minds permit them to see such things from a protected (elevated) distance that renders them immune to their effects." Ibid., 98.

76. Moreau de Tours, *De la contagion*, 5.

77. Sighele, *Littérature et criminalité*, 174.

78. Ibid., 175.

79. Ibid.

80. Proal, *La Criminalité féminine*, 15.

81. Talmeyr, "Le Roman-feuilleton," 203.

82. Ibid., 204.

83. Jules Langevin, quoted in Thiesse, "Mutations et permanences de la culture populaire," 85.

84. Puibaraud, *La Femme criminelle*; Julien Chevalier, *L'Inversion sexuelle*.

85. Icard, *De la contagion du crime*, 12.

86. Ibid., 13.

87. Moreau, *Le Code civil*, 6–7.

88. Ibid., 290.

89. Mareille, *La Plaidoirie sentimentale*, 349.

90. Cruppi, *La Cour d'Assises*, 43.

91. Macé, *Un Cent-Garde*, 229.

92. Signorel, *Le Crime*, 7.

93. Cruppi, *La Cour d'Assises*, 296.

94. Garçon, *La Justice contemporaine*, 628.

95. Ibid., 627.

96. Mareille, *La Plaidoirie sentimentale*, 327–33.

97. AVP, D2 U8: 92, March 23, 1880.

98. APP, BA 1612.

99. *La Lanterne*, April 9, 1880, APP, BA 1612.

100. *Le Figaro*, April 9, 1880, APP, BA 1612.

101. Garçon, *Du crime*, 23.

102. See *Le Figaro*, Feb. 23, 1887; *Gil Blas*, Feb. 26, 1887; *La XIXème Siècle*, Jan. 7, 1889. APP, BA 1165, Dossier Macé.

103. Stallybrass and White, *Politics and Poetics of Transgression*.

104. Goron, *L'Amour à Paris*, 5.

105. *Le Petit Moniteur*, June 14, 1888. APP, BA 1165, Dossier Macé.

106. Ibid.

107. Sighele, *Littérature et criminalité*, 193.

108. Gautier, "Le Monde des prisons (Notes d'un témoin)," 417, quoted in Harris, *Murders and Madness*, 90.

109. Stendhal followed the outlines of a fait divers of July 22, 1827: the Berthet affair; Flaubert used the story of Delphine Couturier, the wife of a doc-

tor who poisoned herself in 1848 after being abandoned by her lover rather than endure the boredom of rural life; and Zola incorporated the celebrated Fenayrou affair of 1882 in his study of crime and heredity.

110. Emile Zola, "Experimental Novel," in Ellmann and Fiedelson, eds., *Modern Tradition*, 274.

111. Sighele, *Le Crime à Deux*, 163.

112. Ibid., 168.

113. *Faits divers. Crimes, délits, accidents de l'année 1882.*

114. Perrot, "Fait divers," 913.

115. Amaury, *Histoire du plus grand quotidien*, vol. 2, 656.

116. Barthes, *Critical Essays*, 185–86.

117. See, for example, Walkowitz, *City of Dreadful Delight*; Davis, *Society and Culture*; Stallybrass and White, *Politics and Poetics of Transgression*.

118. Radway, *Reading the Romance*; Armstrong, *Desire and Domestic Fiction*; Davidson, *Revolution and the Word*.

119. For interesting discussions of the effects of literary formulas, see Cawelti, *Adventure, Mystery, and Romance*; Porter, *The Pursuit of Crime*; Doane and Hodges, *Nostalgia and Sexual Difference*.

120. Kayser, *Le Quotidien français*.

Chapter 2

1. Ouerd, "Dans la forge à cauchemars mythologiques."

2. See Stephen Heath's discussion of plausible texts: A readable text, he argues, is one "which repeats the generalized text of the social real institutionalized as Natural," a discourse "that copies the discourse assumed as representative of Reality by the society." Heath quoted in Porter, *The Pursuit of Crime*, 115.

3. Steedman, *Landscape for a Good Woman*, 12.

4. See, for example, the collection of articles in "Legal Storytelling."

5. Farge, *La Vie Fragile*, 8.

6. Ibid., 7–8.

7. See Lailler and Vonoven, *Les Erreurs judiciaires*; Lacaze, *Des enquêtes officieuses*; Saillard, *Le Rôle de l'avocat*; Martin, *Crime and Criminal Justice*. The presumption against the defendant was further exacerbated by the fact that until 1897, the *instruction* was secret (that is, the accused was not privy to the information gathered against her, nor was she accompanied by a lawyer during the interrogations), and the defense lawyer might not see the file until just before the court appearance. Critics of these policies argued that the protracted isolation of the defendant awaiting trial led to full confessions if not suicide attempts.

8. For an interesting discussion of the construction of stories and versions of stories, see Smith, "Afterthoughts on Narrative"; Schafer, "The Court of Documents."

9. Cruppi, *La Cour d'Assises*, 72.

10. AVP, D2 U8: 211, Nov. 12, 1886.

11. AVP, D2 U8: 40, Sept. 19, 1875.

12. AVP, D2 U8: 40, Oct. 19, 1875.

13. AVP, D2 U8: 288, Jan. 30, 1892.

14. This same information was included in the prosecutor's summation but was dropped from the indictment.

15. AVP, D2 U8:144, Mar. 29, 1883.

16. AVP, D2 U8: 38, July 9, 1875.

17. Ibid.

18. In a later interrogation, she elaborated a bit on this story, claiming that when she sat down to eat her lunch, Charrier began sweeping, raising dust to annoy her and commenting on the perfections of other women.

19. Cruppi, *La Cour d'assises*, 76, 139; *Le Petit Parisien*, "Juges et criminels," Sept. 2, 1880; Lailler et Vonoven, *Les Erreurs*, 146. Critics of this interrogation referred especially to the close connections between the men chosen as Présidents de la Cour (presiding judges) and the prosecutors.

20. *Gazette des Tribunaux*, July 10, 1875.

21. *Gazette des Tribunaux*, June 30, 1878; ellipses in original.

22. *Gazette des Tribunaux*, Feb. 23, 1887.

23. See especially Cambréal, *Le Jury criminel*; Garçon, *La Justice contemporaine*; Bérard des Glajeux, *Souvenirs*.

24. In 1860, 20 percent of defendants were deemed not guilty; in 1869, 22 percent; in 1880, 25 percent; in 1890, 30 percent. Yvernès, *Le Crime et le criminel*, 14.

25. Garçon, *La Justice contemporaine*, 580.

26. AVP, D2 U8: 293, Aug. 10, 1892.

27. AVP, D2 U8: 236, Aug. 11, 1888.

28. De Ryckère, *La Servante criminelle*, 63.

29. Ibid., 33–34. In another example that once again attests to the irresistible appeal of this perspective, de Ryckère explained that women's natural vanity could be manipulated to assist in maintaining prison discipline. He cited an experiment at an Ohio prison that rewarded good behavior with the privilege of wearing different grades of nonprison garb, concluding that such a system would insure rigorous respect for the rules among female prisoners. Somewhere in the midst of his anecdote, de Ryckère acknowledged that this experiment had only been tried with men—a fact that, seemingly, is irrelevant to his argument.

30. Proal, *Le Crime et le suicide*, 122; ellipses in original.

31. An example of the kinds of confused associations that emerge in efforts to define women's essential nature can be seen in the writings of sociologist and philosopher Gabriel Tarde, where he compared ordinary women to male criminals: "so many traits in common with our [male] criminals. . . . The same lack of foresight, the same vanity . . . the same sterility of imagination, the same penchant for imitation . . . but woman, on the other hand, is eminently good and

devoted, and this single difference suffices to counterbalance all of the preceding analogies." Tarde, *La Criminalité comparée*, 48.

32. Ferrero, "Le Mensonge," 149.

33. De Ryckère, *La Servante*, 27.

34. Not only could they fool men, he continues, but because they were habitual liars, they were readily able to discover men's lies. Ibid., 29.

35. Ferrero, "Le Mensonge," 149.

36. Ibid., 138. It is especially interesting that a criminological text written in the 1960s reiterates nearly to the word such claims about women's deceitfulness. Pollack noted that women are trained to deceit because they disguise their sexual responses, conceal their menstrual periods, and withhold sexual information from children. See Pollack, *Criminality of Women*.

37. Ferrero, "Le Mensonge," 138.

38. In French law, women could not bring paternity suits until 1912, a factor that complicated the responses of juries to the crimes of women who felt themselves without legal recourse in cases of abandonment.

39. AVP, D2 U8: 224, Eugénie Belligand, July 26, 1887.

40. *Compte général*, 1900; Benoit, *De l'empoisonnement*.

41. De Clery, *Les Crimes d'empoisonnement*, 5. The emphasis is mine.

42. Proal, *La Criminalité féminine*, 16.

43. Gayot de Pitaval wrote in 1743 (*Causes célèbres et intéressants avec les jugements qui les ont décidées*) that women are poisoners because they "do not have the courage to avenge themselves openly . . . and embrace this means that favors their timidity and hides their malice." Quoted in Dupré and Charpentier, "Les Empoisonneurs," 6.

44. Ibid., 52.

45. Charpentier, *Les Empoisonneuses*, 13. Nineteenth-century medical literature spoke of *l'empoisonneuse* and the hysteric as especially dangerous because both were capable of tricking the doctor. Although neither Dupré nor Charpentier makes this connection directly in his writing, both claim that the women who poison are a particular kind of *dégénérées hystériques*, characterized by moral defects that complement their hysterical suggestibility. They assert "a permanence across the ages of a special criminal-pathological type" for whom poison is the weapon of choice.

46. Dupré and Charpentier, *Les Empoisonneurs*, 7. See also Charpentier, *Les Empoisonneuses*, 9–13.

47. For example, in 1877, A. Bechon, the mother of a newborn, was convicted of poisoning her infant with laudanum and condemned to five years of forced labor, although she insisted throughout that she had given an overdose of medication in error, seeking only to soothe a colicky baby with an ordinary remedy.

48. Robert, *Jane Daniloff*. This book was part of a series entitled *Grandes Repenties et Grandes Pécheresses* (Great [female] repenters and great [female] sinners).

49. "Les Petits Cahiers," 422; ellipses in original.

50. *Gazette des Tribunaux*, May 29, 1891.

51. Lailler et Vonoven, *Les Erreurs*, 405–12.

52. It was not uncommon for criminal anthropologists to link *l'empoison-neuse* to older representations of witches, punctuating their accounts of women's crime with atrocity stories, including descriptions of female pleasure in ferocity, cannibalism, and mutilation.

53. Puibaraud, *La Femme criminelle*, 414.

54. Granier, *La Femme criminelle*, 241.

55. Ibid., 157–58. According to Granier, the poisoning of a woman by a man never occurred, while on occasion degenerate men borrowed women's bowls to hurl vitriol. The use of a woman's weapon identified the offender in this case as medically degenerate.

56. *Gazette des Tribunaux*, Sept. 16, 1881. The defendant, Rosalie Velay, worked in the leather-tanning industry.

57. AVP, D2 U8: 114, Mar. 9, 1881, Alexandrine Breton.

58. "Pendant qu'elles cuisent," *Le Petit Journal*, Mar. 26, 1892.

59. AVP, D2 U8: 200, Apr. 28, 1886.

60. AVP, D2 U8: 144, Mar. 29, 1883, Rose Chervey. See also AVP, D2 U8: 156, Jan. 1, 1884, Amélie Sanglé; AVP, D2 U8: 200, Charot.

61. Evidence of a kind of community solidarity, if not conspiracy, may be seen in the fact that one witness reported that she had heard Melanie say that, if she did not fear justice, she would shoot her husband; the witness later retracted this assertion, claiming that the mayor had forced her to say it.

62. Lailler et Vonoven, *Les Erreurs*, 491.

63. AVP, D2 U8: 75.

64. Ibid.

65. Ibid.

66. Ibid.

67. *Gazette des Tribunaux*, June 29, 1878.

68. AVP, D2 U8: 185, July 4, 1885.

69. AVP, D2 U8: 60, Aug. 5, 1876, Marie Bercet.

70. De Ryckère, *La Servante*, 65–69.

71. Ibid., 145; see also Bouton, *L'Infanticide*.

72. Steedman, *Landscape for a Good Woman*, 5.

73. Davis, *Fiction in the Archives*, 81.

74. AVP, D2 U8: 144.

75. Guillais, *La Chair de l'autre*, 314–15.

76. Gelfand, *Imagination in Confinement*, 54.

77. AVP, D2 U8: 107, Sept. 6, 1880.

78. Steedman, *Landscape for a Good Woman*, 10–11.

Chapter 3

1. Marc, *Consultation médico-légale.*
2. Dubuisson and Vigouroux, *Responsabilité pénale,* 464–66.
3. Boyer, *Thèse de Montpellier* (1880), cited in Schwob, *Contribution à l'étude,* 25.
4. Fouquet, "Le Détour obligé?" 71–84.
5. De Beauvoir, *The Second Sex,* xv.
6. Laqueur, *Making Sex.*
7. Ibid., 150.
8. Moreau, "Sang sur," 151–65.
9. Michelet, quoted in ibid., 159.
10. For a broader discussion of this theme, see Landes, *Woman and the Public Sphere;* and Riley, *"Am I That Name?."*
11. Laqueur, *Making Sex,* 150, 215. Jan Goldstein makes a similar argument about the increasing use of the hysteria diagnosis in the Third Republic as alienists of the Saltpêtrière school participated in the republican effort to strip the clergy of its social authority. "The Hysteria Diagnosis."
12. Borie, "Une gynécologie passionnée," 164–65.
13. According to popular opinion and legal precedents in the opening decades of the century, the mad (*les fous*) could be identified by absurd and inappropriate behavior and by incoherent, excited, or distracted language; they were those who had lost a sense of reality and the control of their persons. Such madness divided loosely into categories distinguished by degree of severity (completely mad, half-mad) or by quality of affliction (gentle madness, fierce madness, dangerous madness). Madness was used interchangeably with "delirium," "agitation," "confusion," "dementia," "imbecility," "idiocy." Although this language had no formal legal specificity, popular consensus held that the mad announced their insanity through a range of widely recognized behaviors. Dupré, *Définition médico-légale de l'aliéné;* Dubuisson, "De l'évolution des opinions," 103–4.
14. For a discussion of the professionalization of psychiatry, see Goldstein, *Console and Classify.*
15. Schwob, *Contribution à l'étude;* De Saussure, "The Influence of the Concept of Monomania," 374.
16. For an interesting discussion of the significance of classification changes in nineteenth-century psychiatry, see Berrios, "Obsessional Disorders."
17. Schwob, *Contribution à l'étude,* 31.
18. Berthier, *Des névroses menstruelles,* 9, 22.
19. Schwob, *Contribution à l'étude,* 17.
20. Berthier, *Des névroses menstruelles,* 8.
21. Ibid., 128.
22. Tardieu, quoted in ibid., frontispiece.
23. Berthier, *Des névroses menstruelles,* 233.

24. Ibid., 8.

25. Ibid., 238.

26. For an interesting recent discussion of these issues, see Allen, "At the Mercy of Her Hormones," 19–44.

27. Loiseau, *Thèse de Paris*, (1856), cited in Schwob, *Contribution à l'étude*, 69.

28. Esquirol, *Des maladies mentales*, vol. 1 (1838), cited in Schwob, *Contribution à l'étude*, 27.

29. Brachet, cited in Schwob, *Contribution à l'étude*, 35.

30. Ball, *La Médecine mentale*, 27.

31. Dauby, *Quelques considérations*, 56.

32. Morache, *La Responsabilité*, 587.

33. Dubuisson and Vigouroux, *La Responsabilité pénale*, 466.

34. Law of 28 germinal, an III. Marcé, *Traité de la folie*, 123.

35. Icard, *La Femme pendant*, 265–66.

36. Brierre de Boismont, *De la menstruation*, 531.

37. Dagonet, *Traité des maladies menstruelles* (1862), cited in Schwob, *Contribution à l'étude*, 47.

38. Legrand du Saulle, *Les Hystériques*, 480.

39. Brierre de Boismont, "De la folie puerpérale," 587.

40. The forensic specialist Ch. Marc was the first, in the 1840s, to use the word "kleptomania" to name theft that resulted from some form of "mental debility."

41. *Annales médico-psychologiques* (1845), 231.

42. Legrand du Saulle, *Les Hystériques*, 441; Lacaze, *De la criminalité féminine*, 66-68; Lunier, "Des vols."

43. For a broader discussion of female kleptomania see especially O'Brien, "The Kleptomania Diagnosis"; Abelson, *When Ladies Go A-Thieving*.

44. Lacaze, *De la criminalité féminine*, 66. In fact, in response to the high social status of the majority of kleptomaniacs, some commentators recommended a new legal category of "civic theft"—that is, the theft of unneeded items by those who had succumbed to *la tentation de l'éblouissement* (bedazzlement)—that would be punishable, not by prison, but by a fine.

45. O'Brien, "The Kleptomania Diagnosis," 70–71.

46. Dubuisson and Vigouroux, *Responsabilité pénale*, 458–59.

47. Tardieu, in Berthier, *Des névroses menstruelles*, 156–57.

48. Legrand du Saulle, *Les Hystériques*, 437–42, 449–50.

49. O'Brien, "The Kleptomania Diagnosis," 72–73.

50. In tracing this history, Gladys Swain argues that it was not until the rupture that began with Charcot and was realized by Freud that it was possible to imagine a different way of inhabiting the body. Swain, "L'Ame, la femme," 107.

51. Harris, *Murders and Madness*, 36.

52. Swain, "L'Ame, la femme," 126.

53. Didi-Hubermann, *Invention de l'hystérie*; Showalter, *The Female Malady*.

54. AVP, D2 U8: 144.

55. For a longer discussion of this case, see Chapter 2.

56. It is interesting that Brouardel bases his concluding statement on physical symptoms: "In sum, [she] is a hysteric. She has sensory disturbances and disturbances in cutaneous sensitivity that leave no doubt in this regard."

57. Laqueur, "Bodies, Details."

58. Ibid., 177, 181–82.

59. AVP, D2 U8: 200. See Chapter 4.

60. Ibid.

61. Ibid.

62. *Gazette des Tribunaux*, Apr. 29, 1886.

63. AVP, D2 U8: 290, Blanche Bertal.

64. AVP, D2 U8: 148. June 27, 1883. A letter from the mayor of the commune where Marie Charrière was raised attested to the family's respectability and to the daughter's episodes of temporary insanity.

65. AVP, D2 U8: 266, Dec. 23, 1890.

66. Lacassagne, *Des transformations*.

67. According to Jan Goldstein, 14 percent of admissions to Salpêtrière were diagnosed as monomaniacs in 1850; this number declined to 10 percent in 1858; 8 percent in 1860; 2 percent in 1865; and none in 1870. Goldstein, *Console and Classify*, 191.

68. Dubuisson, "De l'évolution des opinions," 108–11; Falret, *De la responsabilité morale*; De Saussure, "The Influence," 379–82.

69. Berthier, *Des névroses*, 264.

70. Legrand du Saulle, *La Folie*, 563.

71. Tardieu, *Etude médico-légale*, 188.

72. Ibid., 190. In an interesting effort to qualify the impunity of the criminal pregnant woman, Emmanuel Lasserre provided a cautionary note that exemplifies the mixture of medical theory, moralism, and ideology that characterized so much of the writing about criminal women of this period. He wrote that "in general, whatever the state of nervous instability of the woman, whatever influence the womb exercises over the intellectual and moral faculties after conception, it repels us to believe that the sensitive and loving character becomes perverted and changes into cruelty." *Etude sur les cas de non-culpabilité*.

73. Courtis, *Etude médico-légale*, 157.

74. Imploring the criminal justice system to take account of the physical and moral tempests to which a woman was subject as a condition of her femaleness, he concluded, without irony, "if these principles constitute feminism, then feminism it is." Morache, *La Responsabilité criminelle*, 586.

75. Icard, *La Femme pendant*, 274.

76. For an extended discussion of theories of degeneracy see especially Har-

ris, *Murders and Madness*; Nye, *Crime, Madness and Politics*; and Pick, *Faces of Degeneration*.

77. Courtis, *Etude médico-légale*, 157. See especially Alexandre Paris for case histories that rehearse variations on this diagnosis: *La Folie des femmes*.

78. Portemer, *Les Erotomanes*, 87.

79. See especially Coutagne, *La Folie au point de vue judiciaire*; Icard, *La Femme pendant*; Paris, *La Folie des femmes*.

80. "Rapport Médico-légale."

81. Ibid., 251.

82. Ibid., 256.

83. Ibid., 257.

84. Ibid., 265.

85. Goldstein, *Console and Classify*, 162; Doerner, *Madness and the Bourgeoisie*, 151.

86. Doerner, *Madness and the Bourgeoisie*, 151.

87. Lasserre, *Etude sur les cas de non-culpabilité*, 213.

88. Harris, *Murders and Madness*, 158.

89. Legrand du Saulle, *Les Hystériques*, 483 (my emphasis).

90. Laurent, *L'Amour morbide*, 11.

91. Féré, *La Pathologie des émotions*, 479.

92. See especially Portemer, *Les Erotomanes*; Féré, *La Pathologie des émotions*; Laurent, *L'Amour morbide*; Lyon, *Responsabilité et paroxysme passionnel*; Lasserre, *Etude sur les cas de non-culpabilité*; Ball, *La Folie érotique*; Moreau de Tours, *La Folie jalouse*; Mairet, *La Jalousie*.

93. Cixous and Clément, *Newly Born Woman*, 8.

94. Ibid., 29. The double meaning is evident in French: *règle* translates as "rule"; *règles* translates as "menstrual period."

95. Harris, *Murders and Madness*, 171.

96. Harris, "Murder under Hypnosis." Harris notes that Charcot and the physicians at Salpêtrière regularly refused to acknowledge the implications of their work. While their demonstrations did seem to make hypnotized subjects into human automatons, the Salpêtrière school maintained, nevertheless, that some integral personality persisted in the trance condition, making hypnotized persons only passive participants in criminal activity.

97. For a useful discussion of the complexities of the controvery between Salpêtrière and Nancy physicians, see Harris, *Murders and Madness*, chap. 5.

98. See Jan Goldstein, *Console and Classify*, for a discussion of the political anticlericalism of late-nineteenth-century psychiatry.

99. Laurent, "Les Suggestions criminelles," 631.

100. Harris, *Murders and Madness*, 189.

101. Ibid., 437.

102. Zola, *Au Bonheur des Dames*, 23, 41, 116–17.

103. Lacaze, *De la criminalité féminine*, 66.

104. Nayrac, *Grandeur et misère de la femme*, 107–8.

105. Discussions of erotomania often gave examples of the obsessive worship of the Virgin by priests and, similarly, of women's excessive attachment to their priests. The disease was, in effect, clericalism. In evidence here is the attack on clericalism waged by psychiatrists at the end of the century that Jan Goldstein has discussed in "The Hysteria Diagnosis."

106. Portemer, *Les Erotomanes*, 175; Ball, *La Folie érotique*, 32.

107. Tardieu, *Etude médico-légale*, 171.

108. Ibid., 172.

109. Ibid.

110. Schwob, *Contribution à l'étude*, 72.

111. Proal, "L'Adultère de la femme."

112. Corbin, "Le 'Sexe en deuil,'" 144.

113. Ibid., 143–44. In his discussion of bourgeois male sexuality in nineteenth-century France, Robert Nye has pointed to the fact that male honor had come to be defined in terms of sexual potency and "reproductive fitness," making sexual excess, with its alleged dangers of eventual debility, all the more dangerous. Nye, "Honor, Impotence, and Male Sexuality."

114. Guéneau, "Erotisme et ménopause"; Laurent, *L'Amour morbide*.

115. Villermay, cited in Schwob, *Contribution à l'étude*, 70–71. For an intriguing discussion of a late eighteenth-century medical account of nymphomania see Livi, *Vapeurs de femmes*. Livi cites a similar pattern of temptation and struggle that propels the young woman from a simple attack of melancholia to uterine furor. The dangers included: the abuse of certain spices and aromatics, liqueurs, wines, coffee, chocolate; the reading of certain novels; lascivious painting and sculpture; licentious theater; obscene songs; and especially masturbation.

116. Legrand du Saulle, *Les Hystériques*, 450–51.

117. Many young women, especially those recently arrived in Paris in order to give birth away from their homes, do seem to have been unclear about the kinds of assistance available to them. For a fuller discussion of all of these issues, see Fuchs, *Poor and Pregnant*.

118. Ibid.

119. In crimes of passion, however, premeditation did not rule out a defense of temporary insanity provoked by a surge of emotion. See Chapter 4.

120. See AVP, D2 U8: 291, Anne Marie Ricoul, Oct. 14, 1891. See also Bouton, *L'Infanticide*.

121. Fuchs, *Poor and Pregnant*, 212–13.

122. AVP, D2 U8: 218, Apr. 7, 1887.

123. For a fuller discussion of the canonical nature of this story, see Chapter 4.

124. For similar cases, see AVP, D2 U8: 227, Marie Vasseur, Aug. 23, 1887;

D2 U8: 139, Elisa Bouvignies, Nov. 9, 1882; D2 U8: 48, Marie-Elise David, May 20, 1876.

125. Between 1862 and 1880, the acquittal rate for women tried for infanticide averaged 38 percent; by the turn of the century, half of all women tried were acquitted. And, when juries did convict, in nearly all cases they voted for extenuating circumstances that mitigated the penalty. Fuchs, *Poor and Pregnant*, 206.

126. Michel Foucault, "About the Concept," 17.

127. Goldstein, *Console and Classify*, 181, 183.

Chapter 4

1. Romi, *Histoire des faits divers*, 76.

2. Luhmann, *Love as Passion*, 20.

3. Ibid.

4. Guillais, *La Chair de l'autre*, 240. See also Ruth Harris, *Murders and Madness*.

5. Garçon, *La Justice contemporaine*, 629–30.

6. Monzie, *Le Jury contemporain*, 11.

7. Ibid., 14.

8. Adler, *Les Secrets d'alcove*, 164.

9. *Gazette des Tribunaux*, July 10, 1875.

10. *Faits divers . . . 1881*, 117–18.

11. Lachaud, quoted in Monzie, *Le Jury contemporain*, 17.

12. Guillais, *La Chair de l'autre*, 288–89, 304, 324.

13. Macé, *Un Cent-Garde*, 233. In the case of Blanche Béchard, the magistrate in charge of the pretrial investigation used the indictment to charge the accused with the crime of attempted homicide, but also to identify the criminal complicity of her victim: "One cannot ignore the fact that M. Longne, forgetting all his duties, left his mistress in the most complete [illegible], even though he knew that she was pregnant; he tried to attribute paternity to another man, he urged an abortion . . . [nevertheless], justice cannot leave unpunished an act forbidden in law." AVP, D2 U8: 245, Sept. 29, 1888.

14. Escoffier, *Les Crimes passionnels*, 5–7; Toulouse, *Les Conflits intersexuels*, 293.

15. McMillan, *Housewife or Harlot*, 17. According to the jurist Louis Proal, public opinion generally misunderstood the actual meaning of the legal excuse, a term of art that attenuated guilt but did not eliminate it. Proal, *Le Crime et le suicide passionnels*, 260.

16. Escoffier, *Les Crimes passionnels*, 6.

17. Ibid.

18. See Juratic, "Contraintes conjugales," 107, for a discussion of the differ-

ent social meanings attributed to male and female violence in the eighteenth century.

19. *Gazette des Tribunaux*, Feb. 23, 1887.

20. Macé, *Un Cent-Garde*, 233.

21. Escoffier, *Les Crimes passionnels*, 7.

22. See, for example, Holtz, *Les Crimes passionnels*; Aubry, "De l'homicide commis par la femme"; Proal, *Le Crime et le suicide passionnels*.

23. Proal, *Le Crime et le suicide passionnels*, 285. Emphasis appears in the original.

24. AVP, D2 U8: 185, July 4, 1885, Marie Couffin.

25. *Gazette des Tribunaux*, July 10, 1875.

26. Nye, *Masculinity*.

27. Joseph Sur, *Le Jury et les crimes passionnels*, 23.

28. Goron, *L'Amour à Paris*, 4.

29. Buguet and Benjamin, *Paris enragé*, 171. The ironic tone of this passage is evident in the French original, which relies on a pun on the word *enragé*: it refers either to someone afflicted with rabies or to someone overcome by passion.

30. Monzie, *Le Jury contemporain*, 12.

31. AVP, D2 U8: 144, Emile Perrin, Mar. 30, 1883.

32. AVP, D2 U8: 114, Mar. 8, 1881.

33. AVP, D2 U8: 164, Sept. 25, 1884.

34. See, for example, Tarde, "L'Amour morbide," 589; Proal, *Le crime et le suicide passionnels*; Laurent, *L'Amour morbide*.

35. Tarde, "L'Amour morbide," 593.

36. Proal, *Le Crime et le suicide passionnels*, ii.

37. Ibid., 106, 107.

38. BMD, Dossier: "Criminalité."

39. Granier, *La Femme criminelle*, 106. In a fascinating reprise of this argument, a recent study of crime in France (1959) argued that in male crimes of passion, defendants admit killing because they felt themselves ridiculous, while women admitted to panic that they had ceased to be pleasing or desirable. According to this study, both men and women experience a sense of falling status, but "the man doubts his power to dominate, the woman her ability to seduce." Dhavernas, "La Délinquance féminine," 79.

40. *Gazette des Tribunaux*, May 29, 1891.

41. Sighele, *Le Crime à deux*, 85.

42. Ernest-Charles, *Les Drames*, 190–91.

43. Ibid., 173.

44. Ferrero, "Le Mensonge," 148.

45. Zola, *La Bête humaine*, 149.

46. De Ryckère, *La Femme en prison*, 12.

47. Georges Macé wrote in *Mon Musée criminel*, for example, "What an unfortunate phenomenon, this woman Fenayrou, killing her lover with the same

ease that she deceived her husband, without knowing why! She is perhaps moved by curiosity, seeking sensations that she has not yet experienced."

48. De Ryckère, *La Femme en prison*, 18. Macé echoed these remarks, nearly to the word, *Mon Musée criminel*, 207–8, while Guillot (*Paris qui souffre*) concluded similarly that female prisoners were readily able to distinguish between those women who turned in their lovers for acceptable reasons and those who simply betrayed them.

49. Laurent, *L'Amour morbide*, 51.

50. Granier, *La Femme criminelle*, 219.

51. The discussion of crimes of passion in an evolutionary framework was particularly popular in the 1890s. See especially Courtis, *Etude médico-légale*, 12.

52. Gayot de Pitaval, *Causes célèbres et intéressantes*, 1740, cited in Juratic, "Contraintes conjugales et violences féminines," 104.

53. AVP, D2 U8: 114, 8 Mar. 1881.

54. Courtis, *Etude médico-légale*, preface.

55. AVP, D2 U8: 207, Oct. 6, 1886.

56. Ibid.

57. *Gazette des Tribunaux*, Oct. 6–7, 1886.

58. Ibid.

59. AVP, D2 U8: 122, Oct. 11, 1881.

60. *Gazette des Tribunaux*, Oct. 12, 1881.

61. In fact, the indictment makes no reference to Guillet's charges that Cattiaux took 100 francs from her without asking, was not working, and had lost 600 francs that she had lent him for a business venture.

62. *Gazette des Tribunaux*, Feb. 23, 1887.

63. AVP, D2 U8: 135, June 28, 1882.

64. AVP, D2 U8: 144, Mar. 29, 1883.

65. Proal, *Le Crime et le suicide passionnels*, 113.

66. Ibid., 110.

67. Ibid., 111.

68. Tarde, "A propos de deux beaux crimes," 462.

69. Robert, *Jane Daniloff*, 218.

70. AVP, D2 U8: 218, Apr. 7, 1887.

71. Aubry, "De l'homicide commis par la femme," 275.

72. Granier, *La Femme criminelle*, 158.

73. Proal, *Le crime et le suicide passionnels*, 121.

74. De Ryckère, *La Servante criminelle*, 194–95.

75. Aubry, "De l'homicide commis par la femme," 284. Again, it was the nature of the act and not the sex of the perpetrator that gendered a crime. The magistrate Escoffier, for example, narrated a case in which a man who feared abandonment by his lover lured his victim to a final rendezvous under the false pretext that he was contemplating suicide, and then killed her. Escoffier explained this homicide as an act precipitated by "the pure exaltation of a violent

and cruelly selfish temperament." Both the motives and the devious strategy, "aggravated by the ferocity of its execution," made this case, for Escoffier, a paradigm of the "perfidious character of a *feminine* crime" (my emphasis).

76. Du Camp, *Les Convulsions de Paris*, t. II, pp. 86-90, cited in Krakovitch, "Misogynes et féministes," 87. For a longer discussion of the links between genital disclosure and social danger, see Hertz, "Medusa's Head."

77. Aubry, "De l'homicide commis par la femme," 281.

78. See Harris, "Murder Under Hypnosis."

79. Sur, *Le Jury et les crimes passionnels*, 13.

80. Proal, *Le Crime et le suicide passionnels*, 288–89.

81. Aubry, "De l'homicide commis par la femme," 276.

82. AVP, D2 U8: 68, Dec. 14, 1877.

83. AVP, D2 U8: 176, Feb. 21, 1885. The documents compiled by the police include a full list of the household items that he sold or pawned and the money he raised, including a buffet, three chairs and a table (130 francs), a man's watch (180 francs), a man's overcoat, an armoire, a pair of pearl earrings, two armchairs (25 francs each), and a gun. It may even be the case that Bonnefous's careful account of her financial losses disqualified her act in the end as a crime of passion. She was condemned to two years in prison.

84. Eagleton, *Criticism and Ideology*, 102.

85. AVP, D2 U8: 122.

86. *Gazette des Tribunaux*, Sept. 29, 1881.

87. AVP, D2 U8: 122.

88. *Gazette des Tribunaux*, Sept. 29, 1881.

89. *La Lanterne*, Apr. 9, 1880.

90. Monzie, *Le Jury contemporain*, 20.

91. Ibid., 10. In thinking about these contradictions, Monzie wondered whether there were motives other than love (for example, political conviction), nobler if less universal ones, that ought equally to earn the jury's tolerance.

92. Ibid., 19–20.

93. Quoted in Berenson, "The Politics of Divorce," 51.

94. McBride, "Public Authority and Private Lives."

95. For a discussion of melodrama, see Brooks, *Melodramatic Imagination*, 11–12, 45.

96. Men were also held to precise readings of an implicit code. For example, the lawyer Joseph Sur warned against "false" crimes of passion in which a man killed because he felt mocked and humiliated, not out of "real" jealousy. Sur identified such cases as motivated by vanity, not love. Sur, *Le Jury et le crime passionnel*, 33.

97. When a prostitute attempted to attribute her violence to jealousy, for example, invoking the conventional formula, neither her victim nor the court personnel would take seriously such a claim.

98. See, for example, Macé, *La Femme criminelle*, 20–22.

99. *Gazette des Tribunaux*, June 30, 1878.

100. *Plaidoyers de Ch. Lachaud*, Affaire Thiébault, 98.

101. Ibid., Affaire de La Meilleraye, 325–26; second ellipsis in original.

102. In his study of the criminal jury, Maurice Garçon wrote, for example, that although jurors were lenient toward a murderer, they were severe on the subject of *moeurs*. Thus they might acquit a woman murderer who was jealous in a traditional way, but if the same crime, animated by the same motives, revealed the existence of "sexual depravity," the presumption of leniency would disappear. Garçon, *Le Jury criminel*, 630.

103. Farge, *La Vie fragile*, 41.

104. APP, BA 1612.

105. *Mot d'ordre*, Apr. 12, 1880.

106. *Gazette des Tribunaux*, Sept. 16, 1881.

107. AVP, D2 U8: 285, Marie Croissant, Oct. 26, 1891.

108. AVP, D2 U8: 245, Sept. 29, 1888.

109. For an extended discussion of these issues, see Fuchs, *Poor and Pregnant*, especially chapter 3.

110. Various proposals to modify Article 340 were introduced into the legislature between 1901 and 1910 amid fierce controversy, until the eventual enactment of new legislation in 1912. The new statute listed the specific conditions in which women could pursue the putative father for child support and also identified the limits of this pursuit. In effect, women who could show that the man had promised marriage or had demonstrated paternity in any way, including living with the mother in consensual union at the time of conception, could seek support. The carefully negotiated terms of the law meant that married men remained free of responsibility for their out-of-wedlock children.

111. Strauss, as quoted in Fuchs, *Poor and Pregnant*, 69.

112. AVP, D2 U8: 227, Aug. 23, 1887.

113. Métayer, "La Leçon de l'héroine," 39. For an interesting discussion of melodrama and the woman question in England, see Crosby, *The Ends of History*.

114. Métayer, "La leçon de l'héroine," 44.

115. *Plaidoyers de Ch. Lachaud*, Affaire Marie Bière, 458. The emphasis is mine.

116. Walkowitz, "Melodrama and Victorian Political Culture."

117. *Le Palais de Justice*, 270.

118. Juries were not supposed to consider the consequences of their verdicts, but it was more typically the case that the implications of the verdict weighed heavily with the jury, especially in crimes of passion.

119. Guillot, *Le Jury et les moeurs*, 22–23; Morand, *De l'application des peines*, 29.

120. Escoffier, *Les Crimes passionnels*, 12.

121. Garçon, *La Justice contemporaine*, 628.

122. Sur, *Le Jury et les crimes passionnels*, 13.

123. Guillot, *Le Jury et les moeurs*, 15.

124. The words are those of Garçon in *La Justice contemporaine*, 626.

125. Escoffier, *Les Crimes passionnels*, 8; Courtis, *Etude médico-légale*, 56.

126. Escoffier, *Les Crimes passionnels*, 11.

127. Holtz, *Les Crimes passionnels*, 22.

128. Bourget, *Physiologie de l'amour moderne*, 317.

129. See, for example: Moreau de Tours, *De la contagion*; Aubry, *La Contagion du meurtre*.

130. Reibrach, "Le Poison," 150–71.

131. Puibaraud, *La Femme criminelle*, 407.

132. In the words of Henry Buguet and Edmond Benjamin, "Customs have changed, things have progressed. Henceforward, when the church organ emits its joyous sounds as the Don Juan puts an end to his career in marrying the daughter of a rich chocolatier, Ariane waits at the exit with her small bowl of vitriol, ready to hurl it at his head. . . . The drama ends in the Cour d'Assises where the judges, always gallant, acquit the young woman who sustained this vengeful fury." Buguet and Benjamin, *Paris enragé*, 163.

133. Rabinowicz, *Le Crime passionnel*, 138–39.

134. For a comprehensive exploration of the significance of this case, see Berenson, *The Trial*.

135. Ibid., 27.

136. Pagnat, *Enquête*.

137. Such *enquêtes* could be surveys of popular opinion, but they were also discussions carried on within elites that sought to create, rather than reflect, public opinion.

138. Pagnat, *Enquête*, 30–31. In his own terms, he saw himself as providing a forum for a wide range of perspectives, including the clinical approach of doctors, the familialist perspective of sociologists, that of novelists and dramatists who "cultivated bohemian excess," and the administrative perspective of legislators interested in social order.

Chapter 5

1. Barthes, *Eiffel Tower*; Silverman, *Art Nouveau*, 2–4.

2. Nye, *Masculinity*, 154.

3. Klejman and Rochefort, *L'Egalité en marche*, 82–83; Moses, *French Feminism*, 221–22. Paris in 1889 was also the site of the Socialist Workers' International.

4. Deraismes, *Eve contre M. Dumas*, 70–71.

5. Marcil, *Les Femmes qui écrivent*, 5.

6. Klejman and Rochefort, *L'Egalité en marche*, 58.

7. Steven Hause and Anne Kenney make a similar point in their study of

women's suffrage in the Third Republic. They note that "there was a startling similarity to the theories of Catholics, socialists, and radicals. . . . Conservative attitudes about the woman question girded radical ideology just as it did Catholic and socialist thought." Hause and Kenney, *Women's Suffrage and Social Politics,* 278, 281.

8. Jones, *Women Who Kill,* 14.

9. Lucien LeFoyer, cited in Granotier, *L'Autorité de mari,* 42.

10. Krakovitch, "Misogynes et féministes," 90. By the end of the same year, two anonymous pamphlets appeared: *Le Mal qu'on a dit des femmes* and *Le Bien qu'on a dit des femmes.* Within a year *Le Mal* had undergone five editions while the more benign pamphlet remained in its first edition.

11. Dumas fils, *L'Homme-Femme,* 171, 176.

12. Deraismes, *Eve contre M. Dumas,* 25–26. This pamphlet was reprinted three times in 1872.

13. See especially Moses, *French Feminism;* Hause and Kenney, *Women's Suffrage and Social Politics;* Sowerwine, *Sisters or Citizens;* Offen, "Depopulation, Nationalism, and Feminism."

14. Terrisse, *Notes et impressions.*

15. Granotier, *L'Autorité de mari,* 42, 45.

16. Silverman, *Art Nouveau,* 65.

17. Ibid., 66. Between 1885 and 1900, the number of *lycée* degrees increased from 4,300 to 13,000. In the 1890s women entered the institutions of male higher education; in 1895 there were 842 women attending the facultés; 20 female doctors and 10 lawyers completed degrees in the 1890s.

18. Agulhon, *Marianne into Battle,* 184.

19. Ducreux, *Les Droits de la femme,* 46.

20. Krug, *Le Féminisme,* 6.

21. Toulouse, *Les Conflits intersexuels,* 4.

22. Even feminists worried about the implications of political rights for women. Léon Richer wrote, for example, that "out of nine million women who have reached their majority, only several thousand would vote freely; the remainder would take their orders from the confessional." Quoted in Hause and Kenney, *Women's Suffrage,* 17.

23. Saleilles, *L'Initiative de la femme.*

24. Thulié, *La Femme,* 458. In fact, the claim to superiority in difference was one that appealed to some feminists as well as to their detractors.

25. Roger-Milès, *Nos Femmes et nos enfants.* The cover of this edition depicts a well-dressed woman wrapped in a snake.

26. Offen, "Depopulation, Nationalism, and Feminism."

27. Sée, quoted in Rabaut, *Histoire des féminismes français,* 182.

28. For extensive information on the details of Chauvin's career see the Dossier Chauvin, BMD.

29. *Eclair*, Nov. 17, 1900.

30. Ravail, *La Femme et le barreau*, 46. For another discussion of Chauvin's case, see Frank, *La Femme-avocat*.

31. Ravail, *La Femme et la barreau*, 48. There were other men who similarly exposed the self-serving rhetoric and disingenuousness of their peers. In one of the most forceful examples of straight talk, one lawyer dubbed efforts to restrict opportunities for women as "a monopoly organized against competition." Speaking to the assembled lawyers at the opening of court sessions in Marseille in 1898, he claimed that "the most honest of us will admit our worries about the overcrowding of the liberal professions." He insisted on the hypocrisy of protective and restrictive legislation which left Man dreaming of the charm, delicacy and gentleness of Woman, a fragile flower broken by the slightest breeze, while women, for whom no domestic work was too disgusting, were denied access to the medical profession. Eymin, *L'Emancipation des Femmes*.

32. Ravail, *La Femme et la barreau*, 54.

33. BMD, Dossier Chauvin.

34. Chauvin, *Conférence sur le féminisme*.

35. Chéliga, "Craintes puériles," 8–9.

36. Foucault, ed., *Herculine Barbin*. Robert Nye has also observed that "until recently in European society, charivaris enacted boisterous shaming rituals to reprove nagging or domineering women, hen-pecked or cuckolded husbands, by recalling to them, and to the whole community, their 'true' sex, thus setting right a world which inappropriate behavior threatened to turn upside down." Nye, *Masculinity*, 6.

37. Chevalier, *L'Inversion sexuelle*, 374.

38. Silverman, *Art Nouveau*, 66.

39. Marius-Ary Leblond as quoted in Silverman, *Art Nouveau*, 70.

40. "Feminism," by Albert Delvallé, *Le Petit Journal*, Dec. 31, 1899.

41. Chevalier, "De l'inversion sexuelle," 500–501.

42. Berenson, *The Trial*; Nye, *Masculinity*.

43. Vuillermet, *Soyez des hommes*, quoted in Berenson, *The Trial*, 190.

44. Ernest Lavisse, quoted in Nye, *Masculinity*, 154.

45. Berenson, *The Trial*, 192.

46. Fauquez, *La Bicyclette*, 5.

47. Sarah Bernhardt, quoted in de Loris, *La Femme à Bicyclette*, 32.

48. Pelletier, *Les Femmes en lutte*, 39, 49.

49. Thulié, *La Femme*, 236.

50. Taxil, *La Corruption*, 246.

51. Chevalier, *L'Inversion sexuelle*, 218.

52. Chevalier, "De l'inversion sexuelle," 501.

53. Chevalier, *L'Inversion sexuelle*, 219.

54. Chevalier, "De l'inversion sexuelle," 502.

55. He attributes this revolution to the education of women in the middle and upper classes and to the need to earn a living among the working classes.

56. Deraismes, *Eve contre M. Dumas*, 60.

57. Lourbet, *Le Problème des sexes*, 293.

58. Bourgas, *Le Droit à l'amour*, 23–24.

59. See Scott, "Women Who Have Only Paradoxes To Offer," for an extended discussion of the ways French feminists negotiated through the contradictory implications of the discourse of rights in the period 1789–1945.

60. Ducreux, *Les Droits de la femme*, 55.

61. Roger-Milès, *Nos femmes et nos enfants*, 10–11.

62. Fouquier, *La Sagesse parisienne*, 11. Some of the essays are written as if by a woman.

63. Bourgas, *Le Droit à l'amour*, 86. See also Berenson, *The Trial*, 131.

64. Bourgas, *Le Droit à l'amour*, 3, 7, 102.

65. Corbin, "Le 'Sexe en deuil.'" An interesting example of the biases of the sources is evident in the pamphlet *La Femme-homme*, written anonymously in response to Dumas. The author writes at some length of the fact that men must learn to satisfy their wives sexually, especially when the women are between 25 and 45 years old. The possibility of passionate, erotic feeling in women before or after these ages is explicitly denied. The putative author of this tract is a woman. Nevertheless, throughout this period, books actually authored by men were frequently presented as "from a woman's point of view," after the author had engaged in "numerous conversations with women." In this case, Odile Krakovitch has speculated that the author might be J. Bédarride, a lawyer, who wrote an introductory letter to the text.

66. Corbin, "Le 'Sexe en Deuil,'" 143–44.

67. Nye, "Honor, Impotence, and Male Sexuality," 64.

68. Waelti-Walters, *Feminist Novelists*, 31, 177.

69. Marcil, *Les Femmes qui écrivent*, 45.

70. Deraismes, *Eve contre M. Dumas*, 50.

71. Pelletier, *L'Emancipation sexuelle*, 39.

72. Doane and Hodges, *Nostalgia and Sexual Difference*, 7.

73. Berenson, *The Trial*, 154–56.

74. Le Roux, *Un Homme qui comprend les femmes*. In using the French phrase, Le Roux makes reference to the grievance lists submitted by all of the different constituencies throughout France on the eve of the French Revolution.

75. Ibid., 251.

76. Ibid., 264.

77. Nye, *Masculinity*, 119; Mauge, *L'Identité masculine*.

78. Desmaze, *Le Crime et le débauche à Paris*.

79. Corre, *Crime et suicide*, 270.

80. BMD, Dossier Amour-Psychologie, E. Philippe, "L'Amour qui tue," 1899.

81. BMD, Dossier Amour-Psychologie.

82. Dumas fils, *Les Femmes qui tuent*, 20–23.

83. Ibid., 23.

84. Ibid., 78.

85. Ibid., 140–41.

86. Ibid., 111–12. In 1895, shortly before his death, Dumas sent a letter to Marya Chéliga, which she subsequently published, in which he acknowledged that he had changed his mind and had come to support identical rights for women and men. Chéliga noted that feminists followed his coffin with tears in their eyes, mourning the loss of a friend. "Alexandre Dumas fils et le féminisme," 264–71.

87. Levinck, *Les Femmes qui ne tuent*, 2, 135.

88. Lesueur, *L'Evolution féminine*. Daniel Lesueur was the pen name of Jeanne Loiseau, Mme Henri Lapauze, who was the first woman to be awarded the Légion d'Honneur for literature by the French Academy.

89. Terrisse, *Notes et impressions*.

90. Ibid., chapter 3.

91. Ibid., 123.

92. Adler, *Les Secrets d'alcove*, 165.

93. Pelletier, cited in Berenson, *The Trial*, 121.

94. Granier, *La Femme criminelle*, 200.

95. De Lorde, *Théâtre de la Peur*.

96. Talmeyr, "Le Roman-feuilleton," 223.

97. Bouton, *L'Infanticide*, 173; Monzie, *Le Jury contemporain*.

98. Gaston Jollivet, "Si j'étais juré," *Le Fronde*, Nov. 12, 1901.

99. Ibid. In an effort to realign the popular balance of sympathy, Jollivet argued that the "moral disaster" that befell men deceived by their wives—the horrible doubt about paternity—was, in fact, considerably greater than the misery sustained by wives whose husbands had affairs.

100. Henri Rochefort, "Les Scélérates," *L'Intransigeant*, June 7, 1891.

101. Schaefer, "Children in Moral Danger." See also Donzelot, *The Policing of Families*.

102. Henry Fouquier, "Les Femmes qui tuent," *Le Journal*, Aug. 2, 1901.

103. Nye, "Honor, Impotence, and Male Sexuality"; Offen, "Depopulation."

104. Offen, "Depopulation," 655.

105. Agulhon, *Marianne into Battle*, 164–65.

WORKS CITED

Archival Sources

Archives de la Préfecture de Police, Paris
    BA 127: Congrès international des Œuvres et Institutions féminines
    BA 1165: Dossier Macé
    BA 1612: Dossier Marie Bière
Archives de la Ville de Paris et du Département de la Seine
    Série D2 U8
Bibliothèque Marguerite Durand, Paris
    Dossier Amour-Psychologie
    Dossier Chauvin
    Dossier Criminalité
Journals
    Annales médico-psychologiques
    Archives d'anthropologie criminelle
    Bulletin de la Société générale des prisons
    Grande revue
    Journal de la Société de statistique de Paris
    Revue des Deux Mondes
    Revue encyclopédique
    Revue féministe
Newspapers
    Gazette des Tribunaux
    L'Illustration
    Le Journal illustré
    Le Petit Journal
    Le Petit Parisien

Books and Articles

Abelson, Elaine. *When Ladies Go A-Thieving: Middle-class Shoplifters in Victorian Department Stores.* Oxford: Oxford University Press, 1989.

Adler, Laura. *Les Secrets d'alcove: Histoire du couple de 1830–1930.* Paris: Hachette Littérature, 1983.

Agulhon, Maurice. *Marianne into Battle: Republican Imagery and Symbolism in France 1789–1880.* Cambridge: Cambridge University Press, 1981.

Allen, Hilary. "At the Mercy of Her Hormones: Premenstrual Tension and the Law." *m/f* (1984): 19–44.

Allen, James Smith. *In the Public Eye: A History of Reading in Modern France, 1800–1940.* Princeton: Princeton University Press, 1991.

Amaury, Francine. *Histoire du plus grand quotidien de la IIIème République: Le Petit Parisien, 1876–1944.* Vol. 2. Paris: Presse Universitaire de France, 1972.

Armstrong, Nancy. *Desire and Domestic Fiction: A Political History of the Novel.* New York: Oxford University Press, 1986.

Aron, Jean-Paul, ed. *Misérable et glorieuse: La femme du XIXème siècle.* Paris: Fayard, 1980.

Aubry, Paul. *La Contagion du meurtre: Etude d'anthropologie criminelle.* Paris: F. Alcan, 1894.

———. "De l'homicide commis par la femme: Etude médico-légale." *Archives d'anthropologie criminelle* 6 (1891): 266–87.

———. "De l'influence contagieuse de la publicité des faits criminels." *Archives d'anthropologie criminelle* 8 (1893): 565–80.

Ball, Benjamin. *La Folie érotique.* Paris: J.-B. Baillière, 1888.

———. *La Médecine mentale à travers les siècles.* Paris: Asselin et Cie., 1879.

Baradez, M. L. *L'Anthropologie criminelle et le roman*, discours prononcé . . . pour l'audience solonnelle de Rentrée du 16 octobre 1895, Cour d'Appel de Nancy. Nancy: Vagner, 1895.

Barrows, Susanna. *Distorting Mirrors: Visions of the Crowd in Late Nineteenth-Century France.* New Haven: Yale University Press, 1981.

Barthes, Roland. *Critical Essays.* Trans. Richard Howard. Evanston, Ill.: Northwestern University Press, 1972.

———. *The Eiffel Tower and Other Mythologies.* Trans. Richard Howard. New York: Hill and Wang, 1978.

Beauvoir, Simone de. *The Second Sex.* Trans. H. M. Parshley. New York: Random House, 1952.

Benoit, Dr. Georges. *De l'empoisonnement criminel en général.* Lyon: A. Storck, 1888.

Bérard de Glajeux, Anatole. *Souvenirs d'un Président d'assises (1880–1890).* Vol. 1. Paris: E. Plon, Nourrit et Cie, 1892–93.

Berenson, Edward. "The Politics of Divorce in France of the Belle Epoque: The

Case of Joseph and Henriette Caillaux." *American Historical Review* 93.1 (1988): 31–55.

———. *The Trial of Madame Caillaux*. Berkeley: University of California Press, 1992.

Berrios, G. E. "Obsessional Disorders during the Nineteenth Century: Terminological and Classificatory Issues." In W. F. Bynum, Roy Porter, and Michael Shepherd, eds., *Anatomy of Madness: Essays in the History of Psychiatry*. Vol. 1. London: Tavistock Publications, 1985.

Berthier, Pierre. *Des névroses menstruelles ou la menstruation dans ses rapports avec les maladies nerveuses et mentales*. Paris: A. Delahaye, 1874.

Borie, Jean. "Une gynécologie passionnée." In Jean-Paul Aron, ed., *Misérable et glorieuse: La femme du XIXème siécle*. Paris: Fayard, 1980.

Bourgas, Dr. Michel. *Le Droit à l'amour pour la femme*. Paris: Vigot Frères, 1914.

Bourget, Paul. *Physiologie de l'amour moderne*. Paris: Lemerre, 1891.

Bouton, Réné. *L'Infanticide: Etude morale et juridique*. Paris: Société des Editions Scientifiques, 1897.

Brierre de Boismont, A. F. J. "De la folie puerpérale." *Annales médico-psychologiques* (1851).

———. *De la menstruation; considérée dans ses rapports physiologiques et psychologiques*. Paris: Baillière, 1842.

Brooks, Peter. *The Melodramatic Imagination*. New Haven: Yale University Press, 1976.

Brunetière, Ferdinand. *Questions de critique*. Paris: Calman Lévy, 1897.

Buguet, Henry, and Edmond Benjamin. *Paris enragé*. Paris: Jules Lévy, 1886.

Bynum, W. F., Roy Porter, and Michael Shepherd, eds. *Anatomy of Madness: Essays in the History of Psychiatry*. Vol. 1. London: Tavistock, 1985.

Caignart de Mailly, M. P. *L'Evolution de l'idée criminaliste au XIXème siècle et ses conséquences*. Paris: Société d'économie sociale, 1898.

Cambréal, André. *Le Jury criminel: Comment se forme, délibère et statue le jury de la Cour d'assises*. 1937.

Cawelti, John G. *Adventure, Mystery, and Romance: Formula Stories as Art and Popular Culture*. Chicago: University of Chicago Press, 1976.

Charpentier, Réné. *Les Empoisonneuses: Etude psychologique et médico-légale*. Paris: G. Steinheil, 1906.

Chauvin, Jeanne. *Conférence sur le féminisme en France*. Salle du Glove, March 23, 1898.

Chéliga, Marya. "Alexandre Dumas fils et le féminisme." *Revue féministe* 1 (1895): 264–71.

———. "Craintes puériles." *Revue féministe* 1 (1895): 8–9.

Chesnais, Jean-Claude. *Histoire de la violence en Occident de 1800 à nos jours*. Paris: Editions Robert Laffont, 1981.

Chevalier, Dr. Julien. "De l'inversion sexuelle aux points de vue clinique, anthropologique et médico-légale." *Archives d'anthropologie criminelle* 6 (1891): 500–505.

———. *"L'Inversion sexuelle: Une maladie de la personalité.* Lyon: Storck, 1893.

Chevalier, Louis. *Laboring Classes and Dangerous Classes in Paris During the First Half of the Nineteenth Century.* Trans. Frank Jellinek. Princeton: Princeton University Press, 1973.

Cixous, Hélène, and Catherine Clément. *The Newly Born Woman.* Trans. Betsy Wing. Minneapolis: University of Minnesota Press, 1986.

Compte général de l'administration de la justice criminelle. Annuaire statistique. 1880, 1900.

Corbin, Alain. "Commercial Sexuality in Nineteenth-Century France: A System of Images and Regulations." In Catherine Gallagher and Thomas Laqueur, eds., *The Making of the Modern Body.* Berkeley: University of California Press, 1987.

———. "Le 'Sexe en deuil' et l'histoire des femmes au XIXème siècle." In Michelle Perrot, ed., *Une Histoire des femmes, est-elle possible?* Paris: Rivages, 1984.

Corre, Dr. A. *Crime et suicide: Etiologie générale, facteurs individuels, sociologiques et cosmiques.* Paris: Octave Doin, 1891.

Courtis, Hélie. *Etude médico-légale des crimes passionnels.* Toulouse: Dirion, 1910.

Coutagne, J.-P. *La Folie au point de vue judiciaire et administrative: Leçons faites à la Faculté de Droit de Lyon.* Lyon: A. Storck, 1889.

Crosby, Christina. *The Ends of History: The Victorians and "the Woman Question."* New York: Routledge, 1991.

Cruppi, Jean. *La Cour d'assises.* Paris: Calman Lévy, 1895.

Dallemagne, Jules. *Les Théories de la criminalité.* Paris: Masson et Cie, 1896.

Dartigues, J.-P. *De l'amour experimental ou des causes d'adultère chez la femme au XIXème siècle: Etude d'hygiène et d'économie sociale.* Versailles: A. Litzellmann, 1887.

Dauby, Edouard. *Quelques considérations sur la menstruation dans ses rapports avec la folie.* Paris: Collection des thèses à la Faculté de Médecine de Paris, 1866.

Davidson, Cathy. *Revolution and the Word.* New York: Oxford University Press, 1986.

Davis, Natalie Z. *Fiction in the Archives: Pardon Tales and Their Tellers in Sixteenth-Century France.* Stanford: Stanford University Press, 1987.

———. *Society and Culture in Early Modern France.* Stanford: Stanford University Press, 1975.

Deraismes, Maria. *Eve contre Monsieur Dumas fils.* Paris: E. Dentu, 1872.

Desmaze, Charles. *Le Crime et le débauche à Paris. Le Divorce.* Paris: G. Charpentier, 1881.

Dhavernas, Mary-Jo. "La Délinquance des femmes." *Questions féministes* 4 (Nov. 1978).

Didi-Hubermann, Georges. *L'Invention de l'hystérie: Charcot et l'iconographie photographique de la Salpêtrière*. Paris: Macula, 1982.

Doane, Janice, and Devon Hodges. *Nostalgia and Sexual Difference: The Resistance to Contemporary Feminism*. New York: Methuen, 1987.

Doerner, Klaus. *Madness and the Bourgeoisie: A Social History of Insanity and Psychiatry*. Trans. Joachim Neugroschel and Jean Steinberg. Oxford: Basil Blackwell, 1981.

Donzelot, Jacques. *The Policing of Families*. Trans. Robert Hurley. New York: Pantheon, 1979.

Dubuisson, Paul. "De l'évolution des opinions en matière de responsabilité." *Archives d'anthropologie criminelle* (1887).

Dubuisson, Paul, and A. Vigouroux, *Responsabilité pénale et folie. Etude médico-légale*. Paris: F. Alcan, 1911.

Ducreux, Camille. *Les Droits de la femme dans la société française*. Paris: Alcan-Lévy, 1898.

Dumas fils, Alexandre. *Les Femmes qui tuent et les femmes qui votent*. Paris: Ch. Lévy, 1880.

———. *L'Homme-femme*. Paris: Michel-Lévy, 1872.

Dupré, Ernest. *Définition médico-légale de l'aliéné: Leçon de l'ouverture du Cours de psychiatrie médico-légale*. Paris: Impr. de J. Gainche, 1904.

Dupré, Ernest, and Réné Charpentier. "Les Empoisonneurs: Etude historique, psychologique et médico-légale." *Archives d'anthropologie criminelle* 24 (1909).

Eagleton, Terry. *Criticism and Ideology: A Study in Marxist Literary Theory*. London: Verso, 1978.

Ellman, Richard, and Charles Fiedelson, eds. *The Modern Tradition*. New York: Oxford University Press, 1965.

Ernest-Charles, J. *Les Drames de la possession amoureuse*. Paris: Ernest Flammarion, 1925.

Escoffier, Paul. *Les Crimes passionnels devant le jury*. Orléans: Imprimerie de Georges Jacob, 1891.

Esquirol, J. E. D. *Des maladies mentales*. Vol. 1. Paris, 1838.

Eymin, Alexandre. *L'Emancipation des Femmes*. Marseille: Barlatier, 1898.

Faits divers: Crimes, délits, accidents de l'année 1881. Paris: Jules Rouff, 1882.

Faits divers: Crimes, délits, accidents de l'année 1882. Paris: Jules Rouff, 1883.

Le Fait Divers. Musée National des arts et traditions populaires. Catalogue. Exposition de 19 novembre 1982–18 avril 1983. Paris: Editions de la Réunion des Musées Nationaux, 1982.

Falret, Jules. *De la responsabilité morale et de la responsabilité légale des aliénés*. Paris: Impr. de E. Martinet, 1863.

Farge, Arlette. *La Vie fragile: Violence, pouvoirs et solidarités au XVIIIème siècle*. Paris: Hachette, 1986.

Fauquez, Dr. *La Bicyclette au point de vue de la femme*. Clermont: Daix Frères, 1897.

Féré, Charles. *La Pathologie des émotions: Etudes physiologiques et cliniques*. Paris: F. Alcan, 1892.

Ferrero, G. "Le Mensonge et la veracité chez la femme criminelle." *Archives d'anthropologie criminelle* 8 (1893).

Forster, Robert, and Orest Ranum, eds. *Deviants and the Abandoned in French Society: Selections from the Annales*. Baltimore: The Johns Hopkins University Press, 1978.

Foucault, Michel. "About the Concept of the 'Dangerous Individual' in Nineteenth-Century Legal Psychiatry." Trans. Alain Baudot and Jand Couchman. *International Journal of Law and Psychiatry* 1 (1978): 1–18.

———. *Discipline and Punish*. Trans. Alan Sheridan. New York: Random House, 1977.

———. *Madness and Civilization*. Trans. Richard Howard. New York: Vintage, 1973.

———, ed. *Herculine Barbin, being the recently discovered memoirs of a nineteenth-century French hermaphrodite*. New York: Pantheon, 1980.

———, ed. *I, Pierre Rivière, having slaughtered my mother, my sister and my brother . . .* Trans. Frank Jellinek. New York: Random House, 1975.

Fouquet, Catherine. "Le Détour obligé ou l'Histoire des femmes passe-t-elle par celle de leur corps?" In Michelle Perrot, ed., *Une Histoire des femmes: Est-elle possible?* Paris: Rivages, 1984.

Fouquier, Henry. *La Sagesse parisienne; paradoxes féminins*. Paris: Victor-Havard, 1886.

Frank, Louis. *La Femme-avocat: Exposé historique et critique de la question*. Paris: V. Giard et E. Brière, 1898.

Fuchs, Rachel. *Poor and Pregnant in Paris: Strategies for Survival in the Nineteenth Century*. New Brunswick, N.J.: Rutgers University Press, 1992.

Gallagher, Catherine, and Thomas Laqueur, eds., *The Making of the Modern Body*. Berkeley: University of California Press, 1987.

Garçon, Emile. *Du crime dans ses rapports avec l'art dramatique et la littérature*. Discours prononcé à l'Université de Paris, Faculté de Droit, 1922.

Garçon, Maurice. *La Justice contemporaine, 1870–1910*. Paris: Bernard Grasset, 1932.

Gautier, Emile. "Le Monde des Prisons (Notes d'un témoin)." *Archives d'anthropologie criminelle* 3 (1888).

Gelfand, Elissa. *Imagination in Confinement: Women's Writings from French Prisons*. Ithaca: Cornell University Press, 1983.

Goimard, Jacques. "Quelques structures formelles du roman feuilleton." *Europe* 542 (June 1974).

Goldstein, Jan. *Console and Classify: The French Psychiatric Profession in the Nineteenth Century*. Cambridge, Eng.: Cambridge University Press, 1987.

————. "The Hysteria Diagnosis and the Politics of Anti-Clericalism in Late Nineteenth-Century France." *Journal of Modern History* 54 (June 1982): 209–39.

Goron, Marie François. *L'Amour à Paris*. Paris: Jules Rouff et Cie, 1899.

Granier, Camille. *La Femme criminelle*. Paris: Octave Doin, 1906.

Granotier, Paul. *L'Autorité de mari sur la personne de la femme et la doctrine féministe*. Thèse pour le doctorat. Paris: V. Giard & E. Brière, 1909.

Grisson, Georges. *Paris horrible et Paris original*. Paris: E. Dentu, 1882.

Guéneau, Dr. Noel. "Erotisme et ménopause." *Annales médico-psychologiques* (1875).

Guillais, Joëlle. *La Chair de l'autre: Le crime passionnel au XIXème siècle*. Paris: Olivier Orban, 1986.

Guillot, Adolphe. *Le Jury et les moeurs*. Paris: Imprimerie de Chais, 1885.

————. *Paris qui souffre: Les prisons de Paris et les prisonniers*. Paris: E. Dentu, 1890.

Gullickson, Gay. "The Unruly Woman of the Paris Commune." In Dorothy O. Helly and Susan Reverby, eds., *Gendered Domains: Rethinking Public and Private in Women's History*. Ithaca: Cornell University Press, 1992.

Harris, Ruth. *Murders and Madness: Medicine, Law, and Society in the fin-de-siècle*. Oxford: Oxford University Press, 1989.

————. "Murder Under Hypnosis in the Case of Gabrielle Bompard: Psychiatry in the Belle Epoque Courtroom." In W. F. Bynum, R. Porter, and M. Shepherd, eds., *The Anatomy of Madness*, vol. 2. London: Tavistock Publications, 1988.

Hause, Steven, and Anne Kenney. *Women's Suffrage and Social Politics in the French Third Republic*. Princeton: Princeton University Press, 1984.

Hay, Douglas, et al., eds. *Albion's Fatal Tree: Crime and Society in Eighteenth Century England*. New York: Pantheon, 1975.

Helly, Dorothy O., and Susan Reverby, eds. *Gendered Domains: Rethinking Public and Private in Women's History*. Ithaca: Cornell University Press, 1992.

Hertz, Neil. "Medusa's Head: Male Hysteria under Political Pressure." *Representations* 4 (Fall 1983): 27–54.

Holtz, Louis. *Les Crimes passionnels*. Paris: Imprimerie A. Mellottée, 1904.

Hunt, Lynn, ed. *The New Cultural History*. Berkeley: University of California Press, 1989.

Icard, Dr. Séverin. *De la contagion du crime et du suicide par la presse*. Paris: Edition de la Nouvelle Revue, 1902.

————. *La Femme pendant la periode menstruelle*. Paris: F. Alcan, 1890.

Institut Général psychologique, section de psychologie morale et criminelle, Délibération sur l'action de la presse en matière de criminalité, Paris, 1910.

Jones, Ann. *Women Who Kill*. New York: Fawcett Crest, 1980.

Juratic, Sabine. "Contraintes conjugales et violences féminines: Epouses meurtrières au XVIIIème siècle." *Pénélope* (1986).

Kayser, Jacques. *Le Quotidien français*. Paris: A. Colin, 1963.

Klejman, Laurence, and Florence Rochefort. *L'Egalité en marche: Le féminisme sous la Troisième République*. Paris: Des Femmes, 1989.

Krakovitch, Odile. "Misogynes et féministes, il y a cent ans (I)." *Questions féministes* 8 (May 1980): 85–113.

Krug, Charles. *Le Féminisme et le droit civil français*. Thèse pour le doctorat, Faculté de Droit, Nancy, 1899.

Lacassagne, A. *Des transformations du droit pénal et les progrès de la médecine légale de 1810–1912*. Lyon: A. Rey, 1913.

Lacaze, Charles. *Des enquêtes officieuses et des officiers de police judiciaire qui y procèdent*. Toulouse, 1910.

Lacaze, Henri. *De la criminalité féminine en France. Etude statistique et médico-légale*. Lyon: Impr. de la Revue judiciaire, 1910.

Lailler, Maurice, and Henri Vonoven. *Les Erreurs judiciaires et leurs causes*. Paris: A. Pedone, 1897.

Landes, Joan. *Woman and the Public Sphere in the Age of the French Revolution*. Ithaca: Cornell University Press, 1988.

Laqueur, Thomas. "Bodies, Details, and the Humanitarian Narrative." In Lynn Hunt, ed., *The New Cultural History*. Berkeley: University of California Press, 1989.

———. *Making Sex: Body and Gender from the Greeks to Freud*. Cambridge, Mass.: Harvard University Press, 1990.

Lasserre, Emmanuel. *Etude sur les cas de non-culpabilité et les excuses en matière pénale*. Toulouse: Impr. de Mannal et Gibrac, 1877.

Laurent, Emile. *L'Amour morbide: Etude de psychologie pathologique*. Paris: Société d'éditions scientifiques, 1891.

———. "Les Suggestions criminelles." *Archives d'anthropologie criminelle* 5 (1890).

"Legal Storytelling." *Michigan Law Review* (August 1989).

Legrand du Saulle, Henri. *La Folie devant les tribunaux*. Paris: F. Savy, 1864.

———. *Les Hystériques: Etat physique et mental, actes insolites, délictueux et criminels*. Paris: J. B. Baillière, 1883.

Le Roux, Hugues. *Un Homme qui comprend les femmes*. Paris: Albert Mericaut, 1911.

Lesueur, Daniel. *L'Evolution féminine: Ses résultats économiques*. Paris, 1905.

Levin, Miriam. *When the Eiffel Tower Was New: French Visions of Progress at the Centennial of the Revolution*. Amherst: University of Massachusetts Press, 1989.

Levinck, Anna. *Les Femmes qui ne tuent ni ne votent*. Paris: C. Marpon et E. Flammarion, 1882.

Livi, Jocelyne. *Vapeurs de femmes: Essai historique sur quelques fantasmes médicaux et philosophiques*. Paris: Navarin, 1984.

Lombroso, Cesare, and Guglielmo Ferrero. *The Female Offender*. London: T. Fisher Unwin, 1895.

Lorde, André de. *Théâtre de la Peur: L'Horrible expérience; Baraterie; L'Acquittée; Les Infernales*. Paris: Librairie Théâtrale, 1924.

Loris C. de. *La Femme à Bicyclette: Ce qu'elles en pensent*. Paris: Librairies-Imprimeries Réunies, 1896.

Lourbet, Jacques. *Le Problème des sexes*. Paris: V. Giard et E. Brière, 1900.

Luhmann, Niklas. *Love as Passion: The Codification of Intimacy*. Trans. Jeremy Gaines and Doris L. Jones. Cambridge, Mass.: Harvard University Press, 1986.

Lunier, Dr. L. "Des vols aux étalages." *Annales médico-psychologiques* 4 (1880): 210–42.

Lyon, Aristide. *Responsabilité et paroxysme passionnel*. Montpellier: Impr. de Hamelin frères, 1885.

McBride, Theresa. "Public Authority and Private Lives: Divorce After the French Revolution." *French Historical Studies* 17 (Spring 1992).

Macé, Gustave. *La Femme criminelle*. Paris: Fasquelle, 1904.

———. *Mon musée criminel*. Paris: G. Charpentier, 1890.

———. *Un Cent-Garde*. Paris: G. Charpentier et E. Fasquelle, 1893.

McMillan, James. *Housewife or Harlot: The Place of Women in French Society, 1870–1940*. New York: St. Martin's Press, 1981.

Mairet, A. *La Jalousie: Etude psycho-physiologique, clinique et médico-légale*. Montpellier: Coulet et fils, 1908.

Marc, Ch.-C.H. *Consultation médico-légale pour Henriette Cornier, femme Berton, précédée de l'acte d'accusation*. Paris: 1826.

Marcé, L. V. *Traité de la folie des femmes enceintes, des nouvelles accouchées et des nourrices...* Paris: J. B. Baillière, 1858.

Marcil, René. *Les Femmes qui écrivent et les femmes qui votent*. Paris: E. Dentu, 1889.

Mareille, Vital. *La Plaidoirie sentimentale en France*. Paris: A. Predone, 1907.

Martin, Benjamin. *Crime and Criminal Justice in the Third Republic*. Baton Rouge: Louisiana State University Press, 1990.

Mauge, Annelise. *L'Identité masculine en crise au tournant du siècle, 1871–1914*. Paris: Rivages, 1987.

Maxwell, Joseph. *Manuel du juré: Eléments de science criminelle et pénal à l'usage de la Cour d'assises*. Paris: Flammarion, 1913.

Métayer, Léon. "La Leçon de l'héroïne (1830–1870)." *Europe: Le Melodrame* 703–4 (Nov./Dec. 1987): 39–48.

Miller, D. A. *The Novel and the Police*. Berkeley: University of California Press, 1988.

Monzie, Alfred de. *Le Jury contemporain et les crimes passionnels*. Paris: Alcan-Lévy, 1901.

Morache, Georges. *La Responsabilité criminelle de la femme, différente de celle de l'homme*. [nd]

Morand, Maurice. *De l'application des peines en Cour d'assises.* Poitiers: Imprimerie Blais, Roy et Cie., 1894.

Moreau, Félix. *Le Code civil et le théâtre contemporain: M. Alexandre Dumas fils.* Paris: L. Larose et Forcel, 1887.

Moreau, Thérèse. "Sang sur: Michelet et le sang féminin." *Romantisme* 31 (1981): 151–65.

Moreau de Tours, Paul. *La Contagion de meurtre: Etude d'anthropologie criminelle.* Paris: F. Alcan, 1894.

———. *De la contagion du crime et sa prophylaxie.* Mémoire présentée au Congrès des Sociétés savantes, 12 juin 1889.

Moses, Claire Goldberg. *French Feminism in the Nineteenth Century.* Albany: State University of New York Press, 1984.

Nayrac, J.-P. *La Folie jalouse.* Paris: P. Asselin, 1877.

———. *Grandeur et misère de la femme: Etudes de psychologie normale et pathologique de la femme dans la société.* Paris: A. Michalon, 1905.

Nye, Robert. *Crime, Madness and Politics in Modern France: The Medical Concept of National Decline.* Princeton: Princeton University Press, 1984.

———. "Honor, Impotence, and Male Sexuality in Nineteenth-Century French Medicine." *French Historical Studies* 16 (Spring 1989): 48–71.

———. *Masculinity and Male Codes of Honor in Modern France.* New York: Oxford University Press, 1993.

O'Brien, Patricia. "The Kleptomania Diagnosis: Bourgeois Women and Theft in Late Nineteenth-Century France." *Journal of Social History* 17 (Fall 1983): 65–77.

———. *The Promise of Punishment: Prisons in Nineteenth-Century France.* Princeton: Princeton University Press, 1982.

Offen, Karen. "Depopulation, Nationalism and Feminism in Fin-de-Siècle France." *American Historical Review* 89 (1984): 648–75.

Ouerd, Michèle. "Dans la forge à cauchemars mythologiques, sorcières, praticiennes et hystériques." *Les Cahiers de Fontenay* (Sept. 1978): 139–213.

Pagnat, Ph. *Enquête sur l'amour.* Paris: "Pages Modernes," 1907.

Le Palais de Justice de Paris: Son monde et ses moeurs par la presse judiciaire parisienne. Paris: Librairies-Imprimeries Réunies, 1892.

Paris, Alexandre. *La Folie des femmes enceintes, des nouvelles accouchées, et des nourrices.* Paris: A. Maloine, 1897.

Pelletier, Madeline. *L'Emancipation sexuelle de la femme.* Paris: V. Giard & E. Brière, 1911.

———. *Les Femmes en lutte pour ses droits.* Paris: V. Giard & E. Brière, 1908.

Perrot, Michelle. "Delinquency and the Penitentiary System in Nineteenth-Century France." In Robert Forster and Orest Ranum, eds., *Deviants and the Abandoned in French Society: Selections from the Annales.* Baltimore: The Johns Hopkins University Press, 1978.

———. "Fait divers et histoire du XIXème siècle." *Annales: Economies, sociétés,* ⌣
civilisations (July/Aug. 1983): 911–19.

———, ed. *L'Impossible prison: Recherches sur le système pénitentiaire au XIXème siècle.* Paris: Seuil, 1980.

———, ed. *Une Histoire des femmes: Est-elle possible?* Paris: Rivages, 1984.

"Les petits cahiers de Mme Weiss." *Archives d'anthropologie criminelle* 6 (1891): 418–30.

Pick, Daniel. *Faces of Degeneration: A European Disorder, c. 1848–1918.* Cambridge, Eng.: Cambridge University Press, 1989.

Plaidoyers de Ch. Lachaud. Recueillis par Félix Sangnier. Paris: G. Charpentier, 1885.

Pollack, O. *The Criminality of Women.* New York: A. S. Barnes, 1961.

Poovey, Mary. *Uneven Developments: The Ideological Work of Gender in Mid-Victorian England.* Chicago: The University of Chicago Press, 1988.

Portemer, Dr. A.-E. *Les Erotomanes, étude médico-légale.* Paris: J. Rousset, 1902.

Porter, Dennis. *The Pursuit of Crime.* New Haven: Yale University Press, 1981.

Proal, Louis. "L'Adultère de la femme." *Archives d'anthropologie criminelle* (1900).

———. *Le Crime et le suicide passionnels.* Paris: Alcan, 1900.

———. *La Criminalité féminine.* Paris: Imprimerie de E. Soye, 1890.

———. *Les Médecins positivistes et les théories modernes de la criminalité.* Paris: Soye et fils, 1890.

Puibaraud, Louis. *La Femme criminelle,* extract from *La Grande Revue* (May 1, 1899).

Rabaut, Jean. *Histoire des féminismes français.* Paris: Stock, 1978.

Rabinowicz, Léon. *Le Crime passionnel.* Paris: Marcel Rivière, 1931.

Radway, Janice. *Reading the Romance: Women, Patriarchy, and Popular Literature.* Chapel Hill: University of North Carolina Press, 1984.

"Rapport Médico-légale sur l'état mental de Joséphine Citoleux." *Annales médico-psychologiques* (1880): 250–69.

Ravail, Pierre-Julien. *La Femme et le barreau.* Poitiers: Imprimerie Blais et Roy, 1898.

Rearick, Charles. *Pleasures of the Belle Epoque: Entertainment and Festivity in Turn-of-the-Century France.* New Haven: Yale University Press, 1985.

Reibrach, Jean. "Le Poison." *Revue des Deux Mondes* 107 (1891): 150–71.

Riley, Denise. *"Am I That Name?": Feminism and the Category of "Women" in History.* Minneapolis: University of Minnesota Press, 1988.

Robert, Henri. *Jane Daniloff: L'empoisonneuse d'Ain-Fezza.* Paris: Editions Albin Michel, 1934.

Robinet de Clery, A. *Les Crimes de l'empoisonnement.* Paris: Bureau de la Vie Contemporaine, 1894.

Roger-Milès, L. *Nos Femmes et nos enfants: Choses sanglantes et criminalité.* Paris: E. Flammarion, 1893.

Romi. *Histoire des faits divers*. Paris: Pont Royal, 1962.

Rudinesco, Elizabeth. *La Bataille de cent ans: Histoire de la psychanalyse en France*. Vol. 1. Paris: Editions Ramsay, 1982.

Ryckère, Raymond de. *La Femme en prison et devant la mort*. Paris: A. Storck, 1898.

———. *La Servante criminelle: Etude de criminologie professionnelle*. Paris: A. Maloine, 1908.

Saillard, Paul. *Le Role de l'avocat en matière criminelle*. Paris: Larose et Forcel, 1905.

Saleilles, Raymond, *L'Initiative de la femme dans le domaine du droit*. Paris: Arthur Rousseau, 1901.

Saussure, Raymond de. "The Influence of the Concept of Monomania on French Medico-Legal Psychiatry (from 1825–1840)." *Journal of the History of Medicine* 1 (July 1946): 363–97.

Schafer, Sylvia. "Children in Moral Danger and the Politics of Parenthood in Third Republic France, 1870–1914." Ph.D. dissertation, University of California, Berkeley, 1992.

———. "The Court of Documents: Dossiers and the Dangerous Parent in Fin-de-Siècle Paris." Paper presented at the Ninth Berkshire Conference on the History of Women, Vassar College, Poughkeepsie, N.Y., June 13, 1993.

———. "When the Child Is the Father of the Man: Work, Sexual Difference, and the Guardian-State in Third Republic France." In Ann-Louise Shapiro, ed., *Feminists Revision History*. New Brunswick, N.J.: Rutgers University Press, 1994.

Schwob, Aimé. *Contribution à l'étude des psychoses menstruelles considérées surtout au point de vue médico-légal*. Lyon: A. Storck, 1893.

Scott, Joan W. *Gender and the Politics of History*. New York: Columbia University Press, 1988.

———. "'L'ouvrière! Mot impie, sordide . . . ': Women Workers in the Discourse of French Political Economy, 1840–1860." In *Gender and the Politics of History*.

Seguin, Jean-Pierre. *Nouvelles à sensation: Canards du XIXème siècle*. Paris: Armand Colin, 1959.

Shapiro, Ann-Louise, ed. *Feminists Revision History*. New Brunswick: Rutgers University Press, 1994.

Showalter, Elaine. *The Female Malady: Women, Madness and English Culture, 1830–1980*. New York: Pantheon, 1985.

Sighele, Scipio. *Le Crime à Deux: Essai de psychologie morbide*. Paris: G. Masson, 1893.

———. *Littérature et criminalité*. Paris: V. Giard et E. Brière, 1908.

Signorel, J. *Le Crime et la défense sociale*. Paris: Berger-Levrault, 1912.

———. *La Femme-avocate: Exposé historique, juridique et critique*. Toulouse: Saint-Cyprien, 1894.

Silverman, Debora L. *Art Nouveau in Fin-de-Siècle France: Politics, Psychology and Style*. Berkeley: University of California Press, 1989.

Smart, Carol. *Women, Crime and Criminology: A Feminist Critique*. London: Routledge and Kegan Paul, 1977.

Smith, Barbara Hernstein. "Afterthoughts on Narrative: Narrative Versions, Narrative Theories." *Critical Inquiry* (Autumn 1980): 213–36.

Sowerwine, Charles. *Sisters or Citizens*. Cambridge, Eng.: Cambridge University Press, 1982.

Stallybrass, Peter, and Allon White. *The Politics and Poetics of Transgression*. Ithaca: Cornell University Press, 1986.

Steedman, Carolyn Kay. *Landscape for a Good Woman: A Story of Two Lives*. New Brunswick, N.J.: Rutgers University Press, 1987.

Sur, Joseph. *Le Jury et les crimes passionnels*. Poitiers: Imprimerie Blais et Roy, 1908.

Swain, Gladys. "L'Ame, la femme, le sexe et le corps: Les métamorphoses de l'hystérie à la fin du XIXème siècle." *Le Débat* 24 (1983): 107–28.

Talmeyr, Maurice. "Le Roman-feuilleton et l'esprit populaire." *Revue des Deux Mondes* (Sept. 1903).

Tarde, Gabriel. "L'Amour morbide." *Archives d'anthropologie criminelle* 5 (1890).

———. "A propos de deux beaux crimes." *Archives d'anthropologie criminelle* 6 (1891).

———. *La Criminalité comparée*. Paris: Felix Alcan, 1890.

Tardieu, Ambroise. "L'Affaire Chambige." *Archives d'anthropologie criminelle* 4 (1889).

———. *Etude médico-légale sur la folie*. Paris: J.-B. Baillière, 1880.

Taxil, Leo. *La Corruption fin du siècle*. Paris: Noirot, 1891.

Terrisse, Marie. *Notes et impressions à travers le féminisme*. Paris: Librairie Fischbacher, 1896.

Thiesse, Ann-Marie. "Mutations et permanences de la culture populaire: La Lecture à la Belle Epoque." *Annales: Sociétés, Economies, Civilisations* 1 (Jan./Feb. 1984).

———. *Le Roman du quotidien: Lecteurs et lectures populaires à la Belle Epoque*. Paris: Le Chemin vert, 1984.

Thulié, Henri. *La Femme: Essai de sociologie physiologique*. Paris: A. Delahaye and E. Lecrosnier, 1885.

Toulouse, Dr. *Les Conflits intersexuels et sociaux*. Paris: Bibliothèque Charpentier, 1904.

Waelti-Walters, Jennifer. *Feminist Novelists of the Belle Epoque: Love as a Lifestyle*. Bloomington: Indiana University Press, 1990.

Wajeman, Gérard. *Le Maître et l'hystérique*. Paris: Navarin, 1982.

Walkowitz, R. Judith. *City of Dreadful Delight: Narratives of Sexual Danger in Late-Victorian London*. Chicago: University of Chicago Press, 1992.

———. "Melodrama and Victorian Political Culture: 'The Maiden Tribute of Modern Babylon.'" Paper delivered at the Pembroke Center Conference on Melodrama, Popular Culture, and Gender, Jan. 15, 1987.

———. "Patrolling the Borders: Feminist Historiography and the New Historicism." *Radical History Review* (Winter 1989): 25–31.

Weber, Eugen. *France: Fin-de-Siècle*. Cambridge, Mass.: The Belknap Press of Harvard University Press, 1986.

Williams, Rosalind. *Dream Worlds: Mass Consumption in Late Nineteenth-Century France*. New Haven: Yale University Press, 1985.

Yvernès, Emile. *Le Crime et le criminel devant le jury*. Paris: Berger-Levrault et Cie., 1894.

Zola, Emile. *Au Bonheur des Dames*. Paris: G. Charpentier, 1883.

———. *La Bête humaine*. New York: Penguin Books, 1977.

———. *Nana*. Trans. George Holden. Harmondsworth, Eng.: Penguin Books, 1987.

INDEX

In this index "f" after a number indicates a separate reference on the next page, and "ff" indicates separate references on the next two pages. A continuous discussion over two or more pages is indicated by a span of numbers. *Passim* is used for a cluster of references in close but not consecutive sequence.

156–57; as professionals, 189–91, 244n31; "new woman," 193, 197ff, 206, 214. *See also* Working-class women

Women's education, 180–89 *passim*, 205, 243n17

Women's rights, 181, 185–86, 187, 196f, 201f, 209, 215, 243n22; International Congress on Women's Rights . . . , 180; French and International Congress on the Rights of Women, 180

Working-class women, 20, 21–22, 166, 171, 181, 209

Zola, Emile, 22, 26, 41; *Au Bonheur des Dames*, 126; *La Bête humaine*, 41, 147, 227n109; *Nana*, 22

Library of Congress Cataloging-in-Publication Data

Shapiro, Ann-Louise.
    Breaking the codes : Female criminality in fin-de-siècle Paris /
Ann-Louise Shapiro
        p.   cm.
    Includes bibliographical references and index.
    ISBN 0-8047-1663-3 (cloth : alk. paper). — ISBN 0-8047-2693-0
(pbk. : alk. paper)
    1. Female offenders—France—Paris—History. I. Title.
HV6046.s46 1996   95-37867
364.3'74'094436109041—dc20   CIP

ⓧ This book is printed on acid-free, recycled paper.

Original printing 1996
Last figure below indicates year of this printing
05   04   03   02   01   00   99   98   97   96